TI
FOLLOWERS

"HOLY HELL" AND THE DISCIPLES
OF NARCISSISTIC LEADERS:
HOW MY YEARS IN A NOTORIOUS CULT PARALLEL
TODAY'S CULTURAL MANIA

RADHIA GLEIS

Sage Card Publishing

Copyright © 2021 by Radhia Gleis

THE FOLLOWERS
"Holy Hell" and the Disciples of Narcissistic Leaders: How My Years in a Notorious Cult Parallel Today's Cultural Mania

All rights reserved. No part of this publication may be reproduced, distributed, or transmitted in any form or by any means, without prior written permission from the publisher.

This work depicts actual events in the life of the author as truthfully as recollection permits and / or can be verified by research. Occasionally, dialogue consistent with the character or nature of the person speaking has been supplemented. All persons within are actual individuals; there are no composite characters.

Published by:
Sage Card Publishing
www.radhiagleis.com

Book Cover & Interior Layout: YellowStudios

Paperback ISBN: 978-1-7371258-0-8
Hardcover ISBN: 978-1-7371258-1-5
Library of Congress Control Number: 2021909414

First edition.

Printed in the United States of America

To Jaime Gomez:
"You're so vain, you probably think
this book is about you."

To Jeanne Dalman:
When others said I would never be a writer,
you're the one person who said I was!
Rest in Peace, my dear friend.

CONTENTS

INTRODUCTION

WHAT A RIDE THESE past few years have been. It feels like
the headlights of the year 2020 rushed up behind us,
then suddenly disappeared in our rearview mirror, rammed
our fender, and swerved around us while rageful, drunken
juveniles leaned out their windows, raising their fists and yelling vile expletives. Shocked, confused, and frightened, America is left with little more than red taillights speeding off into
the future. Our maps and GPSs flew out the open window
miles ago, and this journey has no end in sight. Exhausted, our
eyelids strain to stay open as we keep our foot on the pedal
and attempt to navigate the twisted highways and bumpy
backroads ahead. But as though in a recurring dream, it seems
I've been on this road before. I recognize the signposts, the
potholes—the winding, dangerous curves.

I spent twenty-five years of my adult life in a cult, under
the influence of a narcissistic sociopath. I left the group over
twelve years ago, but the post-traumatic stress entombed in my
psyche has been repeatedly triggered by the characteristics of

political and cultural leaders of today; and like Moonies under Sun Myung Moon, Germans under the influence of Hitler, or the Branch Davidians under David Koresh, a percentage of my country has fallen into a cult of personality.

As political elites, corporate puppeteers, and Russian oligarchs continue to spend their dark money, spinning well-coordinated propaganda, the followers don't even suspect that they've been played.

So how is this happening?

It took me twenty-five years to recognize and escape the psychological prison of cult life. But our little cult was hardly on the world stage, with all the gravitas afforded to the most powerful and influential country in the world. We were about 150 men and women insulated within our own small, clandestine community. We called ourselves the Buddha-field. One member, Will Allen, even made a movie about us, called *Holy Hell*.

After they presented *Holy Hell* at the Sundance Film Festival, I heard people say anything from "I get it, I would have joined that group" to "I would never be that stupid; how could anyone fall for that?" There is one common denominator among all the members of the Buddha-field. We would say, "You had to be there!" As I witness a portion of my country having been lured in by a narcissistic sociopath, I'm reminded of what it was like in the Buddha-field. Why did we follow such a leader? What makes people give up their will, their sense of right and wrong—give up their moral compass and family ties for a person or an ideal?

The following is a profound statement from the publisher's summary of *The Most Dangerous Superstition* by Larken Rose: "The vast majority of theft, extortion, intimidation, harassment, assault, and even murder—in other words, the vast majority of man's inhumanity to man—comes not from the greed, hatred, and intolerance that lurks in our hearts. Rather, it comes from one pernicious and almost universal assumption, one unquestioned belief, one irrational, self-contradictory superstition: the belief in 'authority.'"

I set out on this journey to explore these questions. I've read extensively about cult mind control, propaganda techniques, the pathology of narcissists and sociopaths, and the innate human urge to belong. We're all complicated; but there are some common traits that every human being possesses, and I have a burning desire to share them.

I wrote this book because I sought to understand why I made the choices I made in my life, so I could better understand why others make their choices. When it comes to voting for a leader, I usually think I'm sure I know exactly who the right choice should be, so when I see others voting for the opposite, I'm in the "I would never be that stupid; how could anyone fall for that?" camp. But when people say that to me, I feel misunderstood, shamed, and separate. I lose all my compassion and react with the same arrogant, self-righteous judgment towards them.

Before we go down this rabbit hole, let me be clear: This is not a memoir. I have a graduate degree, am an experienced researcher, and I approach this as a science project of sorts. I'm not going to give you ten ways to have a meaningful dialogue with someone in "the other camp." Politics today has gone way beyond a "Let's agree to disagree" scenario. And I don't expect at the end of this journey that we will all hold hands and sing "Kumbaya." This is not about policy or political ideology or even the guru or our political leaders, as much as it is about the followers from the viewpoint of a follower. The Holocaust or any genocide instigated by a narcissistic authority does not happen because of one man. It is the collective consciousness of their followers that supports and enacts those atrocities. And even if a leader is voted out of office, this does not mean those followers will not make a martyr out of them and carry their twisted ideology into the future.

The inspiration for this adventure came from a statement that a woman made during a book club meeting. This little club is a group of men and women, about my age, who read unconventional Christian-oriented books and get together to drink coffee and discuss them. They invited me to the group because the organizer thought I would be an interesting additive, sort of like a weird spice in the soup. One morning we were talking about verses in the Bible that everyone agreed were just nonsense. One woman said, "Yeah, when the priest says stuff like that, I just let it wash over me and ignore it." I thought, *Why? It's bullshit. Why do we let them get away with that? Why do we not challenge them right then and there? Why do we keep returning and let them continue to indoctrinate us without protest?* Then I thought, *Oh, I know. Duh!* I'd let that happen to me for twenty-five years.

When I left that morning I drove to work, and the outline for this book poured out of my mind like a cracked spigot. I thought, *Maybe I can turn my experience in a cult into something useful.* But useful to whom? I wrote the first few chapters about my family and my early childhood, hoping there might be some clues in there that would be helpful to understand why I did the things I did.

As a hobby, I love to buy or gather beads and make them into necklaces. I pick out colors and shapes and string them into patterns. Sometimes I don't like where I'm going and unstring them and start all over again. But you have to start with the first bead. These chapters are like that necklace. One chapter leads to the next. I started from the beginning, because where else would you start?

I read that first chapter to a friend who has known me since I was a little girl. We had a pleasant time reminiscing, but then she got serious. She is a psychotherapist, and after she listened to the chapter, she asked me, "Who is your audience?" "You sound like you're trying to explain yourself," she said. *Oh crap!* I thought. I don't know. I'm just stringin' beads at the moment; you mean now I have to think about this? Maybe I *am* trying to explain myself. Maybe I'm grappling with shame, like when I hear "How could anyone be that stupid?"

After my visit, I thought about it. Who is my audience? What do I want to accomplish with my story? I must admit, for a half-a-second there, I honestly fantasized that I'm writing this for the "other side." Maybe if I wake them up, help them realize they have been duped— manipulated by a narcissist—I could save the world. No doubt that is exactly what they think about me!

Even so, I constantly see strong parallels between my devotion to a cult leader—an authority—whose damaging behavior and influence I willfully ignored, and the followers of other authoritarian leaders. I also see that some of these followers will become disillusioned—literally—and struggle with the same questions I have had to face myself: How could you have believed this guy? How could you have made the moral compromises you did, for so long?

As I conducted my extensive research, I found there is no shortage of material that addresses these questions. I cite excerpts from the *Diagnostic and Statistical Manual of Mental Disorders* (5th edition, abbreviated as the DSMMD); *Combating Cult Mind Control* by Steven Hassan; *The Sociopath Next-door* by Martha Stout, PhD; and a myriad of journals and periodicals, and compare the leader of the Buddha-field and his followers to the startling similarities of other political and cultural leaders.

Recently, I had an encounter with a dyed-in-the-wool supporter of someone on the opposite side. My only thought was, *I truly am living in what physicists call a parallel universe, sharing a starkly different reality.* And then that person added, "But I believe we both really want the same thing." I met her eyes and said, "No—we don't!"

So whom am I writing this to? For now, perhaps I'm writing this just for myself. But as I string my beads, I find little nuggets that might be helpful—maybe for folks like me who think they are also living alone in a parallel universe, or for someone who might be in a religious or political cult and doesn't know how to get out. Maybe for people who feel like outsiders and just want to feel powerful or belong. Maybe there's a bead or two for a mom or a teacher, dealing with a child with dyslexia. Or even the kid who feels different, misunderstood—perhaps shame and isolation. Here's a piece of advice, kiddo: Try not to join a cult.

Here are some beads for people who live with or work for a narcissist, or who have niggling doubts about what their preacher tells them to do, or who, until not long ago, believed their membership in a group made them special.

And here are some precious beads for the people who are beginning to wake up and trickle out of the cult, feeling raw and shaken, and wondering, how did I give up all my principles and allow myself to be—duped? And how can I now forgive myself, heal, and move forward?

SECTION 1

THE JOURNEY

CHAPTER 1

LIFE AS A SNIGLETTE

THE FOLLOWING CHAPTERS ARE not a judgment on my family and friends. I'm not writing this as a tale of woe or sob story. Everybody has a story. Everybody has had pain and suffering. Everybody has reasons for developing the way they did and for making the choices they made in their life. My personal story would be unimportant, except to give insights on common emotional threads that many of us share, that go deeper than the superficial facade of a person's life. This is an exploration, and I'm willing to dive into the nuances of my psyche in an attempt to understand my choices and my world around me.

I was born in 1953, in Los Angeles, California—well, technically Brentwood. You know, OJ's neighborhood. My father,

Stanley Nicholas Gleis—or as his monogrammed shirts read, SNG; folks often called him SNiG—was a trial lawyer. My mother, Kay, was a fashion designer. Kay and Stan reminded me of Katharine Hepburn and Cary Grant. She was a gorgeous redhead, and Stan was your quintessential tall, dark, and handsome man. He was considered one of the "12 Super Lawyers" of Los Angeles, nicknamed "The Big Daddy of Divorce." SNiG was a civil and family lawyer at a time when divorce and family estates of the Los Angeles/Hollywood elite were a big deal. I guess they still are.

He was born in 1909 and raised in Hollywood. I never knew my grandfather. Dad's father, Bernie, a Luxembourgian, died in the 1918 Spanish Flu pandemic, so Dad and his four siblings were left to be raised by a cold, sadistic mother. He lived through World War I, the Pandemic, the Great Depression, and World War II. He was part of the "Greatest Generation." Despite so much pain and hardship, society at the time was intolerant of men who expressed their emotions. From early childhood, he learned to master suppressing his feelings. He was charismatic and had a wicked sense of humor, but when it came to issues like death, pain, or the suffering of others or his own, he was stoic; sometimes even glib.

SNiG put himself through law school and then went off to the South Pacific, a lieutenant commander of a destroyer escort in World War II. He carried the scars of his actions in that war for fifty years before he finally confessed to me at age eighty-one why he was so prejudiced towards Asians. "I hate them," he said. "Why?" I asked. "I have to," he replied, "...or I will have to face what I did." I have a photo of my dad on his ship, and on the side of the hull (like notches on his belt) were decals of Japanese ships, planes, and submarines he ordered be shot down. In those days, getting help from a psychologist or counselor carried the stigma that you were mentally ill. You would never dare even consider it. When his little brother died at a young age, instead of going to the funeral, SNiG went to Vegas. The only time I ever saw my father cry was when my mother died. He exploded like an emotional time bomb. It was as if he was grieving eighty years of pain and loss on a three-day nonstop crying binge.

Kay was born in 1919, in Saskatchewan, Canada, and moved to the US when she was very young. Her mother, Ethel, was Swedish aristocracy (or that's what I was told). Turns out, after I did a search on Ancestry.com, we were neither Swedish nor aristocrats, but Mom and Grandma assumed those identities with ease. According to our genetics and ancestry we are Norwegian and Danish on my mother's side. I felt it was only fair to call my brother Nick and asked him to call the King of Sweden and take us off the royal guest list.

Grandma was a concert pianist (well again, that's what we were told; who really knows? But she did play a mean piano). Mom's father, Harry Railson, was a silent picture actor under Cecil B. DeMille, and a horse breeder. That I know because I have pictures of him on the Hollywood sets. According to Mom, Grandpa was busy philandering with many Hollywood silent picture starlets, including Theda Bara, one of Hollywood's original sex symbols, while Grandma was on the road a lot. So they dumped Kay off at her uncle's thoroughbred farm in the El Cajon Valley. She was an artist, as was everyone in the Railson family—more sensitive and creative than my father—but neither of my parents was grounded in what psychology refers to as *secure attachment*.

Mom's baby brother, my uncle Bob, was one of the original designers of Disneyland. (That's how we got the half-round bar off the original Mark Twain steamship from Disneyland in our lanai.) Mom also had an older brother, Bill, but he died when I was young. Kay was ten years younger than Stan. She left home at sixteen, worked as a model, and put herself through Chouinard Art Institute. While Stan was off circumventing the South Pacific, Kay was developing her own sportswear line, under the label "Georgia Kay." After the war my father became her lawyer and eventually her husband.

My mom's dad and her younger brother Bob were the benevolent men in my life. Unlike my dad, who stopped carrying me or showing much physical affection by the time I was eighteen months old, Grandpa never put me down till the day he died, when I was eight. The most vivid memory I have of that day was his skin—it was grayish-yellow. I stood in the shadows, staring into that silent room with everyone around him. I knew in my heart I would never see him again. I couldn't understand how one minute he could be my adoring champion, carrying me around the garden to see the baby bunnies, checking the chicken coop for eggs, chasing Queeny, the little bantam rooster, around the yard, and be so cold, gray, and lifeless the next.

My parents were challenged with their own grief. In the nineteen fifties it was preferred that children be seen and not heard. And as a rule, adults didn't include young children in the grieving process. I think they thought death was too hard for a child to comprehend, so instead of lending any comfort, or explanation, they just ignored me. I stood there alone while they attended to him. I could feel his death in the marrow of my soul. I don't remember crying or making a sound. Perhaps

I was already learning how to be stoic around tragedy. It affected me with the searing memory of my grandpa as a cold, empty shell, and it left a hole in my heart that never healed.

Uncle Bob was handsome and rugged. He resembled Steve McQueen and had the same King of Cool demeanor. He was a boxer in the Navy, and I loved to listen to him tell stories of his adventures. He was an artist, a designer, a chef, and an inventor, and a horseman who rode bulls in the rodeo. He had a beautiful way with animals and gave me an appreciation for cats and dogs and horses and all wildlife. I loved Uncle Bob deeply. He would come visit Mom, especially when my father was "out." They would smoke and drink and talk into the wee hours of the night. He was funny and light-hearted and a brilliant storyteller. They would laugh and turn up the music, and Mom seemed happier when Bob was home.

One of my favorite memories was when I would dance on Uncle Bob's feet to Frank Sinatra or my favorite—Bobby Darin's "Mac the Knife." Bob knew all the lyrics, and we would sing them together while dancing on the black-slate floor of the grand, sky-lighted family room, which we called the lanai. Life seemed a little safer when Bob was around. He died when I was in my early teens. I remember him saying his life was finally fulfilled, just before he had a stroke at age fifty-one. I visited him in the hospital. He was paralyzed and couldn't speak. Yet he spoke to me with his desperate eyes, and I felt his fear and frustration over his helpless predicament. He died two days later. I don't know if I cried. I felt as paralyzed as he was. But I remember writing a poem to express my grief. I read it to my mother. She said it was beautiful and cried. But she was too gripped by her own grief to be very aware of mine.

My parents were in an interesting economic class. It wasn't the middle class or the super-rich; it was what I would call the entrepreneur class. Neither parent worked for anyone at a nine-to-five, J O B, but they did not have their wealth handed to them on a silver platter either. Although we were not super-rich, we hung out with lots of the super-rich. My brother Nick and I went to private schools. I was presented as a debutante. We were members of Rivera Country Club and the Balboa Bay Club, and we attended polo matches, parties, and other frivolity with the Los Angeles elite.

The problem with entrepreneur parents was that their name and financial reward relied strictly on their own merits; consumed with their work, their parenting skills were deficient, to say the least. If you ever saw the series *Mad Men*, that was my parents and the era I grew up in. In hindsight, I think if, as a child, I had confronted them with their lack of parenting, they would have probably said, "Well...we had you; what more do you want? We know you're only three, but you're on your own." At least at three, that's what it felt like. I had a governess, named DoDo, and many housekeepers, but when Kay and Stan left for work and Nick went off to school every day, I was pretty much left alone without the family unit to develop my own *secure attachment*.

I will not get into the nitty gritty of my life, but it is important to lay the groundwork for those who might be curious why an intelligent girl with all the privileges afforded to me would find herself involved in a cult for twenty-five years. This is not everybody's story. There are all kinds of complex reasons that people join cults, or follow leaders, which I will enumerate as I string these beads. But this is my story, and the assorted details of my life may shine some light on why I joined a cult and what

I was looking for. On the surface some might have looked upon my life with envy; however, as the old saying goes, "Not all that glitters is gold."

A couple of years ago, I was in a writer's workshop and one assignment was to write a poem starting with "I am from…" then fill in the blanks with quick images from my life. The following sums up a lot without going into graphic details.

I am from the Well-To-Do

I am from the well-to-do and private girls' schools. I am from tall, skylit ceilings and black slate floors. I am from chlorine-scented swimming pools, my mother's Norell perfume, Marlboro Reds, and perfect Rob Roys. I am from a sea of green ivy that lines the long driveway. I am from a tall pine tree that kept me company when I was alone. I am from Swedish smorgasbords and drunken nights. Grandmother's pork sausage, cornbread stuffing, and needles in my brother's arm. I am from guns on the coffee table and strangers in my bed. I am from dinner table conversations about law and fashion design. I am from communion wafers on my tongue and switchblades at my throat. I am from cotillion with Jeff Bridges and rides in a yellow Rolls-Royce. I am from debutante balls and fox hunting fields, Baccarat crystal menageries and needlepoint pillows. I am from pianos, flutes, and oil paint. I'm from the well-to-do.

In the fifties and sixties, like in *Mad Men*, cigarettes, alcohol, misogyny, and bigotry were just a part of the social mores of the time. Both my parents smoked, I'm sure, while my mother was pregnant. And alcoholism was just referred to as "cocktail time." My friends still say, "Well, it's five o'clock somewhere in the world." Everyone from that socioeconomic era knows what that means. That's the cue, even today, to break out the booze.

Dad was in his mid-forties and Mom was in her mid-thirties when Nick and I were born. That was old to be having children in those days. They both lived in a world of adults. I recall very few of my mother's friends having babies, so she didn't have the soccer-mom camaraderie with her peers, like other mothers had. After a long day at the office, she came home, fixed herself a drink, and shared her day with Dad; or if he was down in Newport Beach, shackin' up with the judge's wife, local girlfriends of hers would often pop by. After all, it was five o'clock, and the Mark Twain bar was open for business.

If you wanted to survive at all in the Gleis family, you had to be an adult. Even if you were only three. So instead of playing alone in my room with child development toys, I learned the difference between a Ramus Fizz and a Gin Fizz. And God help us, if Stan had gin that night, you would be tested. I would crawl up onto the adults' laps and mimic the conversations. I remember one night when my parents' friends Peggy Lester and her husband came to visit. Mom and Dad were getting dressed, so I answered the door. I reached up and turned the giant doorknob and said, "Good evening, Piggy Westa. Pwease come in, can I fix you a dwink?"

SNiG had absolutely no instinct for children. He was brilliant, but unlike my mother, the "aristocrat," he was unfiltered. He swore like a sailor; though come to think of it, he was a sailor. And like chips off the old block, my brother and I adopted more of his personality than Mom's. If he was SNiG, we were SNiGlettes. One time he was on the phone, swearing heartily at one of his clients. "Oh, Jesus Christ, that son of a bitch..." he said. DoDo warned him not to use that language in front of the children. He answered, "Oh for Christ's sakes, they don't know what these words mean." Later that night he told Nick, who was about five or six at the time, to go to bed. Nick replied, "Oh, for Christ's sakes, you son of a bitch."

I rest my case.

When I was born my parents had read Dr. Spock's famous books on parenting. What an idiot! Upon Spock's suggestion Mom and Dad told Nick that I was his baby, and he took it literally. He felt the responsibility of parenting at age two and a half. He would wake up early, drag me out of my crib, put his jeans on me, and feed me—anything. Spoons full of sugar, corn flakes, whatever. He towed me around in his wagon to visit the neighbors and show them his baby to get us cookies. I crawled after him as fast as he could run, and Icky was my first word. Not Mommy or Daddy—Icky. He was my world. He was my parent. But as he got older, he changed. He was temperamental and he would often take it out on me. DoDo told me that once, we were in the backseat of the car driving home from our grandma's house. She said I was curiously quiet, and when she looked in the backseat, Nick was holding a knife at my leg.

As he got older his temperament got more violent. By the time I was fourteen my brother had me tie him off as he shot crystal meth into his vein. I was terrified. Terrified for him and terrified of him. This was in our home with our parents in the next room. I was worried that he would kill himself and scared to tell anyone because I thought he would kill me.

On another occasion he was showing off to his friends. He pulled out a switchblade, grabbed me from behind, and held it to my throat. They all laughed. Especially his psychotic friend Rick. One time, Rick's girlfriend had just gotten a kitten. Rick fell asleep, and the kitten jumped up on his chest. He got so angry he threw it up against the wall and killed it. One night I woke up with Rick on top of me in my bed as I lay sleeping. He pressed his hand over my mouth and told me to be quiet. He had the intention to rape me, but Nick was calling him from the other room, so he stopped.

On another occasion, Mom and Dad were out of town. When I came home, Rick was in the house, but Nick wasn't there. I hated Rick and didn't trust him in the house alone. I asked him to leave until Nick got back. When Nick returned, Rick told him I kicked him out. Nick took me into the other room, pushed me down, got on top of me, and beat the shit out of me. Another night I came home unexpectedly. I walked into the lanai and there was my brother, buck naked and pointing a gun at me. A real gun. He had many. He burglarized houses in the neighborhood, stole cars, and sold drugs for local mobsters. He would sneak out at night dressed in a suit with a gun tucked in a shoulder holster under his arm. I lived in fear most of my young life. I was afraid of his violent temper; I was afraid of the people he hung around with; and I was afraid he was going to kill someone or get killed.

Nick violently fought with my father, and they didn't speak to one another for over a year. One Christmas he was arrested for drug possession and made a ward of the court. This was not the Icky I had known and loved. This was not my protector, my only secure attachment. He had become the one I felt I needed protection from.

Nick finally grew up, and with the help of Uncle Bob and boarding school, he grew out of his drug use, delinquency, and violent behavior. He became a successful photographer and left that world forever. Many years later, when I was about thirty-five years old, my mother and I were at lunch with a family friend who had a young daughter. Kay launched into a speech on how to be a good parent. I was shocked. I said, "You don't know me, you know nothing about my life." My mother literally put her fingers in her ears and said, "I knew, I just don't want to hear about it."

I went to private Catholic school until they finally asked me not to come back in eleventh grade. That was their way of politely kicking me out. I had some handicaps in my primary and high school years. I had dyslexia and probably a touch of ADHD, which unlike today, no one had ever heard of in the fifties and early sixties, so it was just considered a disciplinary issue. To compound the problem, DoDo was Danish and loved her coffee. Apparently, the Danish felt it was perfectly fine to give coffee to children. DoDo put coffee, milk, and sugar in my sippy-cup. I come to find out, over sixty years later, that I have a genetic mutation that causes me to be a slow metabolizer of caffeine. So I really don't know if it was ADHD or Folgers. That factor alone had a lot to do with how I became a nutritionist, but I'll save that story for later.

At around first grade my personality took a permanent turn. I was small for my age, but I was never a child. "Precocious" is what the adults liked to call it. When I walked into class, usually jacked up on coffee and sugar, and was forced to sit quietly in those little desks and listen to a nun whah-whah like the teacher in a Peanuts cartoon, it was BOOORRING! Hey, it was really the first time I had a tribe of children to play with. Also, as I have now come to understand, my brain was taking in about ten times more data than the rest of the kids.

Couple that with dysgraphia, a condition in which 27 looks like 72 (really sucks on a math test), and, when attempting to read, my eyes could not adjust to the lines on the page. No matter what I understood, I couldn't prove it in test scores. Finally, by the end of the first hour of class, overwhelmed with all of this, I would just fall asleep.

"She's obviously just too young for first grade," the nuns explained to Kay and Stan. So while my newfound colleagues were off to second grade, they put me back to kindergarten. I'll never forget how Sister Eloise Mary, a nasty old nun with pale, transparent skin and little wire-rimmed glasses, grabbed me in the corridor, wrapped her black veil around me like Dracula, and explained to me that I was being put back. What? I beg your pardon. Hey! I know how to make a perfect Rob Roy, for Christ sakes.

The indignation and rejection were too much to bear. There I was with these babies, sitting on a bench next to the sand-box behind the fence that separated me from my peers, playing on the playground. That was it. My first actual life choice. I was either going to give up and crumble into a dysfunctional moron, quietly accepting that I was just too dumb to belong, or I was going to fight these traitors. I chose the latter. A teacher's aide came out to the sandbox and said, "Come on, Linda (that was my name at the time), it's nap time." I looked up at her, and in my small, six-year-old voice, I said, "Fuck off!"

CHAPTER 2

A LONG LONELY ROAD

IN SCHOOL, THEY CONSTANTLY put me in the "slow" kids groups—treated me like a halfwit. Ironically, though, because my mother was a designer and my governess was a meticulous groomer, I was always immaculate—pressed blue uniform, hair tied up in braids with matching navy-blue satin ribbons, emblemed jacket, hat, and white gloves with my leather briefcase—they always picked me to be the model to represent the school at parochial school conferences or when the bishop was in town. While my friends were getting science and history awards pinned to their lapel, I was getting personal appearance and "effort" awards. I guess they thought I needed some kind of award so I wouldn't feel left out. Really? Did they really think I or any child would fall for that? It was humiliating. I just wanted to disappear on Awards Day; not to have to take the walk of shame up to the stage and receive my brown effort-award ribbon.

I had severe test anxiety. Whenever there was a test, between the coffee and the pressure of my inability to read (especially against the clock), I became devoid of frontal cortex function. My heart would race, seeing my classmates putting their pencils down before I could even finish the first paragraph. Every year we had to take the Iowa Scholastic Achievement Tests. I am still haunted to this day by having to fill in those goddamn little circles—choose A, B, C, or D, none of the above. With dysgraphia I may have been going for B and hit C. Or sometimes I'd reach the bottom of the little card and notice I'd skipped a line. "Time's up, pencils down!"

The nuns were so insensitive in those days. I'll never forget how, when I was in sixth grade, they read our scores out loud. Maryliz Benchec—99, Gaea Logan—97, Beverly Bechtold—100, Linda Gleis—2. A two? Not a seventy-two? Okay, I'll accept a sixty-two, but—a two? What were they thinking? Did they not realize that reading that score aloud could scar me for life? Well, it did! At sixty-six years old, even with a graduate degree, I still hear the roar of laughter from that day, echoing in the tarry reservoirs of my memory.

My parents took a hands-off approach to child rearing. They supplied me with tutors, but Dad had a "How come you don't know this already?" attitude. They never helped me with my homework, ever! And that was probably best, because Dad had a chronic intolerance for stupidity. Not that an eighth grader is stupid just because they don't know something, but I think he was concerned about his return on investment.

I remember once, I wrote an essay, and I wanted Dad to read it, cuz I was proud of my thesis, and maybe he would be too. He got through about two sentences and stumbled onto a misspelled word. He screamed, "What's this word?" I told him the word, and he said "That's not how you spell that! How do you spell that word?" I said, "I don't know, how do you spell it?" "Look it up, goddamn it," he yelled. I said, "Why don't you just tell me how to spell it?" He stood up, grabbed my arm, and shoved me into the other room where the bookcase was. "Get the goddamn dictionary," he shouted.

There are dictionaries, and then there was the dictionary at the Gleis house. It was the kind you might find in a public library, perched on its own pedestal because it was so big that you couldn't carry it. It was at least ten inches thick and heavier than a bowling ball. I dragged this thing out, laid it on the table, and thumbed through the thousands of words on the cigarette-paper-thin pages. I couldn't even see the words through my tears.

"Oh, Jesus Christ, Dopey, hurry-up, goddamn it, look it up, look it up." He pushed me aside, grabbed the pages, and impatiently flipped to the right page. He stabbed the word, frantically, over and over, with his short, stubby finger and said, "What's that say, Dopey? How do you spell that word?" I spelled the word in a trembling whisper. He slammed the book, grabbed me by the arm, dragged me to my room, threw me across the threshold, and said. "Now, write it fifty times, and don't come out till you do." So much for my brilliant essay.

I think Stan was allergic to gin. None of my family members were ever falling down drunks. But with gin, like Doctor Jekyll and Mr. Hyde, Dad would turn into a crazy, mean son of a bitch. One time, on the way home from a party (DWIs were sketchy in those days. I mean, come on, a classic song from that era was "One for my Baby and One More for the Road"), he asked my brother and me to sing "The Star-Spangled Banner." We mumbled through the words, and he got so mad, he made us write it fifty times when we got home. "The Star-Spangled Banner"—fifty times. Just let that sink in for a minute. Mom was basically helpless when he was like this. Everybody was, but when we got home, you could hear her scream at him from the other room. I think that was the night she threw a bowl of ice cream at him. He ducked, and it hit the wall. Chocolate Rocky Road slid down the French-blue plaster, slowly making a streak of what looked like shit with little marshmallows in it.

Let me just say this. Mom was very loving and affectionate when she was around. The problem was, she went out of town—a lot! She traveled for weeks at a time to New York, Europe, and Asia throughout the year. And SNiG usually took off to Los Vegas, leaving me with Nick and his gang of delinquents. DoDo was in her late seventies when I was born, so she had only a few good years with us as children. After she left the family, Kay was on deck to take on some maternal duties, like picking me up from school. Many times I sat on the front steps and watched the parking lot empty. One by one, the string of cars circled in front of me, picking up my friends. There I was, in my hat and jacket, briefcase by my side, waiting for someone to remember to pick me up. She would eventually get around to it, or not. I could have taken the school bus, but I was afraid I'd get lost forever. How did the bus driver know where I lived? No one ever bothered to explain that to me.

I remember once, I got very sick. The school tried to get a hold of someone to take me home, but to no avail. There were no cellphones in those days, so it wasn't as easy as it is today.

I had a high fever, so one nun took me upstairs to their private quarters and put me in a nun's bedroom. That was weird. It smelled like mold and frankincense. It had one small bed and a crucifix on the wall. That's it! I crawled into the bed and fell asleep. In my feverish state, I vividly remember dreaming that I had died in that room, that day. I dreamt that I got up from the bed and walked to the window. I looked down at a funeral procession and realized it was mine. I tried banging on the window and yelling down to them that I was up here, and I wasn't dead, but no one could hear me.

A loud knock on the door disrupted my dream, and a panicked nun burst in and got me out of bed. My mom had finally come to get me. It was 7:30…at night. The nuns had forgotten about me, and Mom, having noticed that something was missing when she got home from work, started to investigate. According to her, when she called the school, they told her I wasn't there. Well, eventually, they figured it out. Mom was so upset and frightened she was practically in tears on the drive home. I suppose I could appreciate that she'd worried so much about me, it almost brought her to tears, but it really wasn't about her, was it? I just remember feeling like crap.

The only way anyone discovered there might be something off with me was when I got the lowest score, probably in the history of teaching, on my high school entrance exam. It was so low that the principal wanted to meet me, because she said, "No one could go through eight years of primary school and get a score that low without trying." When I went to her office, I think she was expecting someone with a severe mental disability. And then I walked in, an articulate, perfectly coiffed, mini adult. She asked me a bunch of questions, then recommended I see an eye doctor in Los Angeles, who was exploring treatment for a novel concept called dyslexia.

I got into college the long way around. I went to Brooks Institute, while taking my liberal arts requirements at SBCC, then on to graduate from Art Centre College of Design. I went to art school because I was an artist. That came easily to me. Also, I thought I could never make it scholastically in any other field. In hindsight, I think I would have made a brilliant lawyer, if it weren't for all that reading.

I developed unique skills, however. I don't know, maybe I tapped into the Akashic records. I didn't have a "learning disability." I hate that term; I have a fine ability to learn—it's just different. I repeat what I am learning, over and over, or ruminate. I often talk to myself, teaching anyone whatever I am interested in, even if they are not interested—which makes for challenging social skills. People often ask me, "How do you remember so much information?" As a child, I didn't always play with many kids. I would build little desks and put my dolls in them and teach them. All day long I would teach them what I picked up in school, on TV, or from conversations around me. Repeating over and over, creating stories around the information. So I would retain it. I was probably no more talented than a sophisticated parrot, but that was my idea of fun.

I remember at one point when I was in college, I had never read a book in my life. I had developed the tenacious skill of dialoguing with the teacher. I'll never forget one day, when I was walking out of a history class. We had to read several books that semester, and I hadn't read any of them. As I opened the door to leave, the teacher said, "You're very articulate; you must be very well read." I stopped, turned to her, smiled, and said, "Yeah!" My issue with reading was a dark, shameful secret. Deep down, I always felt that I was a fraud. I remember, in my anthropology class, I had such a running dialogue with the teacher, he told me I didn't have to take the final because, he said, "he knew what I knew." As I think about it, I'm sure I was annoying to the other students. I have read lots of books since then, and now that Audible is available, I listen to many.

I know—I said that I'm a clinical nutritionist. So I will skip ahead for a minute to explain how that happened. I'll be back.

Like many practitioners, my vocation as a Board-Certified Clinical Nutritionist and wellness counselor started with my own health challenges. As an airbrush artist it never occurred to me that blowing rainbows out of my nose, because of the paint fumes, was a bad thing. I was working at Disney. I had all kinds of health problems: heart palpitations; weight problems; headaches; allergies; hypoglycemia so severe I couldn't function by the middle of the afternoon. I was young, and I thought to myself, *If I feel this way now, I don't even want to know what I will feel like in my forties, fifties, and sixties.*

Besides the toxicity and the stress, I was mainlining on coffee and junk food, and my heart palpitations were an enormous concern. I'd had them most of my life. In high school I would ask my friends to hit me in the chest to knock my heart rhythm back into place. They never hesitated to lend medical assistance. Punch me in the chest. What are pals for? They would place one hand on my chest, yell "Clear!" and pound me with the other. It worked! My family physician, who was the chief cardiologist for Santa Monica Hospital, put me on phenobarbital, a highly addictive barbiturate. Great! It slowed my heart rate down; I barely had a heartbeat.

Then I discovered a chiropractor/nutritionist in Malibu who came highly recommended, and she saved my life. When she asked if I wore a mask when I used the airbrush, I replied, "A mask? No, how could I smoke?" She asked me if I drank coffee. "Yes," I said, "about six cups a day." As soon as I cut back on the caffeine, my heart palpitations stopped. (Who knew?) Apparently, I wasn't phenobarbital deficient. She put me through a detoxification program, then taught me how and what to eat and turned me on to the dietary supplements I needed. I feel better now, in my sixties, than I ever did in my twenties.

This nutritionist inspired me. Her solutions were so simple. *I'm an educated woman,* I thought. *How come I did not know this?* We're so programmed to lay our common sense at the feet of the Gods of medicine. Years went by, and by this time I was in the Buddha-field. My entire lifestyle was different. I had an impeccable diet, I was meditating and exercising every day, and I felt terrific. *People need to know this,* I thought. They need to know how to care for and feed their bodies to stay healthy and avoid drugs and disease.

At that point my art career was taking off, and I had come to a crossroads. Should I drop my career as an illustrator and study nutrition? I was offered a position as an art director for a textile company. It was a great gig. I had a choice: a starting salary of $60,000 a year (that was a lot in those days), plus bennies, a company car, and annual trips to Europe OR test urine in a lab for fifty bucks a week. Hmmm, WHAT...was I thinking?

I needed to talk to Mom. Talking to her about this scared me to death. Mom was a successful designer, but she always thought I had more talent than she. She basically put me through art school and supported me in every artistic endeavor. What would she think if I told her I wanted to do this airy-fairy nutrition thing over following in her footsteps, with a budding art career?

I went to her house that afternoon, and there she was, sitting at the table playing solitaire with the cat. "So...what did you decide about your job offer?" she asked calmly, as she flipped the cards over, one by one, on the table. "I think I want to study nutrition." Gulp! I persisted. "Besides, my portfolio was stolen." She never looked up. She just calmly, rhythmically, kept flipping the cards. "I had my portfolio stolen once," she uttered, quietly. "All my awards and original artwork... gone." She stopped, laid the last card on top of the straight, looked up at me, and said, "You're not your portfolio. That's what you do, not who you are. You need to do whatever makes you happy." That was the last conversation I had with my mother. She died, suddenly, the next day.

After that, I went back to school to study nutrition. By then I was an adult. I was even older than some of my teachers. I realized that my value was no longer dependent on my grades or other people's opinions of me. I looked at it this way: I have a specific interest, and I am paying these teachers to assist me with my goal.

I used to illustrate my notes. If I needed to memorize the function of the heart, for example, I would draw the organ and teach my phantom students (the dolls in my head) the heart's physiological function. I would even draw on my exams. My notes and exam papers often looked like a page out of an illustrated medical textbook. It may have been way beyond what they expected of me, but that was the way I learned. That was the way I would manage my anxiety. I had a 4.0 GPA. After receiving a score of 2 as a child (Does that even qualify for a GPA?), a 4.0 was something I was proud of. Both my parents were dead, so there were few in my life who even knew about my scholastic accomplishment; and the guru did not want me to go to my commencement ceremony for my graduate degree. All that work—no pomp and circumstance, no celebratory dinner, or even a congratulation; my degree just came in an unceremonious envelope in the mail.

In the late 1980s, although I was in the Buddha-field, I only lived about fifteen minutes away from my family and still had a relationship with them. When my mother died, as her body lay on the floor in her bedroom, waiting for the morgue to pick it up, I got the news, over two hours later, not from my brother or my father, but from a friend of the family. After she died, she was cremated. Dad refused to allow Nick and me to go with him to bury her ashes at the Holy Cross Cemetery. Although I couldn't understand, he was adamant about it, so I respected his wishes.

Months before my father died, he had a major stroke. SNiG was in the ICU. No one notified me for four days. When I went to the hospital, they wouldn't let me in. I told the doctor I was his daughter. This doctor looked me in the eyes and said, "He doesn't have a daughter." Apparently, my brother had a tad bit of resentment about me being in THAT GROUP. Yet, when the time came to unplug SNiG, suddenly I was resurrected, to be the sole family member to do the deed… alone.

My father died a year and a half after my mother, and Nick and I wanted to bury his urn next to hers. We went to the cemetery and found they had no record of where my mother's urn was. After a lengthy investigation, the cemetery discovered she was put in an unmarked plot with other unknown deceased.

"She's in number forty-six at the end of that row," the cemetery director said. My father didn't want to pay for the extra real estate.

As I trot down memory lane, stringing these beads together, it is becoming clearer to me why I may have wanted to create a family that seemed more functional and safer. Ha! In hindsight, that didn't turn out so well. Not that there weren't wonderful memories along the way. But this is a psychological journey, not meant to be a story of a victim. Many of my friends had much more traumatic childhoods than I did. And this is not a comparison to the suffering that so many people in the world have endured. But everything is relative. On the surface, my family was a 1960s, upper class, idyllic American success story. I knew they loved me in their own narcissistic, broken way. I always felt it from my mom, and I found out how much SNiG loved me at his funeral, when all his friends told me how he couldn't stop talking about me. They did the best they knew how. But like in *Mad Men*, dysfunction was the American way back then.

I notice, as I write this, I describe my family in terms of television and Hollywood personalities. That was very much my reality growing up. TV and the movies were how I escaped into a psychological fantasy, living vicariously through the Cleavers, *My Three Sons, Father Knows Best, The Brady Bunch*, and *The Partridge Family*. I never realized some of my life experiences were not all that healthy. It was just life. Just the way things were.

My childhood was both a curse and a gift. Because of my supposed handicaps, I was forced to find other ways to communicate. I rarely had a normal conversation with my father; it was always a deposition. Thus, I learned to be orally articulate. I learned how to present a compelling argument. Many of my friends often laugh and say, like Mikey in the cereal commercial, "Give it to Radhia, she'll say it." I learned how to be demonstrative and bold, especially when it came to defending justice or the underdog. I was chosen by several organizations to represent them on legislative issues in Texas Representative and Senate hearings. I remember one time, just before a huge battle in the Texas Health and Human Services Committee hearing, a friend and colleague who knew me well said, "You have to channel SNiG here." I have little or no fear of public speaking, teaching, or lecturing, even singing in a rock 'n' roll band. As Malcolm Gladwell said in his book *David and Goliath*, people with adversities learn how to fail; therefore, they are not as afraid to step out of the box. The curse arises when that talent of delivering a compelling message is successful, but the message turns out to be false. You have to bear the responsibility.

I also adopted SNiG's stoic, unemotional disposition in times of emergency or death. During the AIDS crisis many of our brothers were dying, and I took care of them up to their last breath. One of my best friends and brothers in the Buddhafield, Raymond, had AIDS, and I cared for him until the end. For months I just handled whatever needed to be done— unafraid and unemotional. At the end he was in the ICU, and the doctor needed to get an answer if he was ready to be taken off life support. I talked to Raymond about it, and he said yes, he was ready. As I stood at the end of his bed, he looked at me, smiled, and said, "You can cry now." I burst into tears. I am a very emotional person and I'm not generally afraid to express myself, but most of the time, the SNiGlette just takes over in times of crisis.

The point to my story thus far is not just about me, but about the post-World War II generation that is running the country right now. I bear that in mind, as I struggle to understand some of these politicians and their constituents. Most of our leaders come from my generation. They were raised by parents from the "Greatest Generation," who, like my father, endured unimaginable pain and fear, and thus learned how to suppress their emotions and cling tightly to their identities. Most of our government leaders come from white, affluent families with Ivy League educations. They were brought up in a *Leave It to Beaver* reality, with entirely different social mores and concerns than the generations that followed.

Secure attachment is a particularly important component to a person's emotional wellbeing. I will explore this further as we go on. I never imagined that the way things were in those days would mold my character, personality, or choices I would make. And then there's the Catholic Church.

CHAPTER 3

FROM THE CATHOLIC CHURCH TO THE ROAD TO NIRVANA

I'**VE COME TO REALIZE** in my journey that when one is running towards something, they're usually running from something. Although I grew up in the Catholic Church, I left Catholicism at the *age of reason*. According to Catholicism, the *age of reason* is seven. And it didn't take a genius or even a child over the age of seven to realize that what these people were indoctrinating was illogical. Catholics are not really taught the Bible. They tell Bible stories, but they're given the CliffsNotes in the form of Catechism. This offers some quick answers to who God and his entourage are and spells out the rules. Follow these rules explicitly to avoid burning in hell for all eternity. Wait, what? That's right, burn in hell for all eternity. "For I am the Lord thy God. God is the first and the last, the beginning and end of everything. God is the creator of all things; God *is* all things. God is omnipotent, omnipresent, and omniscient. God is all merciful, love everlasting"— except if you fuck up! Then burn, baby, burn.

So as a child I thought, let me get this straight. God created you, okay, but God is everything. What?—everything but you? If God is everything, then that would mean that you are part of God. So why would God want to judge, torture, and destroy itself? This Creator apparently knows everything; therefore, it knows that you will fuck up even before *you* know it—and ... is just waiting to condemn itself to suffer for all eternity?

Sounds to me like this all-loving, all-merciful God is both really sadistic and masochistic at the same time. And how can we go against God's will? That would mean that we are more powerful than this omnipotent being. All things are God's will; he is the creator of all things. Therefore, good, bad, or indifferent, he created it. And don't give me this "free will" bullshit. That God apparently isn't interested in taking responsibility either. An omniscient being knows what you will do, before you do it, so here's your option: Don't do it, regardless of what causes you to do it in the first place, thanks be to God; or do it and burn FOREVER! But it is *your* choice. What a deal! And then there's the fine print. Thou shalt not kill, unless it's in the name of God; then you're a hero. Hmmm? Oh, but it's a divine mystery. That's what they say, when they can't get out of an argument with a seven-year-old.

Don't misunderstand me. I'm sure, reading this, you might think I'm an atheist. Not so. I just don't believe in the

Deity yarn. Some burly, old man with a gray beard, up in the clouds, watching and judging our every move, tallying up our virtues and vices, while pulling out marshmallows and throwing kindling on the fires of hell. I don't believe in a personal God. One who takes your side in a football game or is the only "true" God of your church, synagogue, temple, or mosque. That whole concept contradicts their very definition of God. Have you ever noticed that only men write scripture? That would explain why most organized religions—at least the Western ones that originated in the Middle East—believe in a paternal God. He may be all things, but evidently, according to the writers and artists—he's got a dick. I think Michelangelo did Western Culture a huge disservice with his depiction of God on the Sistine Chapel ceiling.

But I must admit, as a child there was something comforting about the church. I loved the peacefulness of the architecture, the stained-glass windows, the candlelight and the smell of frankincense. The music and the ceremonies were calm and otherworldly. A world I could get lost in, despite the life-size replica of that sadistic God's bloody son hanging from a cross over the altar. Catholics are so theatrical. But it was the other paintings and statues I really loved. Mother Mary in her soft blue and white robes with a crown of golden stars on her brow, holding her arms out, inviting me to her embrace. Scruffy old Joseph holding the smiling baby Jesus, as if I was a guest at his first birthday party. Full-sized sculptures and paintings of the saints, always looking up with an expression of bliss on their face, even as their stories told of their suffering and martyrdom. They looked and spoke of a transcendental experience; a direct knowledge of God that enabled them to rise above physical and emotional pain with the courage to endure any of life's challenges.

I believed in the saints and the angels. I wanted to be a saint. Not, "Oh, look at me, aren't I good and a special person," but I wanted the experience they were having. I could see auras and sensed celestial presence at a very early age. I didn't know what an aura was, but I could always see a four- to six-inch white halo of energy outlining everyone, including the priest on the pulpit, at Sunday Mass. I used to think it was Jesus, if it was the priest, or the person's guardian angel behind them. I never shared this with anyone. What am I, nuts?

Like most good Catholics, I received the sacrament of confirmation at age thirteen. The essential part of the Confirmation rite is when the bishop or priest places his hands upon the head of the confirmee. It was the obligation of every baptized person in the Catholic faith to be confirmed, so that the priest could seal the deal with the Holy Spirit. It was sort of a Catholic's bar or bat mitzvah, one's rite of passage into spiritual adulthood. I will point out we do not know exactly when, during his public life, Jesus instituted the sacrament of Confirmation. As St. John tells us (see John 21:25), this is one of the "many other things that Jesus did," which are not in the Gospels. In other words, made up by the Church. Be it as it may, when we are confirmed, we take on a name of a saint. My name was Teresa.

Her story goes something like this: As a Carmelite nun, she lived a cloistered, simple life of prayer, meditation, and service to the sick. In those days a woman's options were limited to whore, domestic worker, or breeder, so considering those prospects, I think she made a wise choice. St. Teresa, we were taught, "had a great intimacy with God." Which when you think about it, put that way, sounds a bit pervy; but nuns did believe they were married to Christ, so who knows? Rooted in her belief of His merciful love, she remained faithful to God for her whole twenty-four years of life. That was the archetype they now confirmed me to follow.

Having muddled my way through eight years of primary school with dyslexia, I inelegantly entered my freshman year in high school. I was fourteen, and to the school's credit, they offered a comparative religions class. We studied Christianity, Judaism, Buddhism, Hinduism, etc. A lay teacher named Mr. Ore taught the class. He considered himself a theologian.

The·ol·o·gy; noun, the study of God.

Wait, would that be God (being all things) studying himself? Just a thought!

Mr. Ore was your classic geek. He had short black hair, a black mustache, black-rimmed glasses, black pants pulled up just below his chest, a black bowtie, with a white, short-sleeve shirt and a pocket pal. One day he was droning on about Hinduism when we came across a word in italics: *Nirvana!* I asked him what this word meant. He said, "Some yogis in India, through a certain practice of meditation, experience God directly—next question?" My life came to a grinding halt. "Is that true?" I asked. "Apparently!" he replied.

That had to be true, I thought. If God was all things and everywhere, then He had to be somewhere in me, and there had to be a way in. Then I immediately thought, *Well, if you know this, Mr. Ore, what the hell are you doing here?* That was the day my life changed forever.

CHAPTER 4

LIFT OFF

SPENT THE NEXT TWELVE years searching for nirvana. This was the sixties, and this kind of exploration was everywhere around me. We were the post-nuclear generation—mid-Vietnam War. Drugs, sex, and rock 'n' roll, especially in Los Angeles, offered the exodus from the shackles of conformity. Especially from the shallow, superficial, *Leave It to Beaver* lifestyle of our parents. This was *"the happening,"* baby, and one was either in it or part of the problem. I was either a far-out, bitchin' chick, stickin' it to the man, or might be left out of this awakening cultural movement. But here's the problem with that. I had one foot in a debutante's satin slippers, sipping tea at a charity event, and the other beaded and barefoot beneath my bell-bottoms in the sands of Topanga Beach.

Although my mother was an archetype of the liberated woman, she didn't really speak to me about how to navigate a life of independence. My parents were willing to pay for my college, but they never taught me anything practical. Oh, I learned how to draw and paint; I knew the ingredients of a Pimm's Cup and how to set a proper table. But I guess they didn't think I would need to know important things, like how to balance a checkbook, that you had to change the oil when the indicator light in the car goes on, or that the IRS is genuinely serious about you paying your taxes…let alone how to carve out a life-sustaining career. It seemed their real goal for me was to look, speak, and act suitably to catch and marry a wealthy man, preferably a lawyer, so SNiG had someone he could relate to. They didn't bother to tell me anything about sex. They were uneasy about that subject themselves. I guess they figured I would get that 411 on my wedding night. They didn't seem to pay attention to the vast movements happening within the culture, either. I was unarmed amid a revolution—women's rights, gay rights, the sexual revolution, racial equality, anti-war, a revolution against the "establishment," against the shallow ideals of the wealthy, white elites.

Coming from a life of privilege and raised in an all-girls, private Catholic school, I knew little or nothing about life. I hung out with my gangster brother and a lot of teenagers who were older than me. Everybody just assumed that I was cool because it was not cool to be uncool. And I wasn't about to tell them or ask questions. That would be uncool! So to be cool and accepted, I acted as if I knew what everybody was talking about. But I didn't—not really. I was told by the nuns, for example, that the greatest gift a woman could give her husband was her virginity. Not that they explained how that happened or

what your virginity was, specifically, or that that first endow-
ment would hurt like hell. I didn't know I had a vagina until I
overheard some girls talking about theirs at summer camp. But
I, like most adolescent girls, couldn't wait to become a woman,
and losing your virginity was that rite of passage. I was barely
sixteen when a twenty-one-year-old quarterback from Valley
State popped my cherry. Today, I would consider it consensual
rape. Sounds like a contradiction in terms.

I was in love with Jimmy. Every girl was. He was handsome and funny and popular in my circle of friends. So I was
honored to bestow onto him my gift, the coveted flower, the
infamous cherry of childhood. My older girlfriends plotted for
me to spend the night with him. It terrified me—but I never
let on. I consider it rape because I did not know what I was
consenting to. He got drunk that night and fell asleep. In the
morning he woke up and looked at me like I was a garage
for his morning wood. He rolled over on top of me and without foreplay, or as much as a kiss, he gave a few forced, painful thrusts and ejaculated. When he came, I seriously didn't
know what that was. I thought it was me. I was embarrassed.
I was afraid he thought there was something wrong with me,
like I was sick or something. Then the phone rang, he popped
out of bed, picked it up, said "Hold on," put his hand over
the receiver, eyed me with an expression like "What are you
still doing here?" and said, "Do you need a ride home?" That
excruciating ordeal was my initiation into the world of "free
love."

As I mentioned, cigarettes, alcohol, misogyny, and bigotry
were a part of the social mores of my early years; but all of that
was changing, like shifting sands. The cigarettes and alcohol
stayed, but marijuana, mushrooms, and psychedelics added to

the equation. Women's lib and sex were dramatically revolutionized with birth control and Roe v. Wade. Racism, misogyny, and bigotry were being challenged at every turn. An explosion of new thought, alternative ways of looking at things, seemed to disrupt the balance of society and often became uncomfortably polarizing.

I think this was the pivotal point in the schism of our society that led us to today and the uncompromising era of MAGA. Neoconservatives blame the adversarial counterculture of the sixties, which dismissed traditional values and religion as old-fashioned, irrelevant, or unprogressive. And I would agree; they are. But I can understand how, if your identity is not only being challenged but torn down and cast aside—if you are told you are wrong, that everything you believe in, everything you stand for, your entire programmed identity is wrong—you might feel threatened. After almost fifty years of this revolution, I'm not seeing too many white, Christian males suffering any more than the rest of us. But when the illusion of who they are in society is being displaced by people who they have been programed to believe are "less" than them, I can understand why the "old ways" would seem worth fighting for. Note: The word "programed" is key in that sentence, and I will delve into that at length as I continue. The white American male fantasizes that they are getting a taste of what women, LBGTQ, and minorities have felt for centuries. And it doesn't taste good. They maintain that liberal degeneration represents a real and present danger to *their* Western civilization.

Perhaps the idyllic *Leave it to Beaver* life, with the man as the breadwinner, while Mom is at home cooking, cleaning, and raising the children, is the vision that "Make America Great *Again*" is trying to recapture. But great for whom? Pregnant women in high heels with a toddler on their hip, standing at the stove in their starched apron, waiting for their man to grace them with his presence? Gays and queers who are forced to remain in the closet, out of sight, lest they be fired, ostracized, or beaten to death? And let's not even talk about transgenders. Abraham Lincoln may have technically freed the slaves, but Jim Crow laws oppressed the African American for another 100 years, making it near impossible to find a place of dignity, let alone equality in society. This MAGA model views anyone with a complexion darker than a latte, a pair of breasts, a foreign accent, or a symbol other than a cross around their neck as a second-class citizen and a threat to their idea of their White, European, Male-Dominated, Heterosexual Western Civilization.

While the left was going in one direction, the ideology of Ayn Rand, Milton Friedman, John Birch, James Buchanan, the evangelical Christians, the Mont Pelerin Society, and the Neoliberal movement simmered below the surface of conservative thought and has now regurgitated to the top of right-wing politics, economics, and culture. By the mid-eighties, during the Reagan era, Neoliberalism—the worship of free-market capitalism—had become the dominant ideology. We get it; we just don't accept it, not then and not now. In the words of Hamlet, "Therein lies the rub."

In theory, or perhaps in a perfect world, one benefit of a democratic society is the existence of institutions that constrain any abuse of one group over another. The federal government is the only power "We" the people have against such abuse. Yet one can understand why ideologues and corporations try to demolish the power that constrains them. If they can't do what they want, the next best thing is to buy and control the restrainer. A relatively small sect, including the Koch brothers, the Mercers, the Mellon family, the Heritage Foundation, the De Vos family, and others, were and still are part of a coalition of financial elites. This elite class doesn't really have a political party, although they tried to get Libertarian off the ground for years. Which would make sense. The Libertarian slogan is "No big government."

As the Liberals encouraged people to question established authority, criticize religion, and reject traditional beliefs, this elite clan realized that aligning themselves with neo-con ideology and fundamentalist Christians could work. The only way to gain control was to start a unified campaign to manipulate public opinion. They bought politicians, litigators, educators, talk radio, eventually cable television, and paid entertainers to arouse the disenfranchised population. While the hippies were listening to the Real Don Steele and rock 'n'roll on the radio, the conservatives and fundamentalists were feeding at the trough of Christian and conservative AM talk radio, where right-wing hosts such as Paul Harvey, Wally George, or Joe Pyne were dishing it out like rabid carnival barkers.

In 1987, after the FCC overturned the Fairness Doctrine—a policy that required the holders of broadcast licenses to present in a manner that was factual (novel idea), equitable, and balanced—the shit hit the fan. Once they removed that pesky little law, talk radio hosts like Rush Limbaugh were unleashed, which inspired a plethora of emotion-driven, batshit crazy, kabuki dancers to rile up the "base" into a mouth-frothing frenzy. Playing the long game, they transformed media in a way no one had ever seen or heard before. This conservative amalgamation financed think tanks and focus groups to fashion a well-crafted campaign to propagate the belief that liberal society had become amoral, adrift, and degenerate. Well played! And in some ways, I don't disagree. Revolutions are messy.

In my teenage years, I did my share of indulgences, including a lot of psychedelics. When I was tripping, I would get into lofty conversations with my stoned compadres about life, liberty, and that pursuit of God realization. For three years I lived with my boyfriend, Larry, in Santa Barbara. Larry and I spent most of our time playing and living a free-spirited life of rock concerts, psychedelics, skinny-dipping in the ocean at midnight, motorcycle rides in the hills, and deep conversations about reality, the Universe, and who we were in it.

This was a time of innocence and wonder. I didn't care for my parents' superficial interests, but I knew that this road would end, and I would have to get serious and start making a living on my own. ArtCenter College of Design was VERY SERIOUS. It focused strictly on commercial art. It was extremely difficult to get in and even harder to stay in; the attrition rate was immense. When I transferred from Brooks, in Santa Barbara, to ArtCenter, in Pasadena, I knew my days of free-spirit, drugs, sex, and rock 'n' roll were over. Larry wasn't ready to give that up, so I left him. In hindsight, I think he was the only man in my life who truly loved and appreciated me.

Soon after graduating from ArtCenter, I took my first proper job with a woman named VG. She was a self-made millionaire (at least on paper), and one of the most talented cons I'd ever met, but that story could be a book on its own. She had several greeting card lines, and a syndicated cartoon strip in over 100 newspapers in the country. She blew into LA one day, looking for an illustrator to complete the four children's books she had just written. She was a writer, but she signed our artwork as if it was hers. Basically, we were her ghost artists. Her last artist had gone cross-eyed.

I was a classically trained commercial artist—an illustrator. I had aspirations of doing movie posters, album covers, and magazine illustrations. Cartooning was beneath me, or so I thought. But it was a paying job, so pride be damned. She handed me $11,000, the key to a Beverly Hills apartment next door to Richard Simmons, and told me to furnish it, including a jacuzzi on the deck, a portable dance floor, and mirroring the entire living room wall. She jumped into her Cadillac convertible and yelled, "Finish the books, I'll be back in a few weeks." In hindsight, I seem to be a magnet for narcissists and cons. Working for her was like *The Devil Wears Prada* without the style. And that is how I was launched into my adult life.

CHAPTER 5

THE RAZOR'S EDGE

BY THE LATE SEVENTIES free love and the "good drugs" had taken an ugly turn. The "me generation" and the growth of cultural narcissism had emerged. Just as I was getting my adult feet wet, the disenchantment with idealistic politics crept onto the cultural landscape. After the assassination of the Kennedys and Martin Luther King, the brutal Manson murders, and the disappointment over the lies of Viet Nam, our illusion of Camelot was dying. Watergate and the resignation of Richard Nixon was the last nail in the coffin of our innocence. Unapologetic hedonism had replaced our flower power. The "free love" movement, which examined the notion that both men and women have the right to sexual pleasure without social or legal restraints, was now being corrupted by greed and marketing.

Pornography came out of the shadows and became a booming industry, and cocaine and harder drugs were the scene now. Even the music that was very much a part of my life transformed and became an obscenely lucrative industry. Gone were the days when some brilliant artists of folk and classic rock 'n' roll used rhythmic prose to express our collective message of peace and love, and many of those artists died along with the ideals. A dissention from the mainstream and popular culture sparked new genres of music that took wildly unprecedented forms of rebellion. Metal and punk rock created intensely amplified music and antiestablishment lyrics. Metal musicians derived inspiration from intellectuals and writers such as Tolkien, Nietzsche, Blake, and Milton. Punk is almost anti-method; speed, volume, and attitude were their style—mostly violent and angry.

If you weren't the black lipped, shocking-pink-spiked-hair, safety pin in your nose, mosh-pit type, there was always disco music: black rooms, strobe lights on mirrored balls circling on the ceiling, an endlessly pulsing, monotonous beat as we gyrated around the room in a cocaine-heightened frenzy. Hippies had become yuppies, and the sought-after hedonistic lifestyles of people like Hugh Hefner and the super-rich Hollywood and pop stars replaced the idols of the original cultural movement. Envy of the rich and famous pushed my generation to heights of ambition and competition. Movies and television reflected dramatic changes in our culture, and Madison Avenue had our psyche in its commercial talons.

There must have been a soul in all that self-indulgence, because many of us were trying to "find ourselves." In true entrepreneurial response, the self-help industry emerged and drove the expansion of this impulse. Scientology, EST, Hare

Krishnas, vegetarianism, and Eastern religious thinking were surfacing in the culture. Healthy lifestyle products became part of a growing economy. Gyms, health-minded restaurants, and little health-food stores were popping up everywhere in LA and Hollywood. Inspirational literature—such books as *Be Here Now* by Ram Dass, *The Mustard Seed* by Bhagwan Shree Rajneesh, or *The Razor's Edge* by W. Somerset Maugham—were being read or revisited. I would say *The Razor's Edge* was the antithesis of Ayn Rand's *Atlas Shrugged*. It was one of the first of many Western novels to propose non-Western solutions to society's ills. Its title comes from a passage from the Hindu sacred literature, the Upanishads: *"The sharp edge of a razor is difficult to pass over; thus the wise say the path to Salvation [Awakening] is hard."* The novel, although published in 1944, reflected an emergence in at least part of the culture of the search for the meaning of life and the dichotomy between materialism and spirituality

After a year in Beverly Hills, VG moved me to Miami. That was her home base, and although she traveled forty-four weeks out of the year, she wanted me there when she got home. I had become her artist, art director, interior decorator, chief cook and bottle-washer, even her lover for half a second. VG was a member of private disco clubs in Los Angeles, New York, and Miami. We would work all day till about ten PM, go out for dinner, then hit the clubs till four AM. She was a great disco dancer, and so was I. She was only six years older than me, and we had become like sisters.

The Miami lifestyle in the late seventies was pure decadence. This was the port of entry for Cuban refugees and a lot of cocaine. The culture was a mixture of boatpeople living under the freeways and super-rich drug cartels. Life in the fast lane! Despite my wild and adventurous escapades, I was not happy. Having met no one on my journey who had experienced God directly, disheartened I abandoned my search for nirvana. Oh, I read about it, and I listened to people telling me about this saint or that enlightened being in some distant time and place, but no one could look me in the eye and say, "I experience God directly." Until one night.

Life in the fast lane was not all it was cracked up to be. I loved to dance, and when I was out on the dance floor, under that mirrored ball, doing the Latin Hustle with some Cuban on his way to New York, I would lose myself for a few hours. But then the dawn came, VG and I would throw last night's pickup out of bed, and there I was alone and somewhat bitter that God had forsaken me.

One night I was at dinner with a friend. We were deep in conversation about life, liberty, and the pursuit of God realization. I was teaching him everything I had learned about that subject since I was fourteen, whether or not he wanted to hear it. Why? Cuz that's my style. I was recounting an epiphany I had once while on acid when I was seventeen. I described how I'd been watching colorful trails coming off my hands as I waved them back and forth, when I realized that my mind never stops. EUREKA! I thought to myself. *What is thought? Where does it come from? Wow, man, I think I may be onto something. Is this intangible voice in my head—God? This may be the secret to finding God within. If I just keep thinking about God and how to get there, perhaps my mind will eventually unlock the door.* I had the rude awakening sometime later that actually, the opposite may be the formula. Rats! I was starting to get this ruminating thing down, especially while on cocaine.

I was getting around to telling my friend of my great disappointment of not finding anyone who experienced God directly, when he said, "You need to meet Malila." "Who?" I asked. "Malila, she's this beautiful woman in South Miami who claims she experiences just that, God directly." He gave me her information and told me she gave Săt Săng every Thursday night at her house. "Săt Săng?" "Yes!" he said. "It's an Indian word meaning 'sharing of truth.' It's open to anyone," he told me, and suggested I check her out.

The following Thursday night came, and I drove to her little white house in South Miami. When I arrived, the streets were full of cars. I was late. Outside the house, on the front porch, was a sea of shoes. I took the hint, pulled mine off, and quietly slipped in the front door. The living room was packed. Wall to wall, people were silently sitting on the couch, in chairs, and cross-legged on the floor. There wasn't a vacancy anywhere, except an enormous wicker chair in the corner; so I sat in it. Everyone in the room shouted at me. "That's Malila's chair!"

Note: first spiritual faux pas—never sit in the guru's chair. That's like walking into a classroom and sitting at the big desk in the front of the class. I quickly jumped out of the chair and went tripping through the people, thinking *How do you like me so far?* until I nudged my way between two hippies wearing white cotton Nehru shirts, sitting in perfect *padmasana—* lotus position—on the floor, in front of the big wicker chair. We sat in silence for God knows how long (probably about four minutes). It seemed like hours, as my ankle bones were painfully becoming one with the hard wood floor. Some had their eyes closed, but not me. I kept staring at the wicker chair, expecting this Malila-Goddess to magically appear.

Nothin', bupkus, just an empty chair. Then out of the silence, one after the other, people in the crowd spoke in a vernacular I like to call the "Oh wow! Syndrome." "Oh wow, man, it's so beautiful!" *Really?* I thought. *More data dude, what was sooooo beautiful?* They just kept talking in this sickening, blissed-out, stoney, pseudo-spiritual jargon, saying absolutely nothing of relevance.

I had given what I considered a polite amount of time before I was ready to get up and quietly stumble my way out of there, when suddenly in a gap of silence, a woman's voice with a thick Spanish accent broke through from the back of the room. Sitting on the dining room table next to the living room was this gorgeous, thirty-something, blonde, ethereal female, dressed in loose, white linen pajamas. She was different than the rest of the spiritual mockups in the room, who had been droning on about nothing. This was Malila. No doubt. This was the woman I came to hear, and my mind shut up for the first time in my life. She wasn't afflicted with the "Oh wow! Syndrome." Her discourse was clear, humorous, and intelligent about her direct experience of God through the meditation practice she called "The Knowledge."

After her long sharing, everyone stood up and stretched. Soft ambient music played in the background, and several young women in colorful cotton pajamas and stoles scurried to the kitchen to get the "prăsăd." Prăsăd was food made while bathing in the love of God. It was customary to practice "open-eye meditation" during this time, where we would stare into each other's eyes for—EVER, then receive the offering from the tray of fruit, nuts, homemade dessert treats, or whatever vegetarian delight was available, while continuing to stare or "connect" till the next tray would come around, and we'd start the whole process over with someone else.

Malila was unapologetic and moved in a peaceful, loving stillness even when she was being playful. She seemed to float in grace and otherworldliness. All that time, I never saw her out of character. I didn't know what this "Knowledge" was, but as the line goes in *When Harry Met Sally*, I wanted what she was having. So I came to the little house in South Miami to Malila's Săt Săng every week. I felt like I had finally found people who understood my yearning. Even though they were still uncomfortably blissed-out, stoney weirdos, I felt I had found my tribe.

Malila was a big fan of Jesus, but she wasn't a "Christian," in the organized sense. She was disappointed in modern Christianity and how they distorted Jesus' teachings. Primarily the one about "Repent, for the kingdom of heaven is at hand." Repent, meaning, return, it's right here, not after death or in the heavens above, but within, and "The Knowledge" was the way in. She was touching right into my preconceived notions. I had no reason to disbelieve her, but I was agnostic about it. She sure was passionate and genuinely appeared to be experiencing something. I had experienced no one who lived that passion, at least not while not on a mind-altering drug. So why question her? Her stories were tales of hope and inspiration, something I'd had little of in my life, so far. And so I became an "aspirant"—one who aspires to "God realization."

Malila made her living as a certified hypnotherapist. I saw her once a week. I really liked hypnotherapy. We would work on things that were troubling me, and she would take me back in time to a place that matched the feelings I was having in the present. I would explore that past and the related repressed feelings and saw the patterns I may have brought with me into my adult life. I got a lot out of it. By the time I left a session, those things I was dealing with somehow resolved themselves. I could see myself and my child-self with more compassion and love. I felt heard, and she made me feel okay, for once in my life.

I had been with her for about a year and a half when she announced that she would give a "Knowledge session"— otherwise known as "an initiation"—in which she would open one's "third eye," teach the four techniques of meditation, and God within would be revealed. Prior initiates would speak in Săt Săng about the profound experience of the techniques of the "Knowledge." They would see the light of the Universe inside them, hear the word of God and the celestial music within, and taste the ambrosia of the Divine, the "nectar" that would make them drunk with unconditional love. Similar to the stories of the saints I had studied in my past. Finally I had come to the end of my search, and I felt a mixture of terror and excitement at the same time.

On the night of the Knowledge session, I arrived at the house, dressed in white. Shoes were strewn about on the front porch. I took mine off, as usual, and tried to open the door, but it was locked. I knocked softly. Malila answered. She was particularly blissed-out that night, and she asked me, "What do you want?" I said, "I want to know God." She looked at me and said, "You are not ready yet, but there will be other initiations—keep coming to Săt Săng," and she shut the door.

My heart stopped. It felt like it fell out of my chest in slow motion and plunged into an inky pool of black liquid. For over a decade, I had been seeking. At last I had come to the door of my journey's end, only to have it slammed in my face. Tears rolled down my cheeks in rivulets, as I gathered my shoes and crawled off the cold porch and away from that house, bare-footed. I don't know how I got there, but I found myself on a golf course. Walking on the fairway under the moonlight, bawling and pleading with God. I walked and walked on that dew-drenched lawn till after three AM. Racking my brain to understand why I was not acceptable. This reeked of first grade. But how much more ready could I be? Where did I go wrong?

Not a tear was left by the time I exhausted myself into submission. Maybe this is just a test of my faith, I thought. Okay!…okay, I can take it. Whatever it takes. This is God, after all. You can't just walk in and experience God directly, even if you have been searching your whole life, and maybe I just hadn't reached the level of devotion needed. I did sit in the guru's chair. And with all the indulgences of my past, purity was not my strong suit. In hindsight, perhaps it was my personality. When everything I say comes in the form of a dissertation, it's hard to look humble. The words of Saint Teresa echoed in my mind: "Patience obtains all!" Maybe this was my razor's edge, I thought. Well, St. Anthony locked himself in a cave for years, forced to be tortured by demons, before he had union with God. So fine—I'll be patient.

CHAPTER 6

ON THE ROAD TO DAMASCUS

WHEN THE APOSTLE PAUL converted to Christianity after allegedly meeting Jesus, he was literally on the road to Damascus from Jerusalem. But the expression "Road to Damascus" also refers to a sudden turning point in one's life, and this chapter describes my turning point.

Not long after that dreadful night in Florida and my failure to initiate, I moved back to LA. Life with VG was getting unbearable. Narcissists always start out with the con, luring you in with empty promises, and once they have you—in her case sequestering me in another state—they can do what they want: use, abuse, and exploit you. I don't think they are even aware of it. Most narcissists feel that just being in their presence is reward enough to sustain you. She paid a pauper's wage and my finances were in dire straits, so I needed to go home.

There I was, back in Brentwood with Kay and SNiG. I felt empty and lost living in LA again. I missed my pack of weirdos. At least with them, we talked about deeper things than the virtues of buying wholesale and meeting my next wealthy suitor. One night a friend of the family's came over to borrow a cummerbund from SNiG. He was going to the annual Hunt Ball. I was helping him tie his bowtie when he said, "You ride, don't you?" I said, "It's been a long time, but yes. Why?" "We're going foxhunting tomorrow morning," he answered. "Do you want to join us?" "Fox hunting?" I said. "Where—down Wilshire Boulevard?" He laughed and said, "Well, technically, we hunt coyote, and tomorrow it will be on the Ahmanson ranch in the Valley. It's formal attire, so get your britches out and dust off your boots. I'll pick you up at seven-thirty." *Okay,* I thought, *this should be interesting.*

The family friends picked me up in the morning, and we drove out past Thousand Oaks to the Ahmanson ranch. Los Angeles and the cityscape disappeared behind us as we snaked up the winding road, past miles of rich, green rolling hills and sprawling oak trees. I was reminded of my time in the hills of Santa Barbara, on the back of Larry's motorcycle. We approached a cluster of horse trailers in the middle of an open field. Riders in full regalia, with black velvet hard hats, black coats, yellow vests, and white stock ties, and a few men wearing scarlet coats were mounting their horses. There he was— the huntsman, David, dressed in his scarlet coat with blue collar, and black shiny boots with brown cuffs. Every detail of the hunt attire is significant and determines your rank in the field. In those days, only men could wear scarlet. Women who had achieved equal skill and rank were only permitted to wear blue coats.

David resembled Lloyd Bridges, and seated on his seventeen-hand steed, blowing his horn and commanding this elite field of horses, hounds, and riders, he was just too romantic for me to ignore. He was considerably older than me and resembled my uncle Bob. I know—I can see Freud stroking his beard as I recount the tale. I knew it, and Mom knew it. But even though he was older and not in the class my parents were hoping for, I was fulfilling my latent *National Velvet* tendencies. Horses were often my escape as a child. I loved them, and Mom told me that Grandpa and my uncles had put me on a horse before I could walk.

David was a famous steeplechase champion, the huntsman for a hunt club, and a wrangler for Hollywood. I dated and eventually moved in with him at his ranch in the Valley. I was smitten with him and his Uncle-Bob-like, last of the great manly man's character. He was simple, yet possessed skills that most men, especially those urban cowboys in the club, only dreamed of. Those men were rich and usually full of themselves, but in the hunt field, they were all like little boys admiring their hero. I helped David school some of his stunt horses for films and was his chief staff, known as a whip, for the hunt club. We even wrangled in a fox-hunting scene in a *Murder She Wrote* episode. He and I were both mounted marshals in the 1984 Olympics. That was a spectacular honor I'll never forget. Those were the days of fantasy and simple country living.

Although life on the ranch was thrilling and being out in nature with the animals was good for my soul, David had limited interests, and I didn't have many other friends. Some considered I was "sleeping with the help." Seriously? When I wasn't with my horses, I would go into the hills and meditate. I didn't feel comfortable about doing it in front of anyone around the ranch. It wasn't really their schtick. I was so hungry for deep, spiritual connection.

For a while I secretly attended the Church of Religious Science/Science of Mind, a New Age church. I would speak to Malila by phone occasionally and tell her how I missed Săt Săng. One day she called and told me about a friend of hers who had been initiated and was giving Săt Săng at his house in Hollywood on Sundays. His name was Michael Basleon. He was a stage actor, and a lovely, kind gay man.

I started going to his house every Sunday. There were only about three or four of us who attended regularly, but at least it was something. One Sunday Michael introduced an attractive man in his late thirties, named Michel, who was visiting from Florida. Michel was like this golden boy, wearing tight jeans and nothing but a little colorful vest. Michel was short but well-built and had a soft glow of bronze radiating off his bare muscles. We shared Săt Săng that night and afterwards we all went into the kitchen for some tea and prăsăd. The gatherings were a lot less formal at Michael's house. Michel, Michael, and I had a very pleasant encounter, talking and drinking tea for quite some time. I didn't see Michel again until two years later.

Meanwhile, back at the ranch, things were splendid. I loved living a simple life in the country with David, the horses, and the other animals. But I was wondering if this was what I wanted for the rest of my life. I was torn. Not long after that I found out I was pregnant. When I told David, he froze like a deer in headlights. He was already a grandfather, and he stated that under no circumstances would he ever marry again. I was a freelance artist, and in no way able to support myself and a child. I tried to talk to him about my options, but he would not contribute to any commitment or solution. I thought about this old man and this tiny, one-bedroom house (the entire house would have fit in my parent's lanai), and I couldn't imagine this would be my last stop. I begged him to help me make this critical decision. He said nothing. I looked him in the eyes and said, "If you make me make this decision alone, I will, but I will never forgive you." So I decided; the process was brutal. He paid for the abortion, and we never spoke of it again.

I met a woman, a television actress who was a recent member of the hunt club. We got to know each other, and the one thing we had in common was spirituality. We loved our conversations because no one else in either of our lives was interested in these deeper thoughts. She lived in a fabulous condo in Hollywood and she offered me the opportunity to live in her loft. One day, shortly after that invitation, David came in grumbling about the owners of the hunt club. It was time for his contract renewal and awards for the various ranks. He had suggested to the committee that I deserved a scarlet coat. He had argued that because I had represented the club in the Olympics; I was one of the best whips they ever had; and I'd won multiple steeplechase races representing the club, I deserved that honor.

They said no. He threatened to quit if they didn't bend this archaic, sexist rule. While honored and grateful that he was sticking up for me, I was also pissed that these pretentious little boys seemed threatened by me, that they wanted to keep me in my place, even though I had worked hard, without pay, for years, to help David raise and train the hounds for their sport. A scarlet coat was petty, perhaps, but it was the principle of the thing. It was precisely at that moment that I blurted out, "I'm tired of the politics; I will move out." I used that silly incident as my excuse to quit. David and I looked at each other with shock. I could see by his face he knew this was the end of our relationship. I realized that I had just moved on and left him and my *National Velvet* life forever.

I moved into my friend's condo, and we lived a fun but wild life. One day I received a phone call from a guy with a very thick, strange accent. He said he was a friend of Malila's and that he had a letter from her. I suspected the letter was about money. I owed her a little from hypnotherapy and her son was in the hospital, so I assumed she was collecting. I told him to drop it in the mail, but he said he had to deliver it in person. I gave him my address, and when he came to the door I took the letter and was about to close the door when he said he needed to wait for an answer. He seemed familiar, but I wasn't really paying much attention. I invited him in, and he sat in a chair while I sat on the couch reading the letter. Just as I suspected, he was there to collect. I explained to him I was working on a job and I should have the money for her in a few weeks. He smiled and said, "I'm sure that would be fine."

I looked up at him and found him staring at me. Then I realized this was Michel, the golden boy I had met at Michael's two years before. I locked into his eyes in the traditional "open eye meditation," and suddenly he turned into light particles. Seriously, he looked like Scotty (in *Star Trek*) was beaming him up. My first thought was *Oh, great, I'm having an old acid flash with this stranger melting all over my friend's chair, and I'm crying poor, as I'm living in this very expensive condominium with a real Renoir on the wall.*

I can't explain the phenomenon; it was strange and very real. I hadn't seen Michael Basleon in a while, so I broke the silence and asked how he was. Michel told me that Michael had died. Apparently he'd been doing a play in New York and had a massive heart attack. I was stunned! In hindsight, I'm not even sure if that was true.

Michel told me he had moved to LA and invited me to an acting class he was giving on Monday nights. He shared some details about the class and encouraged me to check it out. He stood up, held out his arms to hug me, and said, "Well, I guess I came for more than just money." We both chuckled, and he left.

When my girlfriend came home, I told her what had happened and how this guy dissolved into light right there in her living room. I recall vividly how uncanny the encounter was, and I tried to explain it to her. Michel's energy was very much like Malila's. He was peaceful and otherworldly. He was kind and intelligent, with a wonderful sense of humor. He was gay, so I didn't get any vibe that he was hitting on me. He seemed like a safe, interesting new friend.

I avoided going to his class for several weeks. I was working on that project and I guess I was just procrastinating. He would call me periodically, get into a friendly bit of small talk, we'd laugh about whatever, and then he'd try to coax me into coming by laying on some spiritual argument, like "Be sure you aren't denying what your heart really knows it wants." I'm paraphrasing (or come to think of it, maybe not; that sounds exactly like one of his lines). Such was his typical spiritual jargon.

I finally agreed, and I went the following Monday. There were about twelve, maybe fifteen people in the class. I noted that Michel had several psycho/spiritual and actors' work-shop books, from Ouspensky and Gurdjieff to Strasberg. He put us through very interesting but intense exercises. I have a vague memory of the exercise I took part in that first night. I don't remember the specifics, but I remember crying in front of all those strangers.

After class I was heading to my car when three initiates came up to me. They were friendly and sweet, and I took an instant liking to them. They told me they recognized me as a sister—that they felt like they had known me for ages and that I belonged with them. They invited me to Săt Săng at their house on Thursday. I told them I had just signed up to the Science of Mind seminary classes on Thursdays. They laughed. "Science of Mind? That's exactly what it is," they said. "Of the mind. You can't find God through the mind. Learn to drop your mind/ego to experience God directly." I liked them, and I felt we had just shared a deep experience in the class exercise. I agreed to come on Thursday.

And so it began—a twenty-two-year journey into what seemed like an endless Fellini film.

SECTION 2

THE BUDDHA-FIELD

CHAPTER 7

"THE KNOWLEDGE" AND THE "SHAKTI SCAM"

THE GOLDEN BOY HAD several names throughout the years: Jaime, Andreas, Dorothy, Cindy, Bob, Jeff, and Puff (as in the magic dragon). I kid you not. That was when he was incognito. It seemed more conspicuous to me, but the numerous name changes were an example of his developing paranoia. He probably had a few more names after he fled to Hawaii, but his real name was Jaime Gomez, LOL, hardly a fitting name for how he thought of himself. His final selection was "RayJi," which literally means God King, so from here on, I will call him—Jaime Gomez.

In the beginning, Jaime was just a seed of what he would eventually become. Back in the early days in LA, he appeared to be independent and self-reliant. His disciplined spiritual life inspired me from the start. I just wanted to hang out with this guy. At first it was never about him; it was all about the four meditation techniques known as the "Knowledge" (he later changed the name to the "Knowing"), how to aspire to it, get ready to receive it, and how to devote your life to it. This was the topic of all Săt Săngs, and the initiates would spend hours every week describing their experiences in significant detail. My Knowledge session (initiation), during which he showed me the techniques, was in 1984.

The experience was profound and confusing at the same time. It was not what I expected. I don't really know what I expected, but it shattered my Catholic perception of a God experience. On the night of the initiation, he pressed his fingers onto the center of my forehead and my closed eyes. It hurt like hell; then I became nauseous. At first there was nothing but pain and darkness. I saw a tiny pinhole, and sharp rays of light flashing though it; then suddenly the hole opened, and a startling blast of light burst through.

MentalFloss.com describes what's really happening when we see stars after rubbing our eyes or when our eyeballs are pressed: "Spurts of seemingly random intense and colorful lights known as phosphenes appear due to electrical discharges from the cells inside our eyes that are a normal part of cellular function." But this wasn't like the usual light you see when you rub or press on your eyes. After the light explosion, it started rushing towards me inside, as though I was flying down a wormhole in outer space. Colors and geometric shapes whizzed by. It reminded me of the old Dolby Sound System ads in theaters before the show. It was exhilarating and nauseating at the same time.

The day after, I emerged and walked outside. Everything was in light particles. It could have been eye damage; who knows. But the trees and the plants were sparkling, and the colors were brighter, with luminous hues—similar to my LSD experiences, only softer, and more subtle. The nausea subsided, and I had a feeling of bliss and a warm, floating stillness. Note of caution: Don't try this at home.

My experience was very much coming from within. I don't believe it had anything to do with Jaime. And in the beginning, he didn't imply that it did. He taught us that our direct experience of God-within was our "Divine birthright" revealed through meditation—that no one can give this to us because it is already who we are, and God's grace only shall determine to what magnitude it will manifest. He even said at the start of our initiation that he had nothing to do with it. He was just the assistant, "the midwife," as he put it.

Although the experience was very real, it was temporary. Sometimes it would last for an hour, sometimes only for a few minutes, sometimes not occur at all. And each person had varying degrees of transcendental ecstasy. Some confessed to me they experienced nothing—ever. Yet, even though they didn't experience a damn thing, they would mimic what they heard in Săt Săng and share how incredible their experience was. I get it! If every initiate in the room is describing these fantastic experiences of the Divine light, music, the holy word, and the nectar—and bear in mind there were a lot of benefits to being an initiate within the hierarchy of the community—you were not about to be the only "Holy Company *in the Knowing*" (as it was referred to) who didn't experience the "Knowing." No one wants to be the dud.

I could connect to those techniques and get that experience in fluctuating degrees, and not all the time. It was random, with no rationale. I believe those who didn't experience the "knowing" might have been afraid to admit it to Jaime. I know for me, one night I was walking him home from class and I asked him about my meditations. He whirled around in a sudden tirade and accused me of being ungrateful and full of ego. I wasn't surrendered enough, he said, and my selfish desire for a higher experience was preventing me from having one. That was the first, and last, time I ever brought that up to him. But I sadly believed it, and I judged myself harshly, as a failure, when experiences were dry.

The Buddha-field considered themselves a "mystery school," a body of initiates who had dedicated themselves to preserving, protecting, and perpetuating the age-old mystery teachings. Before our initiation we would take our vows. We vowed to stay devoted and practice the daily meditation, never reveal the techniques to anyone, practice selfless service, stay true to the "master's" teaching, and keep "holy company," which was how we referred to ourselves.

There was a hierarchy within the group. The original initiates "in the Knowing" had moved to West Hollywood from Florida and lived together in an enormous house they called Harper House, where Săt Săng was held. Jaime may have been the guide, but the real disciplinarian was Ben, Jaime's first disciple from Florida. He was hell bent on creating a modern-day ashram, right there in the heart of West Hollywood. Jaime lived in a small apartment by himself, a few blocks away. He still had guys cook and clean for him, and do his errands, but he drove his own car and frequently indulged in the West

Hollywood gay disco scene. I didn't realize until much later that he was a textbook narcissist.

I will support the examples of this in the upcoming chapters with pedantic dribbles of academic rhetoric, just to put things in context. Each section is preceded by a sentence or two in bold italics taken from *The Diagnostic and Statistical Manual of Mental Disorders* (5th edition), the standard used by mental health professionals. The DSM-V describes narcissism and sociopathy as follows:

> **Narcissistic personality disorder** *is a pervasive pattern of grandiosity (in fantasy or behavior), need for admiration.... Exploitation, Entitlement, Empathy-Impairment.*

> **Antisocial personality disorder (sociopathy)** *is a pervasive pattern of disregard for and violation of the rights of others.*

> **Malignant Narcissistic Personality Disorder:** *Includes Psychopathy. [which is] defined as a lack of empathy not just empathy-impairment.*

> **Narcissists use excessive charm and are always plausible and convincing when peers, superiors or others are present (charm can be used to deceive as well as to cover for lack of empathy).**

Jaime was humorous and seemed to be wise, in the beginning, and he encouraged us to get out of our comfort zone. If you couldn't sing, he would push you to sing as if no one was listening. If you couldn't dance, he would dance with you. He created games and exercises wherever we were. For example, in the film *Holy Hell,* the scene of us all dancing around in the forest depicts an exercise in which we were exploring being forest creatures. What was it like to be a squirrel, or an eagle, a mouse or a wolf? We would become those creatures. Really feel what it was like to see the world from their perspective—predator or prey.

Later, we would discuss our experience. We explored such questions as: When does our personality reflect those characteristics in our lives? When were we being a predator? When did we feel like prey? How did we bring those assumed identities into our daily lives, and how could we be more aware of them when they took over? These were characters—masks we took on to learn from. We were searching for our authentic selves rather than the identities we wear in society to fit in.

We also became trees or seaweed, or other aspects of nature, fantasizing being cut down or polluted so we could empathize with our world, to love it more compassionately. Sometimes we would do an exercise in which we would go through the death process and be reborn. Jaime gave us the opportunity to explore being playful and curious—uninhibited, unashamed. This differed from the traditional spiritual teacher or priest, who had made me, and others, feel shame and suppress our playful, natural nature. Jaime never took part himself, however; he would just observe.

We trusted him and allowed him to push us beyond our boundaries. And in spite of him, we got a lot out of it. We were doing the hard work of self-examination and deep reflection while trusting him and each other to be that vulnerable and open. Most people spend their lives avoiding looking at themselves and facing the false identities they have come to depend on. Many folks spend a lifetime in distraction and addictions to one thing or another so as not to see who they really are; the light *and* the dark side of our dual human nature. The problem was he never allowed us to go beyond that. He never allowed anyone to graduate. He just used our group exercises as a tool to manipulate us. He figured out that lowering or removing our boundaries could be of benefit to him.

Evidently, when one is trying to get sexual or other favors, to gratify their own insatiable ego, boundaries can be a hazard. Train your victims to be willing; *complicit*. Jaime used the word "surrender" a lot. We even had a beloved song we sang all the time. "Surrenderrr when love comes calling, surrenderrr there'll be no more falling, your heart knows when it's time to come home, no more misery for you, when you surrenderrr." Blah, blah blah. Doesn't that sound lovely? Almost like a lullaby. "Surrender your ego," he would say; "surrender your desires." Surrender your will, your instinct, your morals, your body, mind, and soul, for the false promise of freedom, enlightenment, and a loving community, for which many of us were searching.

But isn't that what an authoritarian dictator does to their supporters? They offer the promises of freedom, safety, and prosperity; and nationalistic or tribal belonging. In Iran in the 1970s for example, immediately after the revolution, it was clear that most Iranians followed Khomeini to enjoy the freedoms and the "better life" he promised. Most Iranians were misled, however, because at that time few understood Khomeini's real plans and motives. The same is true in other cases of populist favor for authoritarian strongmen. To label MAGA supporters as merely "deplorables" is to neglect their hidden motivations. Supporters of "Making America Great Again" saw Trump as leading them to greater freedom and glory as members of the superior tribe. "We gonna win so much you may even get tired of winning and you'll say please, please, Mr. President, it's too much winning! We can't take it anymore!" Who is he talking to? People who perceive themselves as winners already? No! He has to first convince them they are losers, underdogs, outcasts, victims. Hitler started his vision of a new and better Germany with the premise that the Jews were stabbing Germany in the back. Trump started his campaign with "Other countries are taking advantage of us." He painted a grim and frightening picture: "Illegal immigrants are coming in caravans. They're bringing in drugs, they're bringing in crime, they're rapists."

Authoritarian leaders determine their followers' desires and fears and capitalize on them. They convince the followers that "they alone can fix it." Hitler portrayed himself as this extra-human leader. They lull them into surrender—to surrender their ability to question, surrender critical thinking, surrender their morals, compassion, truth, and justice. The followers are open and willing to be seduced—duped in exchange for lies and empty promises. And if you don't surrender to such leaders, you become the enemy and they will not stop until they destroy you.

Narcissists often fraudulently claim qualifications, experience, titles, entitlements or affiliations which are ambiguous, misleading, or bogus.

Jaime was a complete fraud and a cheat in every aspect. A total con! He even had disciples do the studying and write his dissertation for his Religious Doctorate, so he could get a certificate as a religious pastor. Trump paid for someone to take his SATs, and his sister did his homework. Hitler was an out of work artist. Mussolini was a journalist. Myth-making is a common dictator characteristic. Lies and outlandish stories help build a bigger-than-life persona. Papers published exaggerated stories in which Mussolini wasn't at all tired after threshing for four hours and myths of winning boat races. Vladimir Putin goes face to face with tigers, and even bears fear him. Narendra Modi fearlessly rescues crocodiles. Saddam Hussein had a movie made about how he walked a thousand miles from Syria to Egypt with a bullet in his leg, after his alleged heroic assassination of Abd al-Karīm Qāsim, the Iraqi prime minister. Their followers are eased into a collective suspension of disbelief, accepting their tall tales despite any demonstrable evidence—or even in the face of evidence to the contrary.

In the beginning Jaime's sharing was always about the "Knowledge." He stole these techniques from Prem Pal Singh Rawat, aka Maharajji, another narcissistic cult leader. Jaime was never a disciple of Maharajji; he lied and conned a Premi (one of Maharajji's followers) into giving him the techniques. Later, when it looked as if his guru gig was taking off, Jaime changed the name from the "Knowledge" to the "Knowing." He told a tale about how he went into the cosmos for three days and he needed to change the name, but the truth was he needed to claim it as his own, erasing any connection to any other spiritual leader. At that point things really went downhill.

As the years went by, the group started sharing about their devotion, not to God or the "Knowing," but to him. The "Oh wow, it's so beautiful!" syndrome had morphed into "Oh wow, YOU'RE so beautiful." When Jaime started giving "Shakti," his narcissism fully bloomed. At first, at the end of Săt Săng, people would line up, kneel in front of him, and give him Prasăd, then move on to the next person, as usual. Suddenly, one night he gave "Shakti" by sticking his finger on their forehead and jiggling it, as if it was energy coming from him. Bullshit! Jaime stole this technique from Swami Muktananda, another well-known Indian guru.

When Jaime touched your forehead, one of his helpers pushed against your back from behind. He would shove our heads so briskly and back so far it felt like it would snap off. One time I asked him if the person behind could hold the back of my head, because it was very painful on my neck. I have a congenital fusion of the four and fifth vertebrae. He didn't allow it. I realize now that he had no interest in anyone's comfort but his own—no doubt testing our willingness to suffer for his sadistic pleasure and carnival act. When he would shake his finger on some people's forehead, many would unleash this wild gyration. This is not to say that they didn't believe they were having a genuine experience, but if they were it wasn't because of him. It was all a farce, a collective hypnosis.

Jaime loved these theatrical displays, the more dramatic the better. I hated them, because the experience of the "Knowledge" which, after receiving the techniques, was your own, was being put on the back burner, and Shakti was now a quick, cheap experience that the followers thought they could only get directly from him. So much for the midwife.

The original ideals of these meditation practices and "God-realization" were eroding in front of my eyes. It was quite the spectacle. Sometimes, when I witnessed people gyrating and shaking, I just wanted to tell them, "Oh pleeeze, knock it off!" Did I ever say that? Nope! Should I have? Sure, under normal circumstances. Would it have done any good? Oh, hell no! Would they have annihilated me? Absolutely!

Because of their own ego-projection, their followers— or at least some of them—resort to antagonistic and slanderous behavior whenever their guru is challenged or shown to be false; hence the unpleasant phenomenon of the slanderous devotee.

The Narcissistic Delusional Guru—Definition
http://www.kheper.net/index.htm

I was afraid I'd end up like Simon in the book *Lord of the Flies*. Simon is killed by the group after he discovers the truth about the imaginary beast that frightens the boys. He wants to tell the others that the beast is in all of them, is part of them. My analogy may sound a little dramatic, but we all judged and rebuked anyone who crossed or even disrespected our God King. And symbolically, if you left the Buddha-field, the message was you were dead, at least to your community.

Narcissists excel at deception and should never be underestimated in their capacity to deceive.

Jaime used to give a "Knowing" session every year, but after he started the Shakti scam, he gave only one more session; then he stopped offering it all together, for eighteen years. Yet he used it as a dangling carrot over people for all that time, just to keep them on the hook and under control. The elders who were initiated used it as a ranking privilege, and some were not as impressed by Shakti. That's when he upped his game, and his charade became more sophisticated.

He stopped giving "Shakti" in the public Săt Săng room for all to see. He moved it into a private room with one or two members of his closest entourage assisting. Because some people were not experiencing anything from his Shakti (not a wonder), he would make them kneel in front of him and close their eyes. Then he used a flashlight and flickered it back and forth on their eyelids, while he jiggled his finger on their forehead. Upon seeing the light, they were astounded, some to the point of tears. They would come out of the Shakti room, crying and smiling and ready to tell the tale of how they saw "the light." They saw the light all right—furnished by Eveready. Did the witnesses of this come forward and tell what they knew? Nope! I was not aware of this till years after I left the Buddha-Field.

One time he pulled that parlor trick on me, only with a twist. Swami Muktananda often talked about the "blue pearl" in his books. According to him and other swamis, the essence of the soul sometimes manifests in blue light inside you. During a Shakti session, Jaime shined a blue light on my eyelids. The next day he called and asked me if I saw the blue pearl. "Yes," I said. I felt so special. Few people saw the "blue pearl;" that was reserved for the highest, most revered disciples. As W. C. Fields used to say, "Never give a sucker an even break!"

But Jaime's shenanigans are microscopic compared to the hustlers in history who have led to so much misery and human suffering. Jim Bakker; creator of the PTL (Praise the Lord organization), was convicted of fraud and conspiracy charges after illegally soliciting millions of dollars from his followers. Former president of the National Baptist Convention, USA, Inc. Henry Lyons was convicted for racketeering and grand theft. Sun Myung Moon, leader of the Unification Church, was imprisoned for criminal tax fraud in the 1980s. Or how 'bout David Yonggi Cho, founder of Yoido Full Gospel Church, who was sentenced to three years in prison for embezzling 13 billion won (the equivalent of US $12 million) in church funds, in 2014? Trump's inventory of scandals and fraudulent activity reads like Bernie Madoff's Christmas list. He routinely exaggerates his net worth; he inflates his assets to lenders, yet grossly undervalues his income when declaring taxes. "It really feels like there's two sets of books—it feels like a set of books for the tax guy and a set for the lender," said Kevin Riordan, a finance expert and real estate professor at Montclair State University who reviewed Trump's records.

The illusion of all those buildings with Trump's name on them makes it appear that he has a vast empire of real estate, but his secret to his asset mirage is to create a brand and license it. Take, for example, the Trump Ocean Club International Hotel and Tower in Panama City. Trump doesn't own it. Roger Khafif owned it. Khafif couldn't get financial backing, so he licensed the Trump name, which cost him more than a third of the money raised. Straining under $2.2 million in unauthorized debts run up by Trump's management company, who paid undisclosed bonuses to its executives and withheld financial information from Khafif, he was finally forced to declare bankruptcy, while Trump made money.

This example of Trump as fraudster is the tip of the iceberg. Given his Mafia ties, multiple bankruptcies, tax evasion, hiring undocumented workers to avoid paying union benefits, violating casino operating rules, antitrust violations, refusing to pay workers, Trump University scam, using donor money to buy up his own books, masquerading as a publicist to brag about himself, violating 501(c)3 self-dealing rules by creating a phony charity foundation, decades of illegal dealings with Cuba, quid pro quo exchanges with Russia and Ukraine, paying off porn stars, and so many sex and pedophilia scandals, it's hard to keep up. But like those of us in the Buddhafield, none of that matters to his followers. Members of a cult of personality convince themselves that the leader is exceptional and therefore can do exceptional things. Stepping outside the parameters of social norms (or the law as the case may be), is rationalized as just smart business, and bucking the system is what makes tough-guy, authority figures powerful. Devoted followers refuse to see the little men behind the curtain.

CHAPTER 8

MEMOIRS FROM FELLINI

SOMETIMES WHEN YOU'RE STRINGIN' beads, you come to the middle and add the centerpiece; then you have to start stringin' them from the other side to balance it out. Now is an excellent time to start from the end instead of the beginning. Let's first do a quick recap. This is a story about a spiritual community that started in Florida, moved to LA, then to Austin, and finally landed in Hawaii. After twenty-some years it came to light that the conspicuously gay teacher was sexually abusing many of the members. What a surprise! It's a tale as old as civilization. Narcissistic leader turns community of followers into a cult. That about sums it up.

I can imagine professional psychologists must hate it when amateurs define others by using big, diagnostic labels like narcissist or sociopath. But I figure, I spent twenty-five years of my adult life with a narcissistic, sociopathic leader, so I consider myself an armchair authority on the subject. Nothin' like that up-close-and-personal experience to give one a unique perspective. That being said, I will call upon a few professionals to help me out. In the book *The Sociopath Next Door* by Martha Stout, PhD, the author opens with a chilling description of a sociopath.

> Imagine—if you can—not having a conscience, none at all, no feelings of guilt or remorse no matter what you do, no limiting sense of concern for the well-being of strangers, friends, or even family members. Imagine no struggles with shame, not a single one in your whole life, no matter what kind of selfish, lazy, harmful, or immoral action you had taken. And pretend that the concept of responsibility is unknown to you, except as a burden others seem to accept without question, like gullible fools. Now add to this strange fantasy the ability to conceal from other people that your psychological makeup is different than theirs. Since everyone simply assumes that conscience is universal among human beings, hiding the fact that you are conscience-free is nearly effortless. You are not held back from any of your desires by guilt, or shame, and you are never confronted by others for your cold-bloodedness. The ice water in your veins is so bizarre, so completely outside of their personal experience, that they seldom even guess at your condition.

When I left the Buddha-field, a cascade, like dominoes, of other pillars of the community left, one by one. When suddenly those elders were no longer there, it was very noticeable, and their departures created a firestorm that collapsed the community in a matter of weeks. A narcissistic sociopath will turn those who support him against those who do not. War broke out between the "innies" and the "outies." In Trump fashion, Jaime demonized me and anyone who opposed him, and he used subterfuge at every turn to cover up his lies, sexcapades, and deception.

After we ran him out of Austin, one member put together a website, and many ex-members shared their stories using fictitious names. I shared mine, entitled *Memoirs from Fellini*. Wikipedia describes the style of the film director Federico Fellini as "a blend of fantasy and baroque images with earthiness." Whatever that means. Being familiar with Fellini's work, I think he would have loved the fantastic, bizarre earthiness of our eccentric little community. I chose the title *Memoirs from Fellini* because all I could remember were flashbacks of my last two decades, like bizarre, Fellini-style vignettes somewhere between his *La Dolce Vida* and *Satyricon*. We were a fabulous lot of characters—artists, musicians, dancers, designers, chefs, and wellness practitioners. Many were gay men.

A friend of mine called us "the cult of the beautiful people." And we were. Most of us were young, and fanatical about our health and bodies. Although Jaime was pathologically vain, contrary to what audiences may interpret from the film *Holy Hell*, most of us were just passionate about our health because he taught us that what we put in our bodies could alter our energy and reduce the experience of the meditation. We were sugar-free, gluten-free, dairy-free, caffeine- and alcohol-free, low carb, and organic, and although we did not eat red meat, we ate all other types of protein, at a time when those practices were considered weird and antisocial.

You could only live that lifestyle consistently in a society that supported that lifestyle. For years I was ridiculed by my family for my diet choices alone. To not smoke cigarettes, drink alcohol, or eat crap made my mere existence seem condescending to them. And ya wonder why we didn't go home much! For many of us, our supportive way of life alone had a lot to do with why we stayed for so long. We were living a lifestyle thirty years ago that has only recently become trendy. Whatever anyone thinks about it, it paid off for most of us now in our fifties and sixties.

Ten years after the community in Austin broke up, Will Allen released his film, *Holy Hell*. Imagine watching your lives played out on the big screen, for the first time, in front of hundreds of strangers, at the Sundance Film Festival. None of us had seen any of the film prior to that day. We and the audience of strangers all got to learn the details of our story together.

I supported Will all the way in producing his film. But *Holy Hell* represented his and the other guys' stories more than mine. He interviewed me for about four hours and cherry-picked out about five or six minutes of my footage to create the story he wanted to tell. Dozens of people came up to us after the film's question-and-answer session. Many were crying and disturbed, yet compassionate and grateful that he'd made the film.

Will wanted to tell his story, and I think he did a stellar job through the medium he is best at. Will was always a videographer; that is his passion, his virtuosity. He brought his camera everywhere, not as an obligation or assignment, but as an integral part of him. I deeply appreciate his courage and creative talent. He and I had lengthy discussions about why he was making *Holy Hell*. What did he want to say, and what was his motivation? Who was his audience, and what was his expected outcome? Those are complicated questions that only he could answer. I think one of the significant things about *Holy Hell* was it started this important conversation, and for that I'm eternally grateful.

The ability to compartmentalize is a skill that many sociopaths have. Jaime was a chameleon; he would become whatever you needed him to be. The way he appeared in the film was a theatrical version of him; he was not necessarily always like that. How many times have we seen Trump as a maniacal fool at his rallies, yet many have said, after meeting him one on one, "You know, he's really a nice guy!" It's all theater to a narcissist. Sociopaths have a different personality for every encounter. Especially in front of a camera. Jaime kept a mental dossier on each of us, through his hypnotherapy sessions, and he treated us according to our temperament and tolerance to mind control. This book is, in part, an exploration of the distinctions of mind control and our influences and behaviors as followers. There were about 150 members in the Buddhafield and there are about 150 unique stories.

Because I knew him first as a friend, before he became a self-appointed guru, he knew about my background with abusive males and my lifelong resistance to authority, so he also knew that he could not abuse me the same way he did with others. My case was more subtle. Jaime was another "benevolent male" in my life, my friend. He was intelligent, humorous, and spoke to me more on the level of the culture I grew up in. He touted that although he'd grown up on his family's ranch in Venezuela, his father was a diplomat and he spent much of his childhood in the company of European nobility. Knowing what I know now, in Trump fashion, exaggerations and downright lies are just a part of the narcissistic sociopath's template. But there had to be a modicum of truth there. He seemed too worldly to have made it all up. He was knowledgeable about the classics—art, ballet—and he had a huge mental repertoire of classical music and even knew all the words to the pop music of my parents' era, from Sinatra to Bobby Darin's *Mack the Knife*. Hmm. Freud is scratching his beard again.

Due to time constraints Will had to deliver a thirty-year story in a 100-minute documentary, and the audience must construct their own deductions from the footage. I've seen the film over a dozen times and lived it, and I still see new things every time. I've seen it that many times because I was invited to the Q and A sessions in many cities, six of them at Sundance alone. Even if you didn't see *Holy Hell*, I want to clarify some things here because I've heard erroneous perceptions described in podcasts or from strangers who saw the film.

Let's start with the name "Buddha-field." It had nothing to do with Pure Land Buddhism, as someone on a podcast surmised. I don't even know where our name came from, other than towards the end, that label just sort of stuck. WE gave it that name, not Jaime. Because of his paranoia, he never wanted a formal name for the group. He wanted to remain incognito, clandestine, and undefinable. The teachings were eclectic, primarily Eastern. Jaime stole from Hinduism, Buddhism, Sufism, and Christian mysticism.

Another misconception was that we lived in a commune, or that everyone was "fucking everyone." Just to be clear, no one lived in a commune. Especially by the time we moved to

Austin. Yes, some lived together, but only two or three in a house. Our houses were scattered all over Austin. Some owned their own house, some rented. Ninety per cent of us had jobs or careers. Many of us were in relationships with other members of the Buddha-field. An outside observer would see little or no evidence of a group until we were all together in public, on outings or at the movies. Yes, all 150 of us went to the movies on Friday nights. But we called ourselves a film club when curious onlookers inquired.

No, we were not the "bootiefield," as Demetrious in the film hypes. Everyone was not "fucking everyone." That may be what he was up to, but that was not the general behavior. On the contrary, I know some who left because they thought they had to be celibate, and Jaime was not a fan of marriage or children. "Too much of a distraction from our spiritual discipline," he would say. A distraction from him, I would say. Now that we know what Jaime was doing behind closed doors, it's obvious why he didn't want children in the group. HE knew what he was doing. With children around, it would have been a natural distraction from him and too much of a legal risk if he were caught.

Even today, people ask, "Why don't you sue him?" Sue him for what? He had sex with "consenting" adults. And he made sure they were adults, probably for that very reason. But what could they do about it now, once they realized they had been abused? Like Christine Blasey Ford and many of the women in the "me too" movement, not only is the statute of limitations for rape in Texas ten years, but how are you going to prove it? We couldn't prove it even while it was happening. It would have been his word against ours, and like Trump, he had a lot of delusional followers who would come to his defense, even if they had to lie. And they would, gladly, we all did. Only, to us, it wasn't a lie. We believed him, so we would defend him.

Jaime discouraged some people from being or wanting to be in a relationship, but if you pull back the lens, you can see how even that was a perverse manipulation. I remember one time a senior member of the Buddha-Field scolded some aspirant for wanting to be in a relationship. He said that Jaime had told him that "anyone who wanted to be in a relationship was an asshole, was not serious about their devotion to God and shouldn't be there." And that's true; Jaime did say that—to him. The elder diligently passed that message on to any aspirant within earshot, because that was the "guidance" from the master. But that guidance was meant for the elder. Turns out he was being sexually abused by Jaime at the time.

If Jaime was getting sex from any of the guys who were in a relationship, he would use his hypnotherapy sessions for his own ends. While they were under hypnosis he would lie to them or their partner about how the other either didn't want a relationship or that the partner was corrupting them and keeping them from their enlightenment. Obviously, the master had an ulterior motive to keep his sexual devotees pleasuring him alone and didn't want them distracted by another relationship. Did that older "Holy Company in the Knowing" tell anyone? Nope, not for twenty years. That's what I meant when I said in the film, "The right hand never knew what the left hand was doing." Even today some people in the group are not aware that that guy delivering the "master's guidance" was a victim.

Recently I met with an old friend who I came to find out was a victim, and that had a lot to do with why he did not move to Austin. My friend had kept that horrible secret for twenty years. Another friend's longtime boyfriend just up and fled one day and tried to convince her to go with him, but never told her why he had such a sudden change in mood and attitude towards Jaime and the group. We now know why. But no one ever had the courage to come forward and talk about it. I know they were afraid no one would believe their story and that Jaime would destroy them and their reputation, like Trump has done to so many.

If you see *Holy Hell*, remember those images are footage from special gatherings, such as retreats. We had a retreat once a year for about five years, in the very beginning. We stopped having formal retreats or "Knowing sessions" when we moved out of LA in 1991. Even though there were about 150 members in the group, only about a dozen spent every day with Jaime. Some may presume from the film that everyone was in ballet. Not at all. Again, maybe fifteen or twenty. And we were not just doing it for him, at least I wasn't; it was for everyone in the community. I was the set designer for all his ballets. For the most part it was fun, at least for me. I had the opportunity to be creative on a giant scale, with an entire cast of characters, costume designers, and a crew. Was it insane? Some of it. But mostly, it was no more challenging than any assignment I had at ArtCenter. We would perform these spectacular ballets as a gift to our community. They were also part of our spiritual discipline. They were challenges and accomplishments while practicing detachment.

I never took part in the garden. Once again, maybe twenty people went to the garden every day, give or take. I took part in financing some garden features, but I owned a clinic and I didn't have time to waste, nor did I have the desire. As a sociopath, Jaime was obsessive, and his routine was pathologically repetitive and all-consuming. Anyone with observation skills knew that once you did a service such as the garden, ballet, cooking, bodywork, etc., it was a life sentence. Some folks really loved gardening, creating a beautiful place that resembled a paradise on Earth. Some did it out of actual spiritual discipline. We loosely subscribed to the three main paths of yoga: Raja (royal; the "Knowing" was Raja yoga), Bhakti (devotion), and Karma (work or action). Some practiced Bhakti yoga, some practiced Karma yoga. Some just jockeyed for position. It was very special to be close to the "master," and the garden was in his backyard.

I've heard podcasts extrapolate about Julian's elaborate fruit salads. For those who did not see the film, Julian was one of Jaime's minions and sexual victims. He used to make elaborate, and I mean elaborate, fruit salads for Jaime, using fruit as his palette to create beautiful, detailed images, like De Vinci's *Last Supper*. The film conjures up the fantasy of the villainous master, bellowing out his maleficent laugh as he sadistically grinds up those beautiful works of art in the blender. (By that time Jaime didn't do any work. He wouldn't lift a finger to make a cup of tea for himself, let alone work a blender.) It was Julian's decision to make those salads like that. We were a creative lot! This was Julian's way of expressing himself artistically and showing his love. But he did find it genuinely hurtful to learn that Jaime wasn't actually eating his creations.

We weren't aware at the time that Jaime has no ability to appreciate anything. Remember the words of Stout: *"The ice water in [the sociopath's] veins is so bizarre, so completely outside of [others'] personal experience, that they seldom even guess at your condition."*

But if we think of those works of fruit art more like a Tibetan sand painting (a Buddhist meditative practice representing the transitory nature of material life), it might be a little easier to comprehend why it was not that thoughtless for one of Jaime's entourage to make a smoothie out of those salads, rather than leave them to rot, only to be chucked in the compost. We may have been practicing detachment, but we weren't impractical.

When I met Jaime, I wasn't looking for a "master." I was looking for a teacher. The most effective way to handle me was to make me feel special. Regarding his personal health and legal issues, I was one of his confidants and advisors. Sort of his consigliere. Imagine what that does to one's ego to be the advisor to the "master." I kinda understand what Michael Cohen must have felt like. When the most powerful figure in your world comes to you for advice, it does something to your head. I bought and owned Jaime's house and handled a lot of his legal and health affairs. Just to be clear, I selected, closed, and put the down payment on his house. Although it was in my name, I did not pay the monthly mortgage. And when they sold the house, he paid me what I had put down. Probably only to cut ties with me. Did I make a profit on the house? No, but I didn't lose money, either. At the end, I could have sued him for a lot of things that I will not go into details about. But I didn't.

Some are curious about my name, Radhia. I was called by my given name, Linda, for about twelve years while in the Buddha-field. At times he would throw out different names in class to see if they would stick. One time he mentioned the name of the Roman empress Agrippina. "That's an admirable name," he said. But with his weird accent it sounded like uglypenis. I rejected it. Funny story—and an interesting choice! Agrippina was incredibly powerful and was Nero's mother (Nero being the Roman emperor most often compared to Trump). Nero tried to murder her three times—accounts vary—but was eventually successful. So, if we liken Jaime (unconsciously) to Nero, he was suggesting a matricidal name. Hmm, come to think of it, Jaime tried to have me taken out three times. I'll get to that!

One day as I was leaving a cleansing session, he said to me, "Goodbye, my Radha." Radha was the name of Lord Krishna's lover. That name was very special. It was an honor, I thought, and I accepted it. Later that day I received a phone call from him. "I want to tweak your new name a bit," he said. He didn't want people to identify me as a Hindu. "Let's change it to Radhia." I liked that better so Radhia became my name.

Why did I keep the name? Not because of him or my past or some romantic or spiritual attachment. I made it my legal name many years ago, and when the judge asked me why I was changing my name, I said, "Because I like it!" That's it. I never liked the name Linda, and when I was called Radhia it felt right. No mystery. I found out years later that the real reason he tweaked my name was that Radha was the nickname he called the guy he was sexually abusing at the time and didn't want him to get jealous. Nothing Jaime did or said had genuine intention.

Class is where Fellini would have gotten inspired. That, along with our elaborate ballet productions for no one and our high holy day, Halloween—every gay man's fantasy for the night. Contrary to what podcasters interpreted from the film, Jaime always played the male leading dancer in his ballets, never the female. Every year we had an extravagant Halloween party of elaborate skits and gay parades. It was always a lot of fun.

In over twenty years, I only recall him dressing as a woman once, as a drag queen on Halloween. (Most of the gay men dressed in drag on that night.) Another time, much later, when he was really starting to lose it, he came to a Halloween class night dressed as some female Indian saint, *Divine Mother*. That footage was shown in *Holy Hell*. I don't think anyone in the room that night did not think that was one of his weirder moments. I recall a lot of whispering in the shadows about it. But I can understand why one could deduce from the film footage that that was the way he was all the time. Nonsense.

Yes, he wore Speedos to swim and sunbathe, and get this... when he sat in the sun in his Speedos I guess his crotch would get too hot, so they made this cut-out pud-protector from a sponge to lay over the *divine rod* so as not to get scorched, or cause a herpes breakout. In the beginning he wore tight (and I do mean tight) jeans and extra-small-size tank tops (to show off his muscles). Within a few years he changed his ensemble to little silk boxers and fluffy caftan-type, loose silk pants. He said it was because any other fabric was too heavy on his now delicate mortal coil, due to the Shakti energy that was barely keeping him in his body.

Whenever he would eat a meal, he would sit in his custom-made chair that was carried anywhere he was, and his attendants would serve him on his custom-built tray. He very often spilled on his tank top, so as a joke someone (come to think of it, might have been me) gave him a bib for his birthday. Of course, the joke quickly became a useful idea, and besides being favorite Christmas or birthday gifts from us, he had the costume designers make him matching bibs for his boxers and pants.

I recall him walking in on a ballet dress rehearsal once and screaming at the costume designers over some detail in the latest version of his lead ballerina's tutu. He had just come in from having lunch, wearing his special orthopedic walking shoes, white tube socks pulled up to his calves, loose, dark blue silk boxers with a yellow and red happy-face polka-dot pattern, a wife beater, and a white terry-cloth bib with a red and white striped tie embroidered on it.

He stood on stage berating the costume designer about the merits of good fashion design. I could not resist, while holding my clipboard and peering over my glasses at his ensemble, and remarked something like, "...and this is your idea," as I gestured up and down with my index finger, "of high fashion?" He caught himself, and I will say, he and all of us cracked up. You could play with him if you dared, but very few did. I did speak to him in that cavalier style a lot in private.

As years went on his illness was becoming more obvious to the elders. He was just a ridiculous clown a lot of the time. I loved him but at the same time was disappointed with him. He had become sort of a crazy, eccentric uncle. But he was our crazy eccentric uncle. So whatcha gonna do? Throw him out?

It may seem that I'm trying to make our situation less dramatic than depicted in the film or that I'm in denial. My intention is to paint a broader perspective than the vision of *Holy Hell*. I've heard people say, "Such an obvious freak would never fool me." But I want to show the Buddha-field through a wider lens. I've come across many cults in my life, and I would have said the same thing. "How could anyone not see through that?" And yet, there I was for twenty-five years. Even if I could see through it, why did I stay? How many times have I heard Trump supporters say, "Yeah, he's a lying, braggadocious creep, BUT..." Those three letters have come to form the most dangerous word in American history. "But" is our bridge to insurrection and may lead to the fall of democracy as we know it.

At the time that I left, I didn't leave because I found out Jaime was having sex—not to mention coerced sex. I didn't even hear the details of his sexual abuse until many years later. I left because of his hypocrisy, his lies, his deception, his subterfuge and coverup. Like Adam Schiff said, in his closing argument on day three of Trump's first Impeachment Trial: *"Right matters, truth matters; if not, we* are lost."

For me, as a female, Jaime's abuse was obviously not physical; it was about the deceit. Most of us were sincere seekers. Most of us truly tried to live a virtuous life of selfless service and devotion to something higher than ourselves. So his lies and betrayals were the worst abuse of all. A spiritual rape.

Some narcissistic sociopaths prey on sensitive, empathic individuals; others just prey on the emotionally damaged. Many of us had a childlike innocence and gullibility about us. The more sincere, humble, and less ambitious we strived to be, the easier it was for this clever sociopath to manipulate us for his own gain and pleasure. That is the hypocrisy and depravity of Jaime's crimes. And that is what is so heinous about other religious and political leaders' crimes. Especially religious leaders—so called "men of God." The past president of the Fundamentalist Church of Jesus Christ of Latter Day Saints, Warren Jeffs, for example, was convicted of child sex charges and sentenced to life plus twenty years. How many parents trusted him and put their children in his hands? A parent may never allow their children to be alone with a regular man, but a "man of God," by our very perception of him, implies not only absolute trustworthiness, but it's considered an honor to be in his presence.

Among many other such examples, here are two more. Indian religious leader Swami Premananda of Trichi established an orphanage for destitute children and various programs of support for the local poor and uneducated. During the early 1990s Swami Premananda's reputation grew, and people came in vast numbers for his "blessings" and advice. He was convicted and sentenced to two life sentences for the rape of thirteen girls and murder of a Sri Lankan, who had lived for a short period in the Ashram in 2005. But his followers have made a martyr out of him and are still writing about his innocence and how he was framed. In Snohomish, Washington, cult followers of Theodore Rinaldo called themselves "The Group," and many reported he referred to himself (and others in The Group) as sons of God. Rinaldo was convicted of third-degree statutory rape for having sexual intercourse with one minor girl and of taking indecent liberties with another, along with assault, coercion, and intimidating a witness.

But it's not just predatory behavior; it's the lies that pave the way to the ultimate con. These situations are complicated, however, when the followers are willing participants in the lies, refusing to see or accept them, or rationalizing them "for the cause." Communist regimes of the twentieth century, for example, were (in their beginnings at least) led by true believers in Marxism, not conscious liars. For the most part members of the Buddha-field truly believed in Jaime's narrative until the bitter end. A "big lie," as described in Wikipedia, is "a propaganda technique used for political purpose.... The expression was coined by Adolf Hitler, when he dictated his 1925 book *Mein Kampf*, about the use of a lie so 'colossal' that no one would believe that someone 'could have the impudence to distort the truth so infamously.'" Trump's regime was like a mile-long hero sandwich of "big lies." During his time in office, the lyin' king stuffed over 30,000 lies—slathered with condiments of false or misleading claims, deceptions, and coverups—between two slices of fiction, starting with "It was the largest audience to ever witness the inauguration—period. Both in person and around the globe," and ending with "President Trump was reelected by what will be known soon to be a landslide victory unparalleled in this country." Let me repeat that: THIRTY THOUSAND LIES, LIES, AND MORE, *BIG GODDAMN LIES!*

Crimes of fraud or deceit are a terroristic assault on your reality. What do you do with that? Especially when it's a collective deception. When believers are caught in the sociopath's web of false reality, there is little way out. When you go to Disneyland, you are a willing participant in the illusions the park provides for your amusement. You know it's fake, but you will forgo your disbelief to enjoy the fantasy. But what if you don't know it's fake? What if you trust your best friends, your family, your community, and the one person you hold in the highest esteem? And mostly—you're enjoying the ride.

I tried to warn my Trump-supporting friends about his obvious characteristics, but they just said, "Our system is designed for checks and balances." They believed that the other branches of government and the rule of law would keep him from doing any damage. They gambled with a madman because they trusted that there were enough mature, moral, and sane leaders around him who would never let him get out of hand. Trump's enablers in his cabinet and the appalling support from the Republican Congress did not protect us from this scoundrel. On the contrary, they enabled him all the way. It was a collective deceit, in which everyone around him was in on it, either for their own gain or out of their fear of him.

I could see who Trump was from the beginning. So why can't seventy-four million people see it now? It seemed so obvious. Ha! It took me years, and even now as I write this, to understand the gravity of Jaime's manipulation and exploitation and my complacence in it. In a reflective speech at the Auschwitz Memorial in December of 2019, Angela Merkel aired the guilt Germans feel for the Nazi atrocities some eighty years later, by expressing a "deep sense of shame for the barbaric crimes that were committed here by Germans." She called for the crimes to be remembered and for us to "name them clearly." Hindsight is usually a painful sight; for many, denial is more comfortable and convenient. It takes tremendous courage to admit wrongdoing but naming it—owning it—is the best road to healing.

Certainly, in no way was Jaime's deceit as grave as that of Hitler or a president of the United States. But we naively trust in "authority." We believe that our leaders will be held to the highest standards—an illusion that has been programed into us from childhood. We logically assume that in order to be qualified, our leaders have been thoroughly vetted and scrutinized. But what happens when the vetters and scrutinizers we trust to do that task are members of the very cult you need protection from?

Even immediately after the heinous, violent insurrection on the United States Capitol, including calls for the death of the Vice President, Speaker of the House, and lawmakers themselves...even while the dust, teargas, and the stench of human feces smeared on the ruins of historical artifacts still permeated the Capitol rotunda, ONE HUNDRED AND FORTY-SEVEN cult members in our Congress still voted against Biden's lawful confirmation as president that same night—perpetuating the Big Lie that Trump wasn't the loser of the election. We foolishly assume our representatives are required to have the American people's interest at heart. And in the twisted mind of a cult follower, they utterly convince themselves that they do. But when it comes to a cult of personality, the tenets of democracy are abandoned for the leader.

Trump knows all too well that fictional stories can generate genuine emotion, and manipulating emotions is far easier than manipulating facts. As Newt Gingrich said at the 2016 RNC, "Feelings about the truth will be more important than facts." Especially in a country that doesn't have time for facts—and media that is happy to oblige. For years, television and other media collectively aided Donald's awkward portrayal of himself as a brilliant business tycoon, an impresario of the rich and famous. Forbes put him in the $100 million category, for example, when in fact his worth was more like $5 million. By the time they corrected the information, nobody cared.

Once the "Big Lie" has been told, the leader has to follow up with a continuing narrative to support it. And if that fails, bully tactics are rolled out like a three-dimensional game of Twister. One classic technique is deflection. Within minutes, for example, after an aspirant refused to go along with Jaime's sexual propositions and left the room, Jaime was on the phone to his friends, distorting the truth to establish a plausible counter narrative, making the aspirant the bad guy. I often hear people say today, "It's the same on both sides." Because that's what they are programed to think and to repeat like obedient believers. Someone said that to me just after the attack on the Capitol. "Both sides are just as bad." When I asked him what he thought the other side did that was comparable, he stood there silently—eyes wide open—searching for an answer. Then he blurted out, "Oh, come on, the liberals are just as bad, it was ANTIFA that did this." "Do you believe that?" I asked. "I KNOW THAT," he yelled. Then, like an obedient parrot, he said, "Look at what they did last summer."

Ah, whataboutism—the preferred defense. I understand that this guy believes that breaking store windows and setting fires out of anger and frustration over zero consequences for cops kneeling on the throat of a black man till he dies or shooting a black man in the back seven times or shooting a black woman in her bed while she lay sleeping (Wait, notice a pattern here?) is equivalent to insurrection based on the "Big Lie." I realize this is not a lie to the followers. I get it. If we were with Jaime today and he told us this election was stolen, we would have believed it whole-heartedly.

Trump supporters bought into the illusion—suspending disbelief the way we do at Disneyworld. Facts and details are time consuming and complex. Most people were too busy to listen to the whistleblowers and the hours of testimony from credible witnesses at Trump's first Impeachment hearing. They preferred to hear the curated soundbites of what they want to hear through Donald's zippy propaganda tweets and their biased media, which was and still is all too happy to dish 'em out.

Doing research for this book, I watched as much as I could stomach of the entire Impeachment hearings. Is the left media biased? Of course—and most of the time for good reason. For the last four years the liberal networks have had their hair on fire, tripping over an endless stream of jaw-dropping Trump show shenanigans. Wringing their hands and screaming, "This isn't normal!" But the Trump devotees salivate at the sight of Liberals in a total anxiety meltdown. They were deaf to the town criers and fire alarm bells ringing from the walls of Democracy.

During the first Impeachment hearing, the left-leaning media would mostly show clips of the Democrat committee members questioning the witnesses, while the right-leaning media would mostly show clips of the loud, disrespectful clownery and mocking rebuttals from the Republicans. Trump's Republican marionettes had no real defense— hell, they blocked witnesses from testifying. That should have been the base's first clue, and the evidence was undeniable, so the Trump team gave their base a show like a fake pro-wrestling match. The right-wing media and Fox News presented edited clips of partisan baboons like Jim Jordan and Devin Nunes shouting at, berating, and essentially throwing feces at the witnesses—desperately trying to intimidate or discredit them in a performance meant for their dear leader and their base. I know this technique. I did it to a person we suspected was sending threatening letters to Jaime. Three of us went to his house uninvited. I grilled him with intimidating questions, seemingly pounding my chest in some mock performance of strength. I thought it was my job to defend Jaime—to defend my community. I felt heroic at the time, till I found out the truth. Turns out he wasn't the one who sent the letters. Then I could only feel shame. And keep it to myself.

I listened to the actual 2019 Impeachment hearings on C-Span, and I read at least sixty-four chapters of the Mueller Report. Anyone in their right mind would see clearly the validity of the witnesses, the evidence, and the warnings. Yet it was obvious that many Trump supporters I spoke to had not read any of it, and never heard the actual witness testimony. How would they, if they only watch Fox News? Of course they lied and said they read the report and watched the hearing, when I asked them. It reminded me of the elders who lied about their experience of the Knowing. One Trump follower told me that the Impeachment hearings were anywhere from unconstitutional to illegal. They were told the hearings were illegitimate and the witnesses not credible; that people like Adam Schiff had no legal right to be there; and that the whole sham was part of a Democratic coup, "a witch hunt." Huh?—that deliberate wordsmithing is another method of mind control, but I'll get to that.

These surprisingly ignorant comments were from intelligent, educated people who believe in their hearts that what they hear from their media is right. Propaganda is an essential tool for all authoritarian dictators, and media is shameless when it comes to dishing it out. Whatever sells, whatever gets them ratings. Kim Il-Sung, founder of North Korea and grandfather of North Korean Supreme Leader Kim Jong-un, was a master at propaganda. By the time he died an entire country was so steeped in illusion they were quite willing to torture and kill anyone who opposed their dear leader, and his lies have carried forth to two generations of mindless followers.

This is a terrifying collective deception. But I get it. I would have defended Jaime. I would have closed my ears to anyone trying to tell me he was a fraud. I believed what I wanted to believe at the time, and I would have judged harshly and argued with anyone who contradicted him.

It all depends on what you want, and the more you want it, the easier it is to be conned. I wanted to know God, and the more I heard others were experiencing something like what I was looking for, the more I was willing to forgo my disbelief. Did I believe Jaime was Krishna or Jesus? No, but the way he acted in front of me most of the time—blissful, loving, otherworldly—was close enough. I wanted what he was having.

After *Holy Hell* premiered in Hawaii, where Jaime fled with his diehard disciples, many of them refused to see the movie. Fake News, they claimed. Jaime had convinced them that Will was just a jilted lover, and the film was his revenge. Just like Trump supporters who refuse to see the truth. They routinely make the excuse that "others" are the problem: ANTIFA, "the radical left," socialists, etc. Truth or even reality doesn't fit into their adopted narrative.

It's been years now since the truth about Jaime came out, and some diehards are still with him. But it's not him, it's the *illusion* of him that his supporters created, and he cannot sustain it without them. I will say, as Jaime gets older and uglier, he is losing his charisma—his mojo— and his supporters are slowly abandoning him. Let's hope the fool's gold steadily flakes off of Trump's façade and more people see him for the grifter he really was—and is.

CHAPTER 9

NPD, NOT PARTICULARLY DIVINE/NARCISSISTIC PERSONALITY DISORDER

AS I SIFTED THROUGH the textbooks and articles, I felt like an archaeologist on a dig. I carefully brushed off the topsoil of intellectual artifacts to collect the little nuggets and pearls to form my thesis. But in these past few years, history was writing faster than a stenographer on crystal meth. Not a day went by that we were not fire-hosed with breathtaking atrocities committed by the Narcissist-in-Chief. My head was literally spinning (no, seriously, I came down with a mild case of vertigo). My little archaeological dig was regularly deluged with so many veritable illustrations of malignant narcissism I found it hard to keep up. And the parallels with Jaime were unmistakable.

Narcissists hold deep prejudices (e.g. against the opposite gender, people of a different sexual orientation, other cultures and religious beliefs, foreigners, etc).

It did not take long for our little band of spiritual enthusiasts in LA to expand exponentially. We would even advertise in the *LA Weekly*, inviting people to come to Thursday Săt Săng. To my knowledge, none of us were trying to recruit. At least I wasn't thinking in those terms. We were just having such a marvelous time we wanted to share it with everyone. There were rarely any African-Americans, Asians, or anyone other than whites. Consider, however, that in the early eighties, the prevailing demographic in West Hollywood was white, gay males. I don't think any of us were even considering diversity. I found it odd, however, that although Jaime was from Venezuela, could speak five different languages fluently, and seemed to be worldly, he often would make derogatory comments toward Mexicans and Jews, and his opinion of women was prejudiced and distorted, especially if you were not up to his standards. Like Trump, if you weren't at least a "10," you weren't worthy of anything but public insults.

Jaime had the most unusual and contemptuous perception of females. He would make subtle, but crude references to the smell of women's vaginas. I found that extraordinarily ironic, seeing as he preferred anal sex. Then there was his arm candy. Wherever he went in public, he always had his beautiful, blonde female-du-jour by his side (as if he was trying to hide his homosexuality), with a gaggle of Gopis trailing behind. (As described in the Bhagavad Gita, an ancient Hindu religious text, a Gopi is one of the group of cowherding girls famous for their unconditional devotion to Krishna, a major deity in Hinduism.) As Jaime's narcissism grew, I'm sure he fantasized being Lord Krishna. And Krishna must have his Gopis around, waiting on him hand and foot, then sitting at his feet, gazing up at him with ceaseless devotion in their eyes—a fantasy we fawningly obliged.

In Jaime's case, this included both beautiful males and females. It was a coveted gig for many disciples. I think there was an unconscious understanding that the better looking you were and the more you showed your adoration and devotion to him, the more you would be in his favor, and that did have its advantages. Although Krishna is traditionally portrayed as blue-skinned, and Trump is orange, the Gopi syndrome bears an uncanny parallel to Trump's cabinet. The consequences of being less than submissive, let alone adversarial, were far more disadvantageous to your rank and status with both Jaime and Trump. And both would make sure everyone knew; Trump through Twitter spasms and Jaime by "sharing" at the next community gathering. He would expound on the virtues of devotion to "your master" and the karmic downfall of those who will "miss" in this life if they don't show sufficient adoration.

In *Holy Hell*, Will Allen does a short lampoon called *Femme Fatale* about women who, if not devoted solely to the master, were evil seductresses and destined to endure endless incarnations. A general tenet in the Buddha-field was that incarnation was a dreadful thing. The goal was to attain enlightenment in this life, so you would not have to come back and continue to suffer over and over. On people's birthdays we would even sing the traditional Alcoholics Anonymous birthday song, only at the end we would sing, "DON'T keep coming baaaack!"

Let's take a look at this quote again: *Narcissists hold deep prejudices (e.g. against the opposite gender, people of a different sexual orientation, other cultures and religious beliefs, foreigners, etc).* In a study published in the Journal of the National Medical Association entitled "Racism: A Symptom of the Narcissistic Personality," author Carl C. Bell, MD, CCHP writes: "Racist attitudes may be indicative of a narcissistic personality disorder. It is this need for a sense of absolute control which the racist feels justify his self-given right to violate another's 'territory' by either a physical attack, segregation, or discrimination. The 'territory' (in this country) being, for example, the individual's right to adequate health care, education, and housing wherever he can afford it."

Obviously, little needs to be said about Adolf Hitler on this subject, but Muslims, Jews, black and brown people, and residents of the Trump-christened "shithole countries" would likely concur that when it comes to prejudices and racism, he is their poster child. Trump's "very fine people" remark after Charlottesville got David Duke, the Grand Poohbah of the KKK, more aroused than an alabaster porn star with a vat of Viagra. He said, "That's why we voted for Donald Trump, because he said he's going to take our country back." And whose country would that be?

Starting with Birtherism, attacks on President Barack Obama gave Trump the match that lit the fuse and ignited the larger racial disparity that just played out in our nation's capital for the world to see. But Trump didn't start this. The more repugnant aspects of Trumpism existed long before his presidency. He was just the narcissistic, authoritarian leader the followers needed to unleash their dimly veiled racism. Now it's out in the open for all the world to see. For example, Republicans rebuke the John R. Lewis Voting Rights Act and the Violence Against Women Act. That's subtle! They don't even try to hide it anymore.

A nationwide review conducted by ABC News identified at least fifty-four criminal cases in which Trump was invoked in direct connection with racist violent acts. And that was before January 6th, where crazed cult members—flying giant confederate and Trump flags and sporting shirts that read things like "Camp Auschwitz" and "6MWE" (6 million wasn't enough), stormed and desecrated the US Capitol.

Yet Trump, a certifiable narcissist with the relative IQ of a deck chair, had the audacity to say, four days after a twenty-one-year-old allegedly posted an anti-immigrant screed online and then opened fire at a Walmart in El Paso, killing twenty-two and injuring dozens of others: "I think my rhetoric brings people together." Can we just take a moment here and let that sink in? I guess he's referring to funerals. Or how 'bout when he said "We love you, you're very special people" after his devotees committed the most heinous act of treason since the War of 1812?

If you're white or rich, you have automatic access to a "get out of jail free" card, as demonstrated by the domestic terrorists on January 6, 2021, who felt so comfortable in their place in society that they were unafraid to post videos of their actions even as the FBI sought information from the public to make arrests. They even shouted, during the assault on the Capitol, that "Trump sent them." Some claimed that Trump had "invited them into *his* house," as if the president owned the Capitol building. And out of thousands of rioters, those few who were arrested begged their dear leader for a pardon. They are conditioned to believe that he really cares about them and will save them from any consequences. They really do not understand that if he pardoned anyone, it would only be because it served him in some way.

Regardless, the lax policing and slap-on-the-wrist treatment of the January 6th mob has stood in marked contrast to the Black Lives Matter and anti-Trump protestors the preceding summer, who were beaten, tear-gassed, and shot with rubber bullets by the police and Trump's military. Some were even murdered by right-wing extremists, many of whom were found to be the ones who actually broke the store windows and set fires—similar to Mussolini and his followers, whose homicidal mob terrorized northern Italy and vandalized newspaper offices and social clubs. To date we have seen relatively few consequences for our little brand of American fascists for those crimes or their actions during the insurrection, where it was found that many of the cops and even Republican lawmakers were in on it. Senator Ron Johnson of Wisconsin said, "he did not feel threatened by the pro-Trump mob that raided the Capitol in January, but the Republican would have been concerned if the invaders were "antifa" or Black Lives Matter activists." He said, "the insurrectionists were mostly "people that love this country, that truly respect law enforcement, would never do anything to break a law". "Good ol' boys, never meaning no harm" was their attitude. Similar to, "grab 'em by the pussy," was just locker talk.

Narcissists believe they are untouchable, inhabitants of a special reality, one parallel to ours but never met. Outrageous behavior is the narcissist's hallmark. They can manipulate unsuspecting, and usually respectable, people into their criminal or pseudo-criminal activities. For four years Donald's followers watched their mob-boss show 'em how it's done. Ignore subpoenas—no consequences; evade taxes—just smart business, and no consequences; obstruct justice—no consequences; violate emolument clauses—no consequences; rape and sexual assault—no consequences. The cult members in power said, "No one is above the law! Except—while you are president," giving him carte blanche to break as many laws as he wanted, till he was out of office. "Then let the people decide," the lawmakers said.

The prospect of civil and criminal liability for various offenses, coupled with an addiction to power and attention, no doubt fed Trump's motivation to stay in office, not just for a second term but for decades, like his buddy Putin and other authoritarian dictators. Since the polls indicated that he might fail to win reelection, however, he crafted an alternative narrative of a stolen election, accusing Democrats of major fraud before campaigning even started. For months, Trump laid the groundwork for this strategy. Starting in April he uttered more than 150 claims concerning fraudulent ballots or the alleged dangers of mail-in voting. That chicanery would have been obvious to a child but was not to his followers. And when the majority of the people did decide with their vote, his set-up worked like a charm. "It was a rigged election," the followers parroted, despite all evidence to the contrary. Thus, was an insurrection justified by many of his believers. Trump suckered them into trusting that if they were on his side, there would be no consequences and he would triumph.

In addition to the glaring racist and misogynistic characteristics of a narcissistic sociopath, other qualities are prevalent. This next quote from the DSM-V was particularly disturbing to me and would be to anyone who spent time with Jaime. Although narcissistic sociopaths can be clever wordsmiths, ironically...

Narcissists often miss the semantic meaning of language.

Jaime often mispronounced or used words and idioms incorrectly. We always thought that a language barrier prevented him from grasping certain words; he frequently messed up American expressions and colloquialisms. Yet he had been in America for over forty years. The group would just laugh it off. So I found this quote to be interesting and disturbing, because it is in alignment with the characterization of Narcissistic Personality Disorder.

We make fun of Trump's grammar and syntax blunders—"covfefe," for example—but get this: apparently *covfefe,* out of all of his gaffes, is a real word. Most people think he meant to write "coverage," but "covfefe" is actually a word of Yiddish origin, meaning "a futile search" or "a pointless and false quest." No doubt—to him— it was the equivalent of "witch hunt" for all his jewish supporters. It was originally transliterated from Hebrew as "kabfefe." Maybe he picked up a little Yiddish from the Kushners.

But what about "Tanzaynia" instead of Tanzania; "Beyoncey;" "Nambia," a cross between Namibia and Zambia; "diversary" instead of diversity; "Ulucious" S Grant—that would be Ulysses; "bigly;" "anomous," which might mean enormous or anonymous. And with Trump's very, very large "A-brain," he mispronounces "stankuary" for sanctuary. And let's not forget "Yo Semite" for Yosemite and "Thighland," a Freudian slip, no doubt. There was "Douglas Magarth" and a quote during his classic speech to our armed "forcef;" armed "forcer." "We're holding thousands of Isis fighters right now—prisoners. And we're going to give them to, from where they came—the Europe." Despite these "obselels," "I hope they now go and take a look at the "oranges;" the "oranges" of the investigation, (yibdi yibidi), "the beginnings of that investigation." I'm sure the Buddha-field would get a kick out of Trump's reference to a great religious icon of India, "As the great religious teacher Swami Vive-kamun-nund once said." Uhhh, that would be Swami Vivakananda, and so forth and so on.

Now one may think I'm just making fun of the Donald here. But this is not just a guy who trips over a few words now and then. We all do that from time to time, especially if we're dyslexic or, like Joe Biden, a stutterer. Did I mention this was the president—of the United States? These are not just private word salads that may trip off your tongue after an all-night drug binge at one of Jeffrey Epstein's parties. This grand orator was speaking on the world stage, representing the United States of America. Granted, he could have been caught in a denture slippage in that awkward zone between the Adderall he sniffed and the barbiturate chaser. Or maybe because we know he doesn't read, he doesn't write very well either. But his language woes may be a much more serious sign. Most people either just laughed off Trump's errors or used them as a partisan zinger. Similarly, we just thought Jaime's verbal blunders were cute. Until recently I didn't realize that Jaime's—and likewise Trump's—quirky language gaffes are a sign of a deeper and more serious pathology.

*Narcissists are emotionally retarded with an arrested
level of emotional development; whilst language
and intellect may appear to be that of an adult,
they display the emotional age of a five-year-old.
Sometimes displaying seemingly, limitlessly demonic
energy especially when engaged in attention-seeking
activities or evasion of accountability.*

There were many musicians and singers in the Buddha-field—some professional. I played the flute. We would play instruments and sing popular songs off the top charts, but some disciples, Ben mostly, would change the words to suit our narrative. After a while Jaime started changing the words to more perverse and infantile lyrics. He would make silly faces and puerile gestures, seemingly unaware of his foolish behavior—unbecoming to an "enlightened" soul, for sure.

When we would sing in class or Săt Săng, people would sit at his feet, sing along, and laugh at his every childish, stupid jest while gazing up at him with nauseating devotion. Often, people would work themselves up into a kind of hysteria, crying and laughing. Some would go into pretentious gyrations, shaking and rolling on the floor. Not unlike devotees who speak in tongues or the Pentecostal snake handlers, they acted as if they were possessed by some psycho/spiritual energy. I noticed the more we did that, the more energy he got. So, by around midnight, having fed his insatiable ego all night, he would get a second wind. None of us dared leave until he was damn well ready. And when he did finally call it a night, he would have a collection of his bodyworkers go to his house for a "body adjustment." So...another few hours for them. He would top off the night with someone who read to him in bed.

And then, like a loyal dog, that person would often sleep on the floor at the foot of his bed in case he needed something in the night. Many experts say sleep deprivation is a common characteristic of cults, but I'm not sure that was Jaime's master plan (pun intended). I think he was so drunk on our sycophantic behavior that he just couldn't get enough. This was our routine, for over at least eighteen years before the end, and rarely did anyone dare to leave, much less skip a gathering. The consequences for leaving early were complex—the feeling of being left out, the fear you might miss something, and the certainty you would be judged or criticized for leaving. You would be called into cleansing the next day to work on it, as if the desire to sleep was some flaw in your weak character, and you didn't want to be a spiritual wimp, a "snowflake." Right? (Jaime conducted "therapy" that incorporated hypnosis, which he called "cleansings" to protect him from illegally practicing psychotherapy or hypnotherapy without a license.)

They crave affection and admiration from others, and have a Jekyll and Hyde nature—can be vile, vicious and vindictive in private, but innocent and charming in front of witnesses; no-one can (or wants to) believe this individual has a vindictive nature—only the current target sees both sides.

Apparently, Jaime was often a tyrannical maniac behind closed doors. Did anyone disclose that? Nope. Again...a collective deception. Even my best friend, who lived with me for twenty years and was one of his first entourage, didn't mention his tantrums and cruelties. I thought I knew her better than anyone on Earth. According to her later account, he put her through hell every day, but she came home at night and never said a word. When I asked her recently why she never told me, she said, "Where was I going to go, back to the streets or home to my abusive mother?" She'd had a tragic childhood of abuse and neglect. When Jaime found her, she was seventeen and her family had pretty much abandoned her. At first Jaime was loving to her and gave her a home, a family, and a purpose. After a while he just used and abused her. He often preyed on broken and vulnerable youth, as many sociopaths do.

I heard tales of him flying off the handle, not unlike the stories of Trump. In a fit of rage, Jaime would scream at his entourage and carry on like a spoiled child while in the privacy of home or in his car on the way to an event, then step out in perfect stillness like an angel descending from heaven. Occasionally I witnessed him yelling at a dancer in his ballet class, and when he saw that I was watching, he would wink at me, as if he wasn't serious—just giving a disciple a teaching.

In "The Strange Case of Dr. Jekyll and Mr. Trump," a 2018 article in the *Chicago Tribune*, presented by the editorial board, Trump's dual personality is described:

> Which president will the nation see tonight, today,
> five minutes from now? It's still not a question we're
> accustomed to asking. Or maybe the opposite is true:
> In his 14 months in office, President Donald Trump has
> toggled so frequently between reason and rant, between
> normalcy and lunacy, we're no longer surprised by his
> emotional outbursts. We're inured to the circus in his
> head.

Roberta Satow, PhD, reported in her article in *Psychology Today* that Trump has temper tantrums on a daily basis. "Trump's Temper Tantrums, President Trump seems to find it hard to control his emotions."

They are perfectionists about themselves.

That was the epitome of Jaime. He was extremely disciplined, to the point of obsessive. At first, I interpreted that discipline as devotion. That's what I admired about him. One can't be half-assed in one's devotion to total union with God. Let me be clear: God, not Jaime. Although, come to think of it, if I am to be pure in the hypothesis that God is all things, I would have to admit that even Jaime and Trump are aspects of God. Let's just be content with them being God's shadow side—God exploring himself as malignant, narcissistic assholes—and leave it at that!

The time arc of thirty years in the film *Holy Hell* beautifully illustrates Jaime's physical mutation because of his vanity. He would have his minions secretly go to the drugstore and buy him an assortment of powders and potions, creams and concealers. In addition to his botched Botox, flubbed facial sculptures, and hours at the gym, he would spend time in the bathroom every morning, applying false eyelashes, blow-drying his dyed, thinning hair, and putting on his makeup. He even had disciples try out certain plastic surgeries and procedures before he would consider doing them himself.

I love *Washington Post* columnist Dana Milbank's description of Trump's hypothetical morning schedule:

- 8 a.m.: Hair washing (30 mins)

- 8:30 a.m.: Hair drying (60 mins)

- 9:30 a.m.: Hair combing and spraying (30 mins)

- 10 a.m.: Skin oranging (4 hours)

- 2 p.m.: Makeup application (30 mins)

Would sound better if presented like this:

- 8 a.m.: Executive Time (4 hours)

- Noon: Lunch (1 hour)

- 1 p.m.: Executive Time: (1½ hours).

They may have a constant need for body care.

At first, Jaime was more self-reliant. We loved him and were happy and grateful to him. So what do you do to show your appreciation to a guy like this? Make him cookies? Yeah! Make him dinner? There's a splendid idea! What about carrying his books or his chair? Or drive his car for him? How 'bout a foot massage? You'll have to take his shoes off and then put them back on when you're done. He's sore from his workout? Give him a full massage, or free bodywork. He seems in pain a lot more now—like constantly. He says it's because so much "Shakti" is flowing through his body that it makes his nervous system sensitive and in pain all the time. Or he tells people that the pain he is experiencing is because he is taking on all our ugly karma. Hmm, sounds like Jesus, dying for our sins.

Maybe we should create a team of practitioners and bodyworkers to help him. See where this is going? Everyone started jockeying for position. There were cookie makers and dinner makers. His bodyworker team included massage therapists, chiropractors, acupuncturists, and nutritionists (that would be me). I was also in the set designer, property owner, and legal counsel group. Eventually, he was getting twenty to thirty hours of massage and bodywork a week. Devotees prepared and served all his meals and fancy desserts; drivers chauffeured him in a car with a custom built-in seat; his fashion designers made him special clothes; and they all carted his stuff around like the entourage to an emperor.

One time, followers had to change the position of the couches because he walked by and bumped one corner, then started screaming at people. He told them they needed to bring the old couches back, because he couldn't be bumped. "Are you trying to kill me?" he yelled. After hearing this story, I confronted him about this, and he explained he was just creating scenarios so people could have an outlet to express their love and devotion. I remember making him a cup of tea, and when I handed it to him, he yelled at me because the cup was too heavy. Seriously? This was a guy who could bench press 180 pounds.

After one of his botched silicone injections, he had an adverse reaction, and his face swelled so badly that his lips looked like a duck. He made his driver, Will, hold an ice bag on his face and drive at the same time, because the ice was too heavy for him to hold. "It might throw my arm out," he said.

Vain, petulant, and essentially unable or not deigning to perform the simplest of practical tasks for himself, instead delegating anything resembling labor to lackeys...does this not sound exactly like qualities of our forty-fifth president?

CHAPTER 10

WHAT ARE YOU, NUTS?

IN THE *Diagnostic and Statistical Manual of Mental Disorders (DSMMD),* I found this line the most frightening:

> *If a sociopath is someone who because he is antisocial with no conscience, lies, manipulates and controls people any way he so desires, what is a narcissistic sociopath? The traits and behaviors of a sociopath are chilling enough on their own. Almost unbelievably, a narcissistic sociopath intensifies sociopathy and takes it to another level. People are toys to the sociopath; to the sociopathic narcissist, they are trash. Sociopathy combined with narcissism can be extremely dangerous.*

Narcissists are great con artists. Think about it. They are so good, they succeed in deluding themselves. Clearly, both Jaime and Donald Trump believed in their own utter superiority to everyone else on the planet. This talent for self-delusion may mask a deeply buried insecurity and fear of inferiority—but this isn't a psychological revelation these shallow men are likely to encounter, not being known for their depth of character or practice of self-examination.

One of the extraordinary characteristics of a narcissist is the ability to always turn the tables on you. They flip-flop from benevolent one minute to malevolent the next. They do whatever works for them at the time, but they will never take responsibility for anything. If you dare confront them on their bad behavior, they will always turn it back on you.

The following is a chilling description of a narcissist from the *Narcissism Book of Quotes: A Selection of Quotes from the Collective Wisdom of Over 12,000 Individual Discussions* by Sam Vaknin:

> Does he want to hurt you? Well, now, that would imply that he thinks of you as a human being—a narcissist doesn't. What he wants is to secure supply. If he cannot do it by means of flattery, he will do it by means of cruelty. The goal is to get you to give him what he wants. He doesn't especially care which method he uses, so long as he finds one that works. I know that sounds cold. It is cold. That is the mind of a narcissist. Cold and devoid of empathy. Because he lacks empathy, he probably doesn't know or care if he hurts you, unless he's using bullying as a technique for extracting narcissist supply from you. Even then, he couldn't care less what that does to you,

apart from eliciting the desired response. If it makes him feel better about himself to belittle you, he will do that, but the ultimate goal isn't to make you feel bad, the goal is to perpetuate the myth of his own perfection and simultaneously control you. If by hurting you it gets you in check, makes you take on his failings as your own, and makes you work twice as hard for his approval, it's a bonus for him. If he doesn't need to employ cruelty in order to accomplish either of the above goals, he won't. It's that simple.

As I reflect on the past, I realize that Jaime's sadistic, sociopathic behavior was always there. For example, on Sundays everyone would meet at Harper House and wait for him, sometimes for hours. He did that deliberately; he had absolutely no regard for anyone's time or comfort but his own. He would tell everyone to be at the house at eleven AM and he would show up anywhere between eleven (that was rare, but it was just to keep everyone on their toes) and two PM or later. He would drive up in his car and ask if anyone wanted to go to the beach or on a hike, or if it was raining, perhaps the museum? And then take off. We would rush to our cars and try to follow him.

The group grew, organically and exponentially. First there were sixteen, then thirty-two, sixty-four, and so on; you get the idea. Each of us invited a friend, and in no time it became a sizeable group. At one point in LA we were seventy-five to a hundred people. Imagine, even if you carpooled, how many cars followed him on the outing.

Narcissistic sociopaths are sadistic and toy with your devotion to them. Your welfare and wellbeing are irrelevant.

There were no cellphones or means of portable communication in those days. Many people risked their lives, running red lights and dodging through LA traffic to keep up. He rarely told us where he was going; our struggles were a sick game to him. We kept up with this reckless marathon because (1) we didn't want to miss out; and (2) if we did, he would probably scold, ridicule, or make a public spectacle out of us.

When we would go on retreats, they were supposed to last for a week or two at most, but he would stretch it out and never give us a definitive date of when we would return home. Most people had to call and lie to their families and employers. Many lost their jobs. Yet we were still paying for our food and lodging, as well his and the cost of his entourage. The last retreat we were on lasted seven weeks in Utah. Most people were panicking about money and their employment. He didn't care. We were told to just drop our minds. When we finally returned, he left immediately on a vacation to Hawaii. His minions still collected class money, even though there was no class for two months and most of us were broke and unemployed.

As the community grew, our activities became more frequent and more of an obligation. We all had jobs and careers. But our spiritual routine took up the rest of our time. We had Monday night class, Tuesday night formal two-hour meditation, Wednesday night dinner, Thursday Săt Săng, Friday night movies, and although Saturdays were "free," many people performed one service or another, and Sunday started out with an all-day outing with Jaime and ended up back at Harper House for Ben's Săt Săng. At first, we would usually get out of Săt Săng or class at a reasonable time, ten or eleven at most, and go home. But as time went on and Jaime's narcissism progressed, he would keep us there until one, two, sometimes three AM. I realize now that he needed to keep our time completely consumed so we could not have contact with the outside.

At one point we built a theater for him to do his ballets. *We* built it—with our own hands. Then he would come in and make us tear part of it down and move a window or a wall a few feet. Did I mention this was a gigantic building? I'm sure he got this idea from a story about Yogananda making his disciples move a swimming pool. Nothing Jaime did was original, even his abuse.

Thanksgiving and Christmas celebrations became torturous. In the beginning we would have Thanksgiving dinner, and then a month later we would have another dinner on Christmas Eve. At first it was delightful. All of us would cook and decorate and share a beautiful meal. Afterwards we would dance and sing until about eleven and go home. As the group and Jaime's narcissism grew, however, these celebrations got bigger and more elaborate. We had gotten to be such a large group that we had to rent a hall for the festivities. We lined the tables up in a U-shape, with Jaime and his closest entourage at the front table splayed out like da Vinci's Last Supper. The seating would be predetermined, with name cards marching along the outside of the tables on either side, so we could face each other. The lowest-ranking members and guests would be the furthest away. Unless of course you were having a relationship with a higher-ranking member; then they would often switch place cards when no one was looking to bump you up closer to the action.

One year some clever disciple decided it would be fun to make fortune cookies for one of the desserts. The next year Jaime wanted her to make the cookies again, but this time all the fortunes were to be written around the glories of the master. And from that time on, Thanksgiving and Christmas became a living hell. Each subsequent year, the dinner was dished out and placed on the table in front of you, but no one dared touch it. It sat in front of us coagulating until all the fortune cookies were read aloud one by one. All hundred and fifty cookies. And not all were just one sentence; some were in whole paragraphs, which got more elaborate and sycophantic every year.

When we finally finished our ice-cold repast, Jaime and his entourage would go upstairs for his body adjustments, while the rest of us would clean the tables and clear the room for dancing. When all that was done, he would appear back in the emptied ballroom, and everyone would stand silently in awe at his mere presence. About twenty singers spent months practicing a selection of songs that we rewrote so that the words hailed his glory. After we did our performance (it was usually gorgeous), his typical response was "Humph!"

Then a DJ would play music, and we all would dance till we dropped. It went on and on into the wee hours of the night, and every year the hours would get later and later. On one occasion Jaime disappeared for another hour or so and returned in a black outfit, makeup refreshed and hair coiffed. He got up on stage, took the microphone, and in his dreadfully, creepy bad voice sang, while prancing around like a rock star. Our reaction reminds me of the kind of behavior you might see in North Korea as the sycophantic followers cheer and applaud their dear leader.

Narcissists are control freaks and have a compulsive need to control everyone and everything you say, do, think and believe; for example, will launch an

*immediate personal attack attempting to restrict
what you are permitted to say if you start talking
knowledgeably in their presence—but aggressively
maintains the right to talk (usually unknowledgeably)
about anything they choose.*

Every Narcissistic authoritarian must control their brand—their image within the society—in order to maintain absolute allegiance. They cannot appear to be anything less than infallible. The more power they have, the more ruthless they become towards anyone who may undermine their credibility. I have often heard of this characteristic in celebrities, corporate executives, and politicians, especially narcissistic dictators. Jaime hated anyone taking attention away from him. He couldn't tolerate anyone appearing smarter or more talented than he was. I had money at the time, and my father was a lawyer; thus, I was more familiar and connected with the legal system, so Jaime often chose me to consult with private detectives and lawyers on his behalf. After I consulted with the lawyers and informed him, he would talk to the group in class about the status of the situation and totally make shit up. I would then respectfully correct him. Colossal mistake! He would yell at me and tell me to stop being such a know-it-all.

Sound familiar? Damn you, Anthony Fauci! Stop being such an expert on infectious disease!

Recently, a friend reminded me of those incidents and how frustrated, sad, and angry I was after spending thousands of dollars of my own money to get Jaime the legal answers he needed. I imagine Dr. Fauci went home at night, put a blanket over his head, and sat in the closet, sipping scotch until he could muster up the temperament to go back to the White

House for another press conference. Jaime would offer no thanks, no appreciation; instead—like Trump—he would just slap me down in front of the group for pointing out the truth. My friend reminded me of my humiliation and how I was devastated. I find it interesting that I had to be reminded. Ahh, how the mind filters the uncomfortable things.

They despise anyone who enables others to see through their deception and their mask of sanity.

A few members of the Buddha-field caught on to Jaime's lies and narcissism and tried to confront him. One guy, after writing a scathing letter attempting to disclose Jaime's deceit, realized he could never change anything. So, after losing his job and all his savings, following the last retreat he moved back home to Florida to live with his mother. Jaime told us that the guy was dangerous and mentally ill. He went after him and tried to have him committed. He said he needed to be put on medication. On another occasion he did actually drive one of us to insanity. Jaime was so mentally and emotionally abusive to this man that the guy just flipped one day. He disassociated from himself and started acting as if he was channeling Muktananda. The man used that persona as a way of confronting Jaime and telling everyone within earshot what a fraud he was and how he was creating karma. Jaime did arrange to have him put in a mental hospital for a while, and then sent him away to an ashram in India.

Unlike the days in the Buddha-field, when social media didn't exist, today narcissistic leaders relentlessly exploit social media, often using state-funded troll armies to find and monitor anyone critical of the regime, its leader, or its policies—and then repeatedly belittle, bully, and besmirch critics or label them as "traitor" and "enemy of the state." Jessikka Aro, a Finnish journalist who exposed pro-Kremlin troll factories in 2014, for example, became a victim of their activities herself and was subjected to years of harassment online, including false claims that she was a prostitute soliciting officials from the CIA and NATO, and threats to rape and kill her. In 2006, Anna Politkovskaya, a fearless journalist who specialized in reporting on both sides of the conflict in Chechnya—and a fierce critic of Putin—was shot dead in her apartment. Alexander Litvinenko, another critic of President Putin and a former officer in the FSB and KGB, died a prolonged death from poisoning in London. After Alexai Navalny, Putin's most prominent critic, was poisoned and nearly killed, returned back to Russia only to be arrested and imprisoned as a vain attempt by the Kremlin to scare millions of Russians into submission.

Similarly, after the first Impeachment hearings, Trump staged an angry, vindictive sixty-two-minute White House rant. He fired and attempted to destroy anyone who testified at the hearings.

- Trump forced the career diplomat Marie Yovanovitch out of her position as U.S. Ambassador to Ukraine. As a result of Trump's slanders, she received death threats and a smear campaign against her, perpetrated by his loyal followers.

- Fiona Hill, National Intelligence Council member and senior adviser on the Kremlin and Europe, was attacked, slandered, and mocked by Trump. She endured hateful and threatening calls from his followers, provoked by his public tweets, accusing her of being "a Soros mole in the White House, colluding with all kinds of enemies of the president." The administration forced her to retire.

- George Kent, deputy assistant secretary at the State Department, was mocked and his reputation maligned.

- Michael McKinley, whose career spanned decades at the State Department, resigned just before his testimony at the first Impeachment hearing because of the low morale of the entire department, due to Trump's slander and insults.

- Trump destroyed the reputation of his big donor and Ambassador to the European Union, Gordon Sondland, then removed him from office.

- Lt. Col. Alexander Vindman, Director for European Affairs for the United States National Security Council (NSC), was disgraced, humiliated, and his well-deserved eligibility for promotion to full Colonel, approved way before his testimony, was then denied. He finally retired from office.

- Vindman's twin brother, who also worked for the State Department, was fired and escorted out of the building in disgrace, just for being related to Alexander.

And on and on, ad nauseam. His followers happily accepted this because they embrace the delusion that these witnesses were all just part of the "deep state" (another contrived propaganda catchphrase), and proud that their big strong leader was bucking the system (by system I mean the rule of law and the Constitution), by obstructing justice and "draining the swamp" (and by the swamp I mean longtime, upstanding civil servants). No doubt these actions scared the hell out of Senators who were being asked to follow their conscience and remove the president from office. The families of/and the ten Republicans who finally mustered up the courage to vote for Trump's second impeachment received death threats. The House members were pressured by their own colleagues to resign or be removed from Congress for standing up and protecting the country from future totalitarian threat, and they were promptly torn apart by Trump and his right-wing sycophants and media jackals.

So far, I count one hundred and forty-two people who were in Trump's cabinet, staff, or in service to his office who were fired and publicly humiliated after pointing out the facts. Like Jack in *Lord of the Flies*, Trump gets his most savage media devotees to slaughter these people's reputation. His minions on Fox News, AON, or other fools like Rush Limbaugh, who Trump publicly adorned with the Medal of Freedom, took pleasure in these bully tactics, because—like in *Lord of the Flies*—he aroused the beast in them.

Freud's psychoanalytic theory describes the "id" as the primitive and instinctive component of the personality—primarily governing sex and aggression. It functions entirely according to the pleasure-pain principle; its impulses either seek immediate fulfillment or settle for a compromise fulfillment.

David Nakamura described, in a 2020 article in the *Washington Post*, Trump's post- Impeachment speech in one simple takeaway: "Trump was angry, raw, vindictive, aggrieved—reflecting the id of a president who has seethed for months with rage against his enemies. This was the State of Trump."

"Donald Trump Is A 'Sexual Sadist' Who Enjoys 'Degrading People,'" said psychologist and psychotherapist John Gartner, who contributed to the bestseller *The Dangerous Case of Donald Trump*.

On the *Bulwark Podcast*, Trump-appointed Homeland Security agent Miles Taylor joined Charlie Sykes to discuss the topic: "[W]hen it comes to Trump, cruelty is the point." Taylor went into detail, describing the sadistic and cruel wishes and orders Trump gave his staff. For example, Trump told them to hold back aid for California wildfires because California was not politically supportive of him. "Trump didn't see us as American citizens but more as political pawns, evaluated by our political usefulness," said Taylor. As soon as the officials in Puerto Rico criticized Trump, he cut their funding. It got so bad the staffers were scared to show him the numbers because they knew he would cut them off entirely. He asked people to do things that he knew would violate the law and promised them pardons. "He dangled people's jobs over their heads to get them to do what he wanted, legal or otherwise."

He instructed Homeland Security officials to implement policies that would maim, tear gas, and injure innocent, unarmed civilian migrants coming toward the US border. He told them to sharpen the spikes on top of the wall. He said he wanted them to go through their hands and arms, piercing their flesh. "He has sick bloodlust for innocent people," Taylor said. Trump instructed, "If they throw rocks you will use weapons." He threatened to kill the families of terrorists.

As the president made illegality seem routine, people lost respect for the rule of law and grew ambivalent about it. The blatant acts of insurrection on January 6, 2021 were a perfect example of this ambivalence. "This is, quite literally, how countries fall apart and how civilizations decline," Taylor warned. "This type of demagoguery leads to disrespect for foundational norms that create the unifying principles that undergird the Republic in the first place." It is Trump's followers who enabled him. The vast majority of senior former officials, upwards of 90%, saw what was going on, yet most of them were scared to come out and even today stand silent in the shadows as America splinters at the hands of his deranged followers.

Jaime had a dossier on all of us, with an instant recall he would use as a weapon. For example, if I brought up something that bothered me about what he said or did, he would recall an event in my childhood or recite a dream I had told him in therapy and convince me that I was projecting that onto him. It somehow made sense, and I would find myself grateful to him for making me more aware. Things that would otherwise be ethically questionable, bordering on illegal, became rational and even magnanimous in our minds.

The self-styled "patriots" who stormed the Capitol not only broke the law but did things that were unproductive and shameful—swayed by this false identity that they were somehow heroes for a greater cause. But when questioned as to what that cause was, they had no definitive answer. Some would use abstract words like "We're fighting for our 'freedom.'" Freedom from what? Freedom to not wear facemasks during a pandemic? Freedom to obstruct or change an election because they didn't like the outcome? Freedom to literally shit all over Capitol property? Because it was "their house," they chanted.

Noooo, it's our house, thank you. It does make you wonder, if that's how they treat the prominent House of the

US Congress, what their real dwellings look like. Their leader whipped them into infantile madness. But how far could that have gone? If Eugene Goodman, that courageous Capitol police officer, hadn't lured the angry mob away from the Senate chamber where members of Congress were hiding, another sixty seconds could have easily led to mass murder. How many genocidal events have unfolded in history due to the madness conjured up by a narcissistic authoritarian leader?

Narcissists display a compulsive need to criticize whilst simultaneously refusing to value, praise and acknowledge others, their achievements, or their existence.

Occasionally, when he wanted to do a new ballet, Jaime would look for ideas. One Christmas, I built him a beautiful model of a stage set I thought would be a grand theme for a ballet. Having worked for W.E.D (Disney's theme park division), I was adept at making models, and I made him a very detailed, hand-painted, multi-paneled miniature. He looked at it, said "Hmmph!," then waved his hand in a dismissive gesture. A minion took it and walked away. I later found it in the trash. If it wasn't his idea, it was not only worthless, but he would make a point to humiliate or dismiss you. Sometimes people would do or make lovely things for him, like Julian's fruit salads, for example, and Jaime would eye it and say, "That's pretty—pretty ugly." Everyone would laugh and think he was just playing—or even showing us a lesson—by modeling the opposite of what one would expect any decent human being to say. Now I realize he meant it. But we all just shrugged it off because no one could imagine anyone could be that brazen, that nasty—particularly someone we looked to for spiritual guidance. He must have been joking, right? Nope!

Hitler undermined the judiciary...Called experts "stupid"...Threatened to "whack" mayors who stood in the way of his tactics. Upset about traffic, he called the Pope a "son of a whore"..."Joked" about a woman who was raped...Justified the killing of journalists. "Just because you're a journalist," he said, "you are not exempted from assassination if you're a son of a bitch."

Trump undermined, criticized, and publicly ridiculed not just women, minorities, and the handicapped, but governors; members of the Senate and Congress; the intelligence community; the law enforcement community; members of the press; war heroes; the Department of Justice; Federal judges; members of the State Department, including our American ambassadors—and that's just in this country. Don't get me started with world leaders and dignitaries. And they not only let him get away with it, but his base loved it. That's why he did such outlandish things right out in public, unashamed. As Martha Stout put it, *"Imagine no struggles with shame, not a single one in your whole life, no matter what kind of selfish, lazy, harmful, or immoral action you had taken."*

Like Jaime's followers, I've heard Trump's supporters brush off his derogatory comments by saying things like, "Well, he says what we are thinking; at least he's honest." Or "I'm not a fan of him as a person—he's a pig—but he doesn't sugar-coat anything. He says what he thinks, and that's what I like." Really? Is that what you like? I guess if it's directed to someone else and not you. Someone told me, in reference to Trump's endorsement of bleach as a treatment for the coronavirus, "He was just kidding! You're too sensitive." But watch the clip. He wasn't kidding. Even Anthony Fauci knew he wasn't kidding. After Trump was out of office, Fauci admitted on CNN: "Oh my goodness gracious, I could just see what's going to happen: You're going to have people who hear that from the president and they're going to start doing dangerous and foolish things." And guess what? After Trump made his little "joke," there was a rise in accidental poisonings from disinfectants such as bleach.

Nearly a half a million Americans died from COVID-19 on Trump's watch. So I guess the joke's on him.

There was always about a 50% attrition rate after every Knowing Session. Some folks just didn't experience what Jaime was dishing out, and many confronted him in private about it. I realize now that he took that as a personal insult. Like in the fairy tale "The Emperor's New Clothes," these people were pointing out that he didn't have the mojo he claimed—which he didn't. He would usually talk about them when they left the Buddha-field, making sure everyone knew that they were just losers and will have "missed" the master's grace in this life. And like the Buddha-field followers, Trump's toadies let him do the same or worse and said—and continue to say—nothing. And anyone with the balls to jump ship has been branded by Trump a "loser."

CHAPTER 11

MENTAL GYMNASTICS AND THE ART OF SELF-DEFENSE

MOST SOCIETIES LARGE OR small raise the flag of their beliefs, and you either salute it or you risk being tossed out—forced to trek the barren and lonely wasteland of alienation and non-identity. Here's where the narcissistic sociopath can really implement his skills.

> *Narcissists possess an exceptional verbal facility and will outmaneuver most people in verbal interaction, especially at times of conflict, they are unusually skilled in being able to anticipate what people want to hear and then saying it plausibly.*

Originally, Jaime would say "connect to God's love," but in a few years it became "connect to MY love." I and some elders were confused about this new decree. I asked him about it. He said, "Well, Radhia, some people, *not you* (he knew better, so he knew how to play me), need a living example of God, that they can see, hear, and touch. I am just being that for them." He seriously considered it a sacrifice.

Psychologist Leon Festinger first proposed a theory of cognitive dissonance centered on how people try to reach internal consistency. Festinger said that "[C]ognitive dissonance occurs when conflict emerges between what people want to believe and the reality that threatens those beliefs." He writes:

People have an inner need to ensure that their beliefs and behaviors are consistent. Inconsistent or conflicting beliefs lead to disharmony, which people strive to avoid.

[When cognitive dissonance occurs, they:] Focus on more supportive beliefs that outweigh the dissonant belief or behavior. Reduce the importance of the conflicting belief. Change the conflicting belief so that it is consistent with other beliefs or behaviors.

Cognitive dissonance can cause unease and anxiety, particularly if the disparity between the beliefs and behaviors relates to something that is central to a person's sense of self. "Person's sense of self" bears repeating, because identity is wrapped up in your security, your place in the herd, and those insecurities can be perceived as life-or-death issues. Behaving in ways that are not aligned with your personal values may produce an intense feeling of discomfort.

In a 2019 article in the *Washington Post* entitled: "The psychological phenomenon that blinds Trump supporters to his racism; People sometimes do mental gymnastics to preserve their preferred view of reality," author Kathleen D. Vohs talks about cognitive dissonance in Trump followers:

> In the case of Trump's racist remarks for example— when absorbed by his supporters who do not consider themselves racist—those inconsistencies can be summarized in a sort of syllogism: (1) I do not support racists. (2) I do support President Trump. (3) President Trump has just made a racist remark. Those three facts simply don't fit together comfortably in the mind.

Just as a hungry person will seek food to alleviate hunger, Festinger argued, people who experience mental discrepancies of this sort will work to put them in accord, to reduce the dissonance. And they will often go to extraordinary lengths to do so: "Resolving cognitive dissonance often takes considerable mental gymnastics."

My mental gymnastics went something like this: "Jaime seems to have a posture of Divinity about him; maybe he knows something I don't. Who am I to question? I'm still grappling with my own perceived spiritual inadequacies. And if this is the sure-fire way to nirvana, who am I to question another's needs? They seem to be happy. What have I got to lose? Besides, how far would I get if I tried to question the master?" Cognitive dissonance snuck up on me and made it possible to rationalize the inconsistencies and override my intuition.

The book *When Prophecy Fails* by Leon Festinger gives insights into the motivation and behavior of enthusiastic supporters. In 1956, Festinger and a group of colleagues joined a doomsday cult led by former L. Ron Hubbard devotee Dorothy Martin, who prophesized the world would be destroyed in a great flood on Dec. 21, 1954. She mobilized a group of followers who believed that they would be saved at midnight by embarking on a flying saucer that would take them to the planet Clarion. Contrary to what might be expected, the failure of the prophecy only reinforced the faith of many of the followers. Subsequent prophecies of global destruction (which obviously never happened) only re-energized the faith of the true believers.

Every incident or fact that contradicts one's beliefs can increase a commitment to a false narrative. Festinger concluded from this doomsday example that under certain circumstances—if the prophecy fails and cannot be reversed, for example—a follower, if committed to a cult or set of ideas, may try to alleviate the contradiction between their ideas and reality by "doubling down" and becoming even more committed to the ideas or the ideology to justify the effort they have already expended in devotion to it, rather than acknowledge that they have been duped by a fraud.

The following are just some of the highlights of what is being pushed around the internet. This one is by some guy named "Daniel Divine":

> A peaceful Transition is coming. Trump will not be sworn in as 45th US Pres. on Jan. 20, since US Inc. is no more. Trump will likely be sworn in as the 19th US Pres. before and after US Inc. has fully dissolved on March 4. The US, as a Country, ceased to exist since 1871, when it became US Inc. under the City of London (US flag with gold fringe and tassels attached to it).

Fun fact: There's nothing in any flag code that states the purpose or legality of the gold fringe. Yet if you search the depths of the internet you will find all sorts of conspiracy theories behind the fringe on flags. The most prominent is that the fringe indicates martial or admiralty law—basically that the Constitution does not apply in that area and that whoever is the authority figure in this place has absolute rule. Those who subscribe to this theory fear, for example, that because many courtrooms have a fringed flag, they are under maritime law rather than Constitutional law, and therefore presiding judges have complete say over your fate. I repeat, there is no law or flag code that supports this. Those who subscribe to this theory will often point to executive order 10834 regarding the design of the US flag; however, the text that they cite is completely fabricated. So, there's that! Let's go on with Daniel's fantasy:

> This is the reason you can never get ahead financially and the law is stacked against the average citizen while the elite literally get away with murder and worse. If Biden, Harris, Pence, Pilosi, etc., [sic] are arrested for their crimes against Humanity before Jan. 20, which is very likely, there is no one to assume the Presidency, since Trump was not certified as the Presidential winner by Congress and he cannot remain Pres. US Inc. has dissolved and it will be complete then.

> The EA US military will be guardians of US during the Transition. People will then be shown irrefutable proof that the election was stolen by foreign entities and that Trump was chosen by a landslide. Trump will then assume Presidency as the 19th US Pres. (as last Pres. elected before US Inc. was #18 Ulysses S. Grant, unless,

of course, JFK Jr. reappears and is reelected under GESARA interim gov't) on March 4 or 20, the original Inauguration date. The next 90 days will be chaotic.

And people are wondering what prompted the failed insurrection of January 6, 2021. Divine continues:

> In the coming few hours it is likely all the Media will be taken down because they are not sharing the truth... Then the Emergency Broadcast will have to be used Globally. We need Nuclear Scare event to go to Global Military Martial Law.

> Even if there's a Nuclear threat to SCARE THE WORLD INTO WAKING UP from 3 Gorges Dam area of China revealing all the [S]ex Trafficking worldwide don't be afraid! The end result is a beautiful 5D+ World...

> The entire Nov. 3, 2020 US Election Event was a Military Sting Operation planned many years prior to bring forth the years and years of deception placed on what was thought to be a democracy (fair system). The Intrinsic beauty in this is that everything was rigged and ready for the Steal. Did anyone see [B]iden rallies prior to election. Trump won in an huge landslide, which is why they shut down the vote counting process through the night so they could start the rig, something that has never happened before.

This little screed goes on and on for about another ten pages and we will visit a bit more of Daniel Divine's manifesto again a little later, but here's an interesting excerpt:

We are all party to a monumental lie that it is so big that most will not be able to accept the truth of it for accepting the lie will mean everything once understood to be real would be false! The mental schism caused by this potential between passed beliefs and acceptance of the new reality is called Cognitive Dissonance and it is the reason why the vast majority of people can no longer see through the lies of our times.

Ironically, Daniel is using the Cognitive Dissonance definition to justify his own cognitive dissonance. What do you do with that? You think this madness is going to stop anytime soon? I think not. Conspiracies are a "self-sealing" phenomenon. They present a psychological trap that makes it difficult to untwist these fallacious theories. The more facts push against these fantasies, the more they become evidence of the validity of the fiction in the minds of believers.

The longer a follower is committed, the more difficult it becomes to turn back. Once you start making pro-Trump comments on social media to all your friends, or donate money, sport a MAGA hat, attend a Trump rally, or take a shit on the furniture in the Capitol lobby out of some sort of undefined protest, the easier it is to get swept away by your commitment. And thus the easier it becomes to renounce previously held positions; claim the rule of law is irrelevant; eradicate institutional norms; believe America's international allies are our enemies and Putin and our Cold War enemies are now our friends; and even justify insurrection and cold-blooded murder.

After Biden became president, despite the false claims that the election was stolen and the failed insurrection at the

Capitol, some of Trump's MAGA followers were beginning to become disenchanted with him. But there are still plenty who are willing to double down on their erroneous beliefs, including many high officials and lawmakers. Festinger explained this phenomenon as part of a coping mechanism called dissonance reduction, a form of rationalization. Members often dedicate themselves with renewed energy to the group's cause after a failed prophecy and rationalize with excuses and explanations. They will move the goalpost down the field indefinitely rather than face reality.

Although many MAGA supporters struggled with anger and confusion when their "Storm"—the apocalyptic reckoning they have believed was coming for prominent Democrats and Trump's "deep state" foes—failed, some doubled down with even bigger fantasies, for example that Biden's victory was an illusion and that Trump would secure his rightful second term in office in March. Others clung to the notion that Trump will remain a "shadow president" during Biden's term. Some even floated the idea that the inauguration ceremony was computer-generated or that Biden himself could be the mysterious "Q," of QAnon, who is purportedly a government insider posting cryptic clues about the conspiracy. Sigh!

It's interesting to see what emotions Trump aroused in his committed followers. A study by Katarzyna Jasko, et. al., "Making Americans Feel Great Again? Personal Significance Predicts Political Intentions of Losers and Winners of the 2016 U.S. Election," showed that Trump supporters desired to matter and feel significant (i.e., feeling proud, strong, and important) after a victory; whereas feeling humiliated, excluded, and ashamed after a defeat could predict aggressive reactions. The study showed Trump supporters seemed to mimic his sociopathic behavior. They encouraged hostile and vindictive actions against the president's political rivals (i.e., the slogans "Trump that Bitch!" "Lock her up!" and "Proud to be a hater"). They favored the idea of suing the media, "Trump's enemy of the people," for criticizing their leader or now suing the states for voter fraud, even if there is no evidence.

In contrast, Clinton and Biden supporters demonstrated respect for their political opponents and included them in a political process. While 4.6 million protestors around the nation and the world demonstrated at the Women's March after Trump's inauguration in 2017, no major violence or loss of life occurred. As Michelle Obama put it, "When they go low, we go high."

When Jaime ridiculed me or anyone in public, the followers took it as Gospel and not only did not challenge him but copied his authoritarian disposition.

The Stanford Prison Experiment (SPE) was a famous social psychology study that attempted to investigate the psychological effects of perceived power in a simulated situation. The primary intent of the lead psychologist, Philip Zimbardo, was to focus on the power of roles, rules, symbols, and group identity to validate behavior that otherwise would repulse ordinary individuals. Zimbardo said:

> I had been conducting research for some years on deindividuation, vandalism and dehumanization that illustrated the ease with which ordinary people could be led to engage in anti-social acts by putting them in situations where they felt anonymous, or they could

perceive of others in ways that made them less than human, as enemies or objects.

The students given the position of "guards" were instructed to exert psychological control over the "prisoners." Results of the experiment showed that students quickly embraced their assigned roles, with some guards enforcing authoritarian methods and decisively subjecting some prisoners to psychological torture, while many prisoners passively permitted psychological abuse and, at the officers' request, actively harassed other prisoners who tried to stop it.

I am not suggesting that members of the Buddha-field were that malevolent or abusive to each other. I am suggesting, however, that I understand how it could get to that point. I am seeing our country escalate in violence, abuse, and authoritarian tactics at an alarming pace. When there are relatively no consequences for authorities who commit crimes—such as Trump, his family and cronies, rogue cops, urban militants, and domestic terrorists—it empowers his base to adopt a disregard for injustice and to commit violent acts, which in turn gives them a feeling of pride, strength, and importance.

The subtitle of "Make America Great Again" within the social media cybersphere is "Make Liberals Cry Again." And anonymity on social networks has aroused our shadow side—the vicious beast in us—where otherwise we would be restrained by social norms. Trump and the Republican Party have opened the door to political sadism; the sadistic pleasure in not just being victorious over your opponent but hurting them. And the inability to accept defeat can accelerate violent and abusive behavior. Thus January 6, 2021. The MAGA base and the Republican Party as a whole, especially in the post-election era, have adopted Trump's sociopathic characteristics.

Trump referred to White Supremacists as "very fine people," and he defended a vigilante who crossed state lines and murdered two protestors. I have seen many comments on social media echoing Trump's lead—justifying and cheering their leader's sadistic bloodlust. The mental gymnastics—cognitive dissonance—these followers have constructed is so dangerous that I fear for the life of this country and everything it once stood for.

CHAPTER 12

WICKED WEBS

O, what a tangled web we weave when first we practice to deceive! —Walter Scott

STEVEN HASSAN DESCRIBES A cult continuum in his book *Combatting Cult Mind Control* that includes a destructive/ unhealthy side. Here are some traits he lists:

1. Cults have no guided ethical principles; all goals justify the use of any means.

Ethics? Ha! Here is the definition:

eth·ics /'eTHiks/ *Noun;* The branch of knowledge that deals with moral principles.

And I love how they use it in a sentence: "...neither meta-physics nor ethics is the home of religion."

That's for sure! For starters, Jaime christened himself ReyJi, meaning *God-King,* and our forty-fifth president referred to himself as *the Chosen One, King of Israel.* That should be our first clue that these guys won't be leaning on the pillars of principle. I guess lying is not in the narcissist's ethics rulebook either—perhaps because they have no ethics rulebook. Narcissists have one goal, and that is to serve themselves and their insatiable appetite for self-aggrandizement, by whatever means possible, with no regard to ethics. Out of extreme insecurity, malignant narcissists have to convince themselves they are superior; thus, their means to their goal have no limits or ethical boundaries. Even knowing what they're doing, they may not care due to their lack of empathy for anyone else, and because they are emotional sadists. And it really helps when their followers support their notion of superiority.

One may typically find these individuals selected as CEOs on corporate boards. They're skilled at self-promotion and shine in job interviews—confident and charismatic. Then, once they're in power, like with Jaime, we find out who they really are—arrogant and entitled. Instead of being confident, they're merely impulsive. They lack empathy and exploit others without compunction. They ignore expert advice and treat those who differ with contempt and hostility, while demanding absolute loyalty.

The power of the narcissistic, authoritarian leader can often make good people do bad things. When the leader is malignant and self-serving, behavior that is unethical, even criminal, cascades through the organization, community, or country and becomes legitimized. We need not reiterate the deeds of the followers of Hitler, Mussolini, Charles Mason or Jim Jones—history has already shown us. And January 6, 2021, I fear, may be just the beginning of the crimes and violent "acting out" behaviors of Trump's followers. But when I think back on our behavior at the behest of the guru, although not nearly as heinous, I am saddened and shocked at how easy it was for us to lie and do some of the things we did.

For example, if Jaime needed some "dirt" on a member, we wouldn't hesitate to break into their car or home or computer. He would have someone steal people's mail out of their mailbox. He had his in-house accountant cheat on his tax returns and another write his college dissertation. (Sound familiar?) Many of us would spy on each other, even stalk some people if need be. Like followers of Bhagwan Rajneesh (aka Osho), it was not uncommon for Jaime's devotees to marry foreign members to keep them in the country. Jaime had people lie about having cancer, then publicly announce how he miraculously healed them.

Any woman that got pregnant was forced to have an abortion. I accompanied my spiritual sister, to hold her hand while the doctor performed the procedure. She chose to do it without anesthesia because Jaime convinced her that she could transcend the pain. It was one of the most traumatic experiences I'd ever witnessed. I'm sure upon hearing of her ordeal, Jaime was sadistically flattered that she heeded his "guidance."

My best friend overdosed on cocaine and had a grand mal seizure in my arms, on more than one occasion. Instead of calling 911, upon Jaime's "guidance," I just let her go through it. The memories of those times are seared in my brain with a molten mix of guilt and gratitude that she is still alive. What a confused, mind-controlled fool I was.

One member fell in love with a married woman outside of the Buddha-field. Upon hearing that his wife was having an affair, her husband threatened to expose the group. Although the member broke up with the man's wife, Jaime had someone lie to him, telling him that the husband was in the Mafia and his life was in danger (fake news). He told the member he must flee to Hawaii to protect us all. He just wanted him out of the state. In the meantime, the member had met and fallen in love with another woman. He gave up a successful career here in Austin, took the woman and her young daughter, and fled. When they got to Hawaii he had nothing—no job, no money, and was scared to be found by the other woman's "Mafia" ex. He got into a terrible motorcycle accident and smashed his face and mouth to pieces. He was hospitalized for months. Jaime didn't care, he told him it was his karma and offered to send him some homeopathic remedies. After a couple of years, Jaime convinced him to come back to Austin. Why? I have no idea, other than he couldn't get enough sycophantic, obedient disciples. The man left the woman and little girl in Hawaii, because Jaime said they couldn't come with him, and returned to the Buddha-field. Not long after, both the woman and her daughter were murdered. They never solved the case. The man still carries the pain and guilt and blames himself for their death to this day. He figures that if he hadn't taken them to Hawaii in the first place it would never have happened.

2. Information is manipulated and controlled.

Given Jaime's secrets and backdoor deeds, he ran a tight ship with his hierarchy of minions. No one disciple knew everything. And we didn't have the internet in those days. We shared secrets in whispers, if at all.

Woe betide you if you ever contradicted Jaime, even behind his back; whomever you talked to would definitely tell him about it. Or they would take it to "cleansing" to "work on it." The next thing you knew, you would either be called into cleansing or he would talk about it in a group setting. Therefore no one ever talked to or trusted anyone else about what they saw or felt. Intimidation is one viable technique to control information.

The totalitarian tyrannies of Stalin, Hitler, Mao, Pol Pot, and others relied largely—although not exclusively—on mass terror and indoctrination. In recent decades, however, a less predatory form of authoritarian government has transpired, one better adapted to the globalized media and sophisticated technologies of the twenty-first century. The "soft" dictators control power by quashing opposition and extinguishing checks and balances, while using hardly any violence. Today's political leaders use a vast treasure trove of techniques to manipulate and control their narrative through cable and social media, especially with the help of foreign bots and troll farms.

In America, since the Fairness Doctrine was overturned in the eighties, broadcasters have had free rein to spin the news any way they want. In an article in *The Atlantic* entitled "The Billion-Dollar Disinformation Campaign to Reelect the President: How new technologies and techniques pioneered by dictators will shape the 2020 election," author McKay Coppins makes a startling statement after creating a new Facebook account for his investigation. He writes:

> The story that unfurled in my Facebook feed over
> the next several weeks was, at times, disorienting.
> There were days when I would watch, live on TV, an

impeachment hearing, filled with damning testimony about the president's conduct, only to look at my phone later and find a slickly edited video—served up by the Trump campaign. *Wait,* I caught myself wondering more than once, *is* that *what happened today?*

I was surprised by the effect it had on me. I'd assume that my skepticism and media literacy would inoculate me against any distortions. But I soon found myself reflexively questioning *every* headline. It wasn't that I believed Trump and his Boosters were telling the truth. It *was* that, in this state of heightened suspicion, truth itself—about Ukraine, impeachment, [voter fraud] or anything else—felt more and more difficult to locate. With each swipe, the notion of observable reality drifted further out of reach.

Manipulating information and brand building is the authoritarian leader's most effective tool. Throughout history, leaders have used—or in some cases invented—an ideology to legitimize their power. In the original chiefdoms like Hawaii, the chiefs were both political leaders and priests, who claimed to be communicating with the gods in order to bring about a generous harvest. In North Korea, Kim Sung Il and his policies were responsible for a famine that led to the deaths of one to two million people. When food finally arrived, the message from state media was that it was a tribute to his leadership. Other ideologies include personality cults such as Maoism or Stalinism and now Trumpism. Dictators such as Hitler and Stalin sought to essentially remodel citizens' worldviews by imposing far-reaching ideologies. The new autocrats, however, are more stringent: they aim only to convince citizens of their competence to govern. Donald manipulated the media for years. He used them to build his brand as one of America's royalty—flaunting his illusion of great wealth.

Trump, who had no experience in government, based his entire candidacy upon the notion that he is rich. Somehow conning his followers based on the reasoning that because he is rich, he must also be smart and therefore qualified to be President of the United States. This presented an interesting twist to how his followers could so easily disregard the facts and fall for his seduction.

In *Dictators and their Followers: A Theory of Dictatorship* (University of Warsaw), author Dr. Gustav Bychowski writes:

> There exists a particular interrelationship between the dictator and the subjugated collectivity. The latter submits to the dictator not only because of fear but because it worships him and sees in him an ideal. The members of the group identify themselves with the leader whose image becomes incorporated, as it were, into the collective mind as a kind of new super-ego. That image thus may replace former ideals and principles regulating people's ideas, emotions and activity. They see in him as the embodiment of their own wishes and desires, particularly their desire for greatness and happiness. They believe his promises and in their misery and anxiety rely on him uncritically. They deem him omniscient and almighty, thus regressing in their attitude toward him to the attitude of the infantile psyche toward the omnipotent parent.

Donald deliberately staged his wealth at every opportunity to reinforce the programing, from interviews at his gilded penthouse apartment to the use of props like his private jet prominently displayed in the background at his rallies. His followers are attracted to the façade. Even though it has been proven that he is a repeated failure in business and a confirmed grifter, they refuse to accept the truth. Post-election, even after Biden was declared the winner by the electoral committee, the grifter-in-chief has suckered over two hundred million dollars in "electoral defense legal fees" from his devotees as of this writing.

As the truth rolls out one may ask, what could keep Trump's base still enthralled? To further understand that attraction, Leo Löwenthal and Theodor Adorno, Frankfurt School refugees from Hitler, drew on a Freudian-inspired "mass psychology" to analyze demagogues in the US. Adorno wrote, in his "Freudian Theory and the Pattern of Fascist Propaganda" (1951):

> ... [T]he members of a group stand in need of the illusion that they are equally and justly loved by their leader; but the leader himself need love no one else, he [must] be of a masterful nature, absolutely narcissistic, self-confident and independent.

Hitler, Mussolini, and even Charles De Gaulle fit this model, and like Trump, they drew on mass media, parades, rallies, and film to project themselves as father figures to enthralled nations. Adorno realized, however, that the model only applied in part to American demagogues. What distinguishes the demagogue in this country, he argued of Freud's hypothesis, is the identification between the leader and his followers. Bychowski writes:

The narcissism in question is not only Trump's. More important is that of his followers, who idealize him as they once, in childhood, idealized themselves. Beyond that, the demagogue has a special appeal to wounded narcissism, to the feeling that one has failed to meet standards one has set for oneself. The successful demagogue activates this feeling by possessing the typical qualities of the individuals who follow him, but in what Adorno, quoting Freud, called a 'clearly marked and pure form' that gives the impression 'of greater force and of more freedom of libido.'

In Adorno's words:

> ... [T]he superman has to resemble the follower and appear as his 'enlargement.' The leader 'completes' the follower's self-image. He 'seems to be the enlargement of the subject's own personality, a collective projection of himself, rather than an image of the father'—a Trump, in other words, rather than a Washington or Roosevelt.

Hence, the dick swinging, horned-headdress-bearing, chest-pounding machismo acts at the Capitol on January 6, 2021. Trump gives his followers permission to live out their own fantasy of themselves—sad caricatures of the American Rambo "he-man" archetype that, in reality, are closer to a bloated professional wrestler crossed with a playground bully.

CHAPTER 13

THE MIRROR LIES

The face that pins you with its double gaze reveals
a chastening secret! —*Diane Ackerman*

Narcissists tend to become slanderous or abusive and
engage in much shadow projection when criticized.
They deprecate other teachings and acknowledge
theirs own alone as valid.

EVER NOTICE THAT NARCISSISTS routinely project onto their perceived competitors or enemies the very things they themselves are doing? Jaime did that all the time. In the beginning he would speak admiringly and respectfully about figures like Paramahansa Yogananda, Ramakrishna, and other Indian swamis and teachers, but as his narcissism inflated, he started tearing them down, calling them frauds and perverts. He made up slanderous lies about these once-revered teachers. He spun wild tales of those teachers' perversions and sexual indiscretions. We now know that every story he was making up had an uncanny resemblance to what he was doing himself, behind closed doors. I find it fascinating that Trump's followers accuse Democrats, including Biden, of being pedophiles when there are so many pictures and videos that show the Donald at Jeffrey Epstein's parties, but that little detail doesn't faze them a bit. Ah, cognitive dissonance, it's a wonder drug.

Narcissistic leaders use all kinds of psychological tricks to control their supporters' minds and brand others as enemies. One technique is to block accurate information by deliberately condemning, berating, and repudiating legitimate sources. In May 2019, the *New York Times* created a list entitled "The 598 People, Places and Things Donald Trump Has Insulted on Twitter: A Complete List," and that list has more than doubled by now.

Often this branding takes the form of projection. One of the best explanations of Trump, the Projector-in-Chief, was in a June 2016 article in the *Atlantic* by Kurt Andersen:

> Trump is a man with almost zero ability to empathize or imagine other people's motives or drives. His ego and narcissism are so oversized they warp all his opinions into reflections of himself. Since he has no understanding of anyone but himself, when he tries to attribute motive, needs, or desires in others, they are therefore at best something from himself that he recognizes in them, or simply a reflection of feelings he himself has. In simple terms, one might say his mind is

empty of any thoughts that are not self-referential. And so self-projection is simply a consequence of this vacuity.

Another effective way of branding someone an "enemy other" is called "essentializing"—a technique narcissists typically use to assassinate their opponents' character. Psychologist Gregory Walton explains that essentializing:

[I]mplies that a characteristic is inherent in the person (self or other) rather than the product of circumstance. This is the important difference between using a descriptive verb ("Ted Cruz tells lies") and a noun label ("Lyin' Ted"). Psychological research shows, such minor manipulations of language can convey much more deep-seated, stable and central characteristics about a subject. And these labels preclude other identities.

Negative labeling is no accident. Trump is a master at it. "Crooked Hillary," "Sleepy Joe Biden," "Crazy Bernie," "Little Marco." He gleefully repeats these demeaning nicknames until they stick, and then his followers repeat the same labels like obedient parrots. Trump was a one-trick pony. He used name-calling so often you would think his base would have figured out that this is a classic mind-control technique.

Isaac Bonewits is one of America's leading experts on the ancient and modern occult. Like Hassan, Bonewits lists a number of factors we can use to evaluate whether a suspected group exhibits known cultic dynamics. Two of the characteristics on his list are:

1. Cult leaders focus on controlling, preserving, and acquiring power and information, but share little of these with rank and file members—and none with outsiders.

In the beginning of the Buddha-field we all read and studied many spiritual books. After a few years, Jaime stopped all of that. He discouraged anyone from reading spiritual books and forbade Osho's books altogether; those were his favorite to plagiarize. He kept secrets with his closest disciples, from his legal name and other vital information, his sexual affairs, or who owned what properties and other businesses, to where he kept his cash, how much he had, and how he was declaring for tax purposes—or not.

Besides Trump's many shady business deals, extortions, frauds, hiding his tax returns, and backdoor deals, Trump and his Republican goons were busy destroying as many policies and safety measures put in place by the Obama administration as they could, while we weren't looking—or even if we were. It's not that these actions weren't there if you were paying attention; but his Blitzkrieg of policy destruction was so fast and relentless that it has been hard for any average American to keep up. Especially when these rampages are tucked behind so many other scandals.

In a 2017 article in *The Agenda* entitled "138 Things Trump Did This Year While You Weren't Looking; behind the crazy headlines more conservative priorities got pushed through than most people realize, an exhaustive list of what really happened to the government in 2017" by Danny Vinik, the author spells out in detail:

> What does it look like? There are a few consistent
> themes: Rolling back President Barack Obama's legacy
> on everything from labor regulations to environmental
> protections, and more broadly tearing down rules across
> the government.

Trump's goal was not to be President of the United States. He evidently did not understand what that role entailed. This narcissist's goals were to arouse his supporters to feed his insatiable appetite for self-aggrandizement; to do the bidding of Vladimir Putin and Republican cronies to gain approval; to avoid whatever Putin has on him; and to destroy his enemies, predominately liberals and Barack Obama. President Obama humiliated Donald Trump during his comedy routine at the 2011 White House Correspondents' Dinner after Trump arrogantly took credit for the release of the president's long-form birth certificate earlier in the week. You cannot confront or ridicule a malignant narcissist without grave consequences. And with the power of the presidency of the United States, Trump would stop at nothing. No logic nor reason nor care for anything or anyone will stop this thin-skinned coward's methodical demolition derby. And that played perfectly into the goal of the Trumpublican party.

Donald Trump inspired a culture of divisiveness, cruelty, and revenge. As a classic *Lord-of-the-Flies*-style charismatic leader, he unleashes the beast in others. His followers applaud him, which gives him the fuel to continue his destruction. Leader and followers operate in an ever-intensifying feedback loop of rage and desire for vengeance. The one thing that unites the right and drives the GOP is hatred of liberals. Influenced by powerful propaganda, they hold a strong belief that if Democrats are in power, then it will not be bad or even terrible, but the end of everything they care about. Towns and cities will burn, religion will be outlawed, minorities will take all their hard-earned money, women and homosexuals will be in control, and America as we know it will cease to exist. These horrors have not been presented as metaphors, but as the literal truth. That indoctrination has created animosity that has consumed every policy goal, every ideological principle, and even every ounce of commitment to democracy, if democracy allows for the possibility that liberals might win. We have seen this belief persist, even to the point of denying the 2020 election was legitimate.

Trump is exceptional in his ability to provoke, upset, and irritate liberals. No doubt this is part of his appeal to a certain segment of the population—the ones who have been programed since the seventies that "liberal elites" were laughing at them. Trump fought and fought angrily, resentfully, endlessly driven forward by his hatred of the people his supporters hate. Like kittens who see a lion in the mirror, Trump is the bigger-than-life illusion of themselves—a false reflection of those who believe this lie. That's what the base loves, and every other Republican knows it. So while the country was busy with his multiple scandals, and his cabinet members were being arrested, indicted, and jailed, he was busy tearing down the government and the hard work that his nemesis, Obama, did during his eight years in office. And his followers loved him for it—even if it was against their own interests. Such is the power and madness of cult delusion.

2. Cults have a top-down structure, with a single leader at the top and a small inner circle immediately below. There is a lack of clearly defined organizational rights for members.

The Buddha-field had its hierarchy, very similar to most religious, corporate, or political structures. As with all authoritarian leaders, their loyal toadies have a pecking order. To give the followers their own structure of power reinforces and maintains control of the group. It provides an illusion of power to the powerless and fuels our own narcissistic authoritarian tendencies. Jaime's cabinet went something like this: the "Master;" followed by his immediate entourage (or minions who lived with him), comprised mostly of original older Holy Company in the Knowing —although special dispensation of privileges could be given to an aspirant, depending on how good looking he was and subsequent blowjob aptitude. The next tier (the executive staff) was older Holy Company in the Knowing, followed by his base, the aspirants, and finally newbies. To give you a brilliant example of how life was within the BF, everyone who was a member could relate to the following joke from a devotee called Ivan (an alias):

How many Buddha-fielders does it take to change a lightbulb? Answer: 139!

- One to collect for weekly lightbulb money.

- One to ask who is available for lightbulb service.

- One to tell everyone how Jaime used to change his own lightbulbs.

- Fifty-seven to turn it into an event, buy and prepare food, do major construction on and set up decorations in the venue, set up the PA gear and lights, and clean up afterwards.

- Seventeen to save seats at the event.

- Four to come up with a cover story for the neighbors: saying that we are a "movie club," "acting class," or some other "safe" group of people so "you can just move along now...there's nothing to see...."

- Seven to tell everyone who wasn't invited that there is no function that night and that everyone else is coincidentally out of town and they should go home, drop their mind, and meditate.

- Three who will require countless hours of therapy because the lightbulb being changed triggered some major past life trauma.

- One to write down 17 pages (as dictated from Jaime) about how the lightbulb must be changed in order to be in the highest consciousness and avoid creating karma.

- Seven to argue about the interpretation of those instructions.

- Three to tell all the "new" people how and why the BF method of changing lightbulbs is far superior to all other methods, regardless of how long they've been around, how much better they are, or even in the face of obvious logic or personal experience to the contrary.

- One to make an announcement that we are not to talk about changing lightbulbs directly (because it might promote suspicion) and that we should refer to it as "cleaning the fish tank."

- Six to argue about better code phrases than "cleaning the fish tank."

- One to make a movie out of it.

- Nine to turn it into a Halloween skit.

- One to write a song about it.

- Four to argue that the song lyrics aren't "conscious" enough.

- One to treat the old lightbulb like a holy relic and vow to keep it in a silk bag under their pillow for the rest of their life.

- Three to buy the bulbs, get told they got the wrong ones, return them, and buy new ones at least 4 more times.

- One to actually change the lightbulb.

- Two people "in the Knowing" to supervise the changing of the lightbulb.

- Seven people to "share" about the experience.

- and one to add it to his blog @ www.aboutthetruth.com.

Pathological lying and Jaime's narcissism went hand in hand, so this clever sociopath built his power structure and his coalition of supporters, wicked webs as it were, before many of us caught on to what was actually happening. By that time I was committed, and it was a lot harder to leave.

CHAPTER 14

BIRDS OF A FEATHER

Narcissists often exhibit unusual and inappropriate attitudes to sexual matters, sexual behavior and bodily functions; underneath the charming exterior there are often suspicions or hints of sex discrimination and sexual harassment, perhaps also sexual dysfunction, sexual inadequacy, sexual perversion, sexual violence or sexual abuse.

WHY WOULD SOMEONE SURRENDER their most intimate sense of self to anyone? Jaime was a gay man. In the beginning, rumors arose from time to time of his relationships with other consenting, adult gay men. This was something that one did not openly talk about, because frankly, it didn't seem like anyone's business. As it turned out, many of them were heterosexual, but I didn't find out he was preying on and coercing straight men for years, until the end. He manipulated these men into thinking he was a deity and that to have sex with him would "liberate" them from their bonds of inhibition and thus elevate their spiritual status. Like Trump said, "When you're a star you can do anything—grab 'em by the pussy, anything."

I noticed Jaime never wanted to "liberate" the overweight or less attractive ones, and never the women. We know this in hindsight, and although those involved with him may have their horror stories to tell now, they were not telling them then. There were people who lived with him, and people were with him every night for years, who claim that they did not know what was going on in his bedroom on the other side of the door. Ah! Again, cognitive dissonance; it's like a Magic Eraser.

I asked him about his relationships occasionally, and not unlike Trump, he would flat out deny them. One time, early on, Malila came to LA on a visit from Florida and took me to lunch. She tried to warn me. She said that Jaime was taking sexual advantage of guys in therapy. I asked him about it, and again he denied it. I believed him. He was my pious and humble teacher. He convinced me that Malila was just jealous because she had not attained true enlightenment. This was shortly after I was initiated. I was still in the honeymoon phase. Besides, how far would I have gotten if I had dared try to publicly expose the "master" as a liar, based on rumors and hearsay? I had no proof; there were no complaints, no cooperating witnesses, and no reason at the time to suspect abuse or non-consensual behavior.

Because I am a female, my experience of Jaime's sexual perversion was reduced to his odd and infantile jokes and innuendoes about sex. I came to find out that during his "cleansing" sessions he would have porn running on mute on the TV behind the person while they had their eyes closed. Like his routines with everything, he had his sexual routines. Mondays were with this guy, Tuesday someone else, etc. Due to Jaime's paranoia and lust, which became extreme, he no longer gave Săt Săng in person on Thursday nights. Ben or other Holy Company in the Knowing would give formal Săt Săng. While everyone was out, Jaime would routinely rape Will (the maker of *Holy Hell*) in the same fashion every Thursday night for years. Because I do not wish to cause any further harm to Will, I will spare the details. Suffice it to say, the ordeal was in the most humiliating and degrading manner. I cried when I finally heard the story years later.

Sexual deviancy is very often interlaced with narcissistic sociopathic behavior. And our relationship with sex as a Judeo-Christian culture has an important connection or disconnect to our social behaviors and acceptance.

"...sexual violence or sexual abuse."

At least twenty-five women have accused Donald Trump of sexual assault since the 1970s. Twenty-five! One or two disgruntled or vindictive women, maybe; but twenty-five? The allegations from these women go on and on, with one sordid tale after another.

The following is a court deposition from a woman who was sexually assaulted by Trump and Jeffery Epstein when she was a thirteen-year-old child. Case number 1:16-cv-04642, document 1, Filed 06/20/16 in the United States District Court Southern District of New York, Jane Doe, proceeding under a pseudonym, Plaintiff v. Donald J. Trump and Jeffrey E. Epstein, reads:

Courts have discretion to allow proceeding anonymously where the need for privacy outweighs the public's interest in knowing their identity and any prejudice to the defendants. This litigation involves matters that are highly sensitive and of a personal nature, and identification of Plaintiff would pose a risk of retaliatory physical harm to her and to others.

Exh. A. Plaintiff was enticed by promises of money and a modeling career to attend a series of parties, with other similarly situated minor females, held at a New York City residence that was being used by Defendant Jeffrey Epstein. At least four of the parties were attended by Defendant Trump.

Exhs. A and B. On information and belief, by this time in 1994, Defendant Trump initiated sexual contact with Plaintiff at four different parties. On the fourth and final sexual encounter with Defendant Trump, Defendant Trump tied Plaintiff to a bed, exposed himself to Plaintiff, and then proceeded to forcibly rape Plaintiff. During the course of this savage sexual attack, Plaintiff loudly pleaded with Defendant Trump to stop, but with no effect. Defendant Trump responded to Plaintiff's pleas by violently striking Plaintiff in the face with his open hand and screaming that he would do whatever he wanted.

Exhs. A 11. Immediately following this rape, Defendant Trump threatened Plaintiff that, were she ever to reveal any of the details of the sexual and physical abuse of her by Defendant Trump, Plaintiff and her family would be physically harmed if not killed.

Exhs. A and B.12. Defendant Epstein had sexual contact with Plaintiff at two of the parties. The second sexual encounter with Defendant Epstein took place after Plaintiff had been raped by Defendant Trump. Defendant Epstein forced himself upon Plaintiff and proceeded to rape her anally and vaginally despite her loud pleas to stop. Defendant Epstein then attempted to strike Plaintiff about the head with his closed fists while he angrily screamed at Plaintiff that he, Defendant Epstein, rather than Defendant Trump, should have been the one who took Plaintiff's virginity, before Plaintiff finally managed to break away from Defendant Epstein.

Exhs. A 13, The threats of violence against Plaintiff and her family continued, this time from Defendant Epstein, who again reiterated that Plaintiff was not to reveal any of the details of his sexual and physical abuse of her or else, specifically, Plaintiff and her family would be seriously physically harmed, if not killed.

Exhs. A and B.14. While still under threats of physical harm by coming forward and having no reason to believe that the threats have ever been lifted or would ever be lifted, Plaintiff, who has suffered from stress, emotional distress, mental pain and suffering, among other problems, ever since the assaults, was subjected to daily painful reminders of the horrific acts of one of the perpetrators, Defendant Trump, via mass media coverage of him starting on or about June 16, 2015 that, over a short period of time, became continuous and unavoidable.

Just as Jaime denied his encounters to me so many times, Trump denied ever kissing or groping women without consent. Yet we all heard the tape, in his own words, just days before the election:

> *"I just start kissing them.*
> *It's like a magnet.*
> *Just kiss.*
> *I don't even wait.*
> *And when you're a star, they let you do it.*

You can do anything.
Grab 'em by the pussy.
You can do anything."

Cognitive dissonance: *"People sometimes do mental gymnastics to preserve their preferred view of reality."* And what are the Trump supporter's mental gymnastics?

"It was just harmless locker talk. That's the way all men talk. It doesn't mean anything."

Note, too, the projection behavior we witness from Trump followers who embrace QAnon conspiracy fantasies accusing high-profile Democrats of child trafficking and abuse.

Narcissists undermine and destroy anyone who they perceive to be an adversary, a potential threat, or who can see through their mask. Adept at creating conflict between those who would otherwise collate incriminating information about them. They are also quick to belittle, undermine, denigrate and discredit anyone who calls, attempts to call, or might call them to account.

Like sexual vampires, narcissists often use sex to satiate their lust for ultimate power. Keith Allen Raniere, for example, is an American felon, founder of NXIVM, a multi-level marketing company and cult in which a harem of sexual "slaves" were branded with his initials on their pelvises and coerced into having sex with him. One of the victims was fifteen years old when the abuse began. Similar to the Buddha-field's strict dietary regime, the women in the NXIVM cult were taught to revere him and were ordered to maintain near-starvation diets to achieve the physique he found desirable. As described in the HBO documentary series *The Vow* and elsewhere, operating within the inner-sanctum of NXIVM was a secretive subgroup called D.O.S. — an acronym for a Latin phrase that roughly translates to "Lord/Master of the Obedient Female Companions."

Similar to information gathered in Jaime's "cleansings," the women of NXIVM were required to hand over "collateral"—embarrassing and incriminating information, including nude photographs—that would be publicly released if they disclosed the existence of D.O.S. Jaime had designs on a good-looking heterosexual man in the Buddha-field and convinced a woman to start a relationship with him. Once she got involved, Jaime got her to entice the man into letting her use a dildo on him to get him to like anal sex. At the end of my time in the Buddha-field, Jaime had a member of the group try to seduce me and take nude photos of me. I don't really know what that was about. But years after I left, this person confessed that Jaime set up that seduction. Like Jaime's revolving boys, Raniere also maintained a "rotating group" of fifteen to twenty women and girls with whom he had continued sexual relations. Raniere used psychological manipulation to indoctrinate his followers into obedience.

Both Nancy Salzman, NXIVM cofounder, and Raniere, aka "Vanguard," used egoistic jargon such as "Parasites"—people creating problems where none exist and craving attention— or "Suppressives" who see good but want to destroy it. In the Buddha-field, we used words like "nowhere" or "unconscious." In NXIVM a person who criticized their program called Executive Success, for example, would be considered showing suppressive behavior. Critics faced retaliation and lawsuits, creating an internal culture with no tolerance for dissent.

Salzman, known to the group's followers as "Prefect," was charged with identity theft and altering records to influence the outcome of a lawsuit against NXIVM. Raniere was convicted and sentenced to life in prison for sex trafficking and racketeering. He and his cohorts were suspected of identity theft, extortion, forced labor, money laundering, wire fraud, and obstruction of justice. Raniere stated, "He is not sorry for his conduct or his choices," and—similar to Trump's MO—accused the judge at his trial of corruption and demanded a new trial, which the judge denied twice. As if they all consult the same playbook, when called to comment on the film *Holy Hell*, Jaime told CNN that it was made up, "fake news" as it were.

Trump is facing a defamation suit in the New York State Supreme Court, filed against him by the journalist E. Jean Carroll, who wrote that "Mr. Trump raped her in 1996 in a dressing room at Bergdorf Goodman in New York." He has vehemently denied the allegations, calling Carroll a liar who was just drumming up publicity with the intention of selling her book. And he had the audacity to try to have William Barr, the people's Attorney General at the time, represent him on the taxpayers' dime.

Jaime practiced this pattern of denial, subterfuge, and cover-up against an aspirant who rebuffed him, as soon as the person left the room. Hearing that man's story was the reason I finally quit the Buddha-field.

The burning question on so many people's minds after seeing *Holy Hell* was, "How could anyone stay with that freak?" Not unlike the question that has left me and so many of my female friends asking: How could *any* female vote for a slimy, perverted reprobate like Trump? Well, that's a lot to unpack. But I have a theory. After the #MeToo and #TimesUp movements started, many discussions and old recollections were dragged out of the rusty deposit box of my memory bank.

Cults of any kind usually involve groupthink. A society, large or small, has a set of standards that take a long time to change. During the Brett Kavanaugh hearings, before he was seated as a Supreme Court justice, when Christine Blasey Ford gave her riveting testimony, I thought, oh yeah, that happened to me, only I was thirteen and it was with a perfect stranger. I hadn't thought of it for over fifty years. I hadn't thought about it because in those days, that was just the way it was. Countless female friends of mine have shared their stories of sexual assault or harassment with a curiously nonchalant attitude because that was the standard in those days.

Similar to Ford's description, I was on a road trip with my family, and a guy lured me into his cabin. He didn't succeed in fully raping me, but he pinned me on his bed, and while grinding on me, he tried to rip my clothes off and feel me up. Like Ford, I narrowly escaped. But when I got out of this guy's room, my family had been looking for me. They wanted to get on the road, and they were frustrated that they couldn't find me. After the Kavanaugh hearing, I read comments on Facebook like, "If she wasn't a liar, why didn't she mention it at the time?" Or "She must have been asking for it" or "She's just trying to get her fifteen minutes of fame." Fifteen minutes of fame? After death threats and an excruciating testimony in front of the world? Yeah, that's the kind of fame every girl craves. How could Ford prove it? How could I have proved it?

Not to mention the shame and embarrassment over the entire ordeal.

Did I mention this to my parents or anyone? Oh, hell no. What would have happened? I could imagine my father would have tried to kill this guy; the police would have been called—you get the picture. And it was my word against his. There was no proof. My mother would have wondered how I got myself into such a situation. They no doubt would have blamed me for being so irresponsible. I knew nothing at that age. But somehow I felt guilty, as if I should have known better. Why did I allow myself to be lured into his room? He was flattering; he was good looking. How enticing for a pubescent girl to receive so much attention and affection from a friendly older boy. So why didn't Will or the other guys come forward and tell their tale? Who would have believed them? No one. Who would have blamed them for disrupting our happy little community? Everyone!

When Harvey Weinstein got his ass handed to him over multiple sexual assault allegations, he made the comment: "I came of age in the sixties and seventies, when all the rules about behavior and workplaces were different. That was the culture then." I get it! Under no circumstances do I condone Weinstein's behavior and I hope he picks up a lot of soap in prison, but I understand his comment. Revolutions are messy.

Prior to the seventies, women had very few rights and were treated like property. But many women were waking up with the burning desire to be self-actualized and independent. Helen Gurley Brown, author of *Sex and the Single Girl*, published in 1962, presented the shocking notion that it was okay—even enjoyable—for a woman to live on her own, have her own money, have sexual relationships before marriage or even—wait for it—never marry at all!" Two years later, though, in 1964, Hollywood released an adaptation of the book, starring Tony Curtis and Natalie Wood. It was riddled with sexist comments and made a mockery of the book.

But consider this: In the sixties, a bank could refuse to issue a credit card to an unmarried woman. Women could not serve on juries. They were excluded from the more lucrative professional positions, and women earned fifty-nine cents for every dollar a man earned for the same work. Access to birth control was limited to married women, and the pill was illegal in some states. With birth control a woman could complete her education, enter the workforce, and plan her own life—they couldn't have that.

Many women are still conditioned to believe it is part of their "wifely duty" to have sex with their husbands, even if it is violent sex against their will. Many religious doctrines outline sexual acts as a "duty" for wives. When I was growing up, sex was not talked about. In many cases, our mothers before us were literally told on their wedding day to "Just lay back and let him do his business."

When the #MeToo movement took off, I read comments from men, but also from women, still mocking Hollywood celebrities and other women when they finally told their horrible tales of sexual harassment and assault. Everybody knew the term "casting couch" in those days. Most people looked at it as, that's how *she* got the job, rather than that's what *he* did to her. The finger always pointed at the one they considered that immoral slut—never to him.

Hell, it happened to me. After I graduated from ArtCenter, I got a job opportunity to do a movie poster for a big Hollywood feature film about cocaine dealers. Wow! A chance of a lifetime for a young illustrator. I went to the producer's house. We talked about what images he wanted on the poster. He suggested we take a drive to a head shop on Sunset Boulevard to look at some paraphernalia. We got in his Mercedes and were driving down the Boulevard when he asked me how old I was when I lost my virginity. I was shocked at the inappropriate question, but the next request was even more disgusting. He unzipped his pants, while he was driving, and wanted me to give him a blowjob. When I refused, he looked at me with disbelief and said, "Well this isn't going to work," pulled a U-turn, and took me back to the house. Needless to say, I didn't get the job. Did I say anything to anyone? Seriously? My word against this famous Hollywood producer's? Even if I could prove it, that would have ended this "slut's" budding career before it got started.

In many ways gay men's relationships are like women's. They are often put in situations of subordination to a dominant male, like Jaime. There was no #MeToo movement in the Buddha-field till the very end. So what would have happened to a single guy if he came forward? Would he face the same consequences as Plaintiff Jane Doe, or E. Jean Carroll—or Blasey Ford? Or me, or thousands of victims? You could even end up with an Epstein-style broken neck. Isn't it sometimes just easier to lay back and let him do his business?

So, how does all this relate to the Trump phenomenon? Why did so many women vote for Trump, and how does this relate to cult-think? In the sixties women woke up and thought, *Heyyy, wait a minute...* And so, even though it's taken fifty years, the revolution began. But where did this forward thinking come from? Artists and writers, intellectuals and college-educated women inspired a lot—you know, those uppity "liberals," who were given a taste of freedom and opportunities for self-expression. Then these ideas manifested in Hollywood film, television, and rock 'n'roll music. And where did that come from? California, New York, and the big urban centers, where people were forced to embrace a more diverse culture and open their minds to race, sex, gender identity, and the complexity of society. Unlike the insulated rural, Christian communities outside the city limits. It was and still is a slow awakening in the male-dominant, Christian-controlled South and rural middle America. Thus the gap between the liberals in the coastal states and the conservatives in the middle and southern states widened.

Overall, 55% of whites with a four-year college degree voted for Hillary Clinton over Donald Trump (38%). Among the much larger group of white voters who had not completed college, Trump won by more than two-to-one (64% to 28%). "I love the poorly educated," he twaddled. Of younger women, 63% voted for Clinton. But with women voters aged fifty and older, about half of them were married; and among them, Trump had a 55% to 39% majority. And then, of course, there's the "Becky," American slang used as a stereotype epithet for a white woman, especially one who is unaware or takes advantage of her social privilege. Ever notice the hair color of 90% of the women behind Trump at his rallies? I know—I'm being catty...just sayin'. You think it's just a coincidence? After all, "Gentlemen Prefer Blondes!" "Blondes have more fun" Right? Hollywood and Madison Avenue have programed and conditioned men and women to accept what is considered "sexy" and appealing to men for decades. So that kind of woman can be taken care of by a big strong Daddy figure.

So, what of Trump's promise in 2020 to suburban "wine-moms" that he would get their husbands "back to work"—as if they were all still living like June Cleaver, the stereotypical 1950s housewife from *Leave It to Beaver*? Or that he would protect them from low-income housing—a not-so-subtle dog whistle—by preventing the infestation of those brown ne'er-do-wells from encroaching on their safe neighborhoods? Did these appeals work? Apparently, yes! There was not a big shift in the demographics of white women voters in 2020, despite Trump's reprobate behavior of the previous four years. It was black and Latino women who won Biden the presidency.

Although age and level of education play a clear role in the Trump phenomenon, cultural programing also plays a huge role in the cognitive dissonance of the Trump voter. Recently, I had a startling conversation with a young intern. I was in the lunchroom at work, laughing at some absurd political insanity I was reading on Facebook, when she asked me what I was laughing at. "Do you follow politics?" I asked. "Oh no, I don't care anything about that stuff," she replied. And then, to my horror, she continued, "…but I vote, though." I took a breath and asked, "How is it you vote for something you know nothing about?" She said, "Oh, I just do what my husband tells me; he follows all that." And there it is. I felt like I had just interviewed Alice from the 1950s TV series *The Honeymooners*. The famous expression Alice's husband, Ralph Kramden, used to say all the time, while shaking his fist, was, "To the moon, Alice." In other words, when Alice said something he didn't like, he would threaten to beat her. Everyone thought that was hysterical in those days. I asked this intern where she grew up. "Northeast Texas," she replied. This young woman was studying to be a pharmacist. She wasn't stupid or uneducated by any means. Yet all that education could not break the powerful cultural identification they indoctrinated her with as a child.

I think it is a natural instinct for many females to view their fathers as a protector. And in the Buddha-field, Jaime played the role of patriarch. Things may have been entirely different if the guru was a female. Chances are the group wouldn't have existed. Malila never got her cult off the ground. But that indoctrinated notion that we are safer in a paternal society is a deep and corrosive belief in America. What do we expect? In a Judeo-Christian society, the greatest protector of all—God—is a male. Then, as the ladder descends to the next rung, after the Son of God, we have leaders of the country and churches, CEOs of corporations, then heads of the family—all males.

We all grew up with the reinforcement of paternal security. The Republican Party is the party of keeping the white heteropatriarchy intact. Kristin Kobes Du Mez, a historian and author of the book *Jesus and John Wayne*, states "Christian masculinity is the only thing that can preserve traditional American culture." Trump's supporters love to say how manly he is. They wear "Donald Trump: Finally Someone With Balls" T-shirts at his rallies. Why that dangling piece of flesh between men's legs should qualify them as being superior is beyond me, but this has been the story since the beginning of civilization. It's programed into our genetic makeup, that cavemen were the protectors. And some humans remain unevolved.

Trump's a guy who claims he would stop a school shooting "even if he didn't have a weapon," or apparently a brain. A blustering, braggadocious bully does not make a man—especially a draft-dodging, spray-tanned hypochondriac. But to some, thanks to stereotypes and deep programing, that kind of obnoxious posturing reflects a tough guy who won't let anyone take advantage. And for those who have been duped into believing that they have been taken advantage of by the liberal elite—Trump's your man (and I use the term loosely).

How powerful are these stereotypes? Many of us are still unconsciously programed to judge women by their looks and personality over their achievements and qualifications. Even now, as I write this with my salty language and brazen, sarcastic criticism, I am aware this book will be scrutinized differently because I'm a female. How far do you think Kamala Harris or Elizabeth Warren would get if they were caught saying, "When you're famous, you can do anything—grab 'em by the dick?" Seriously! Think about it. We still have an extraordinarily ridiculous double standard. And a very long way to go.

I've heard people say, "I don't know, I just don't like Hillary Clinton" or "Elizabeth Warren's way of speaking is so annoying" or "Amy Klobuchar is a mean bitch!" Trump deemed Kamala Harris "nasty," followed by more insults characterizing her as not sufficiently nice or compliant—common complaints women experience as they seek power in the corporate and political worlds. What are they running for? Miss Congeniality instead of the President of the United States? In a 2017 political op-ed, a CNN commentator, Mel Robbins, wrote: "Many experts argue that sexism is more acceptable than racism—we accept it; are not as outraged by it or ashamed of it. I believe it."

Jaimele Cottle, in the *Atlantic*, cited this thought-provoking example of "two hecklers at a New Hampshire Clinton rally who waved signs and chanted, 'Iron my shirt!' But if someone had yelled an equivalently demeaning remark at Obama—like, say, 'Shine my shoes!'—the public response likely would have been very different."

There's a long history of white women still needing and wanting to be ahead of Black people, Latinx, Asian, and Indigenous people, however. A vote for Trump came from the desire to stay on top of the racial hierarchy. Similar to low income white populations, who will vote for Trump even if it's against their own interest, white female Trump voters have agreed to accept second-class status with their gender, as long as the Republican Party puts them first with race and keeps them safe.

I admit, for a moment there I judged Elizabeth Warren for her homespun, annoying schoolteacher demeanor and almost didn't vote for her in the primaries, for just that reason. Really? For just that reason? Fortunately, I caught myself and went back to the fact that she was probably one of the most intelligent, experienced, and effective leaders we will ever see. Not unlike Clinton, if we bothered to study the facts and her record of accomplishments. But nope! America prefers to choose the fake illusion of a macho man when picking our leaders. Many still cherish the fantasy of being taken care of by a big, strong, wealthy man. Sounds like the very stereotypical characteristics we accuse women of when we call them gold-diggers. I guess we could characterize American Trump voters as really just trophy wives at heart.

After the movie *Holy Hell*, people were disgusted by Jaime. I heard people ask, "How could anyone let him do that to them?" As if the answer to that question is so simple. Yet we women know all too well that that answer is complicated. Sex to a narcissist is about power and control. And to give over your body and your very private, intimate parts is the ultimate submission. He told some of the men that he needed to soften their energy. Make them more feminine so they would submit more willingly to God.

Will loved Săt Săng. It was his favorite activity. He loved the gathering, the music and dancing, and communal participation. Jaime deprived him of that activity and replaced it with the nightmare of repetitive sexual assault. When he said he wanted to go to Săt Săng, Jaime rebuked him for wanting anything more than him. He told Will that everyone in Săt Săng could only wish to be where he was. He told him that this was a special privilege that his own master did with him. This was total bullshit; Jaime didn't have a master. But fantasy lies like this are part of the malignant narcissist playbook. Jaime was so demented I think he started believing his own fictitious narrative.

It's all about power and subjugation with narcissists like Jaime, Raniere, and Trump. Their weak and fragile ego craves control beyond normal boundaries or desires. And when denied, they turn vicious and dangerous.

CHAPTER 15

EXODUS

Narcissistic sociopaths may try to create dramatic crises to obtain attention to return the focus to themselves. As with patients with antisocial personality disorder, entitlement issues are very important.

ADOLF HITLER EXPLOITED THE economic crisis Germany was facing after World War I. Kim Il Sung starved millions of his own people to death, then magically solved the famine problem to make himself look like a god to gain popularity and power that has lasted three generations in North Korea. One of the most dramatic examples of a crisis that Trump created to divert attention away from his Impeachment hearings was the assassination of Iranian Major General Qasem Soleimani in January 2020. Rebecca Gordon describes Trump in *Salon Magazine*:

"...The president shook the snow globe again, by ordering the assassination of foreign military officials and threatening the destruction of Iran's cultural sites. Nothing better than the promise of new war crimes to take the world's attention away from a little thing like extorting a US ally to help oneself get reelected."

Jaime deliberately created drama wherever he went. He always seemed to find himself in one attention-seeking scenario after another. When we lived in LA, he invited a guy named Kenny to Săt Săng. Kenny was older, unattractive, and a real piece of work. He became infatuated with a young, beautiful girl in the group and wanted to date her (I use that term politely). When she thwarted his advances, he became obsessed. Eventually he started writing very scary, threatening letters and leaving them on her car. He wrote that he believed the cult leader was standing in the way of their love, and if she wasn't so brainwashed, she would want to be with him. The situation escalated when he threatened to have her kidnapped and deprogramed; to kill Jaime and harm me (the girl worked for me) and others; and to bring the group down with the help of the Cult Awareness Network.

I hired lawyers and a private detective to investigate. The investigator found out Kenny was a real psycho. Not that Jaime wasn't; but we didn't realize that at the time. This guy had been a drug addict and institutionalized for seventeen years. He had several arrests for assault and battery and spousal abuse. In hindsight, even though he was a nut job, he wasn't far off in his assessment that we were a cult. I had Cult Awareness Network (CAN) investigated as well. That organization was a nightmare. They were a cult about cults. I read court deposition transcripts from lawsuits by victims of CAN. For a mere $25,000, family members could hire the Network to "deprogram" their loved ones. The deprogrammers would kidnap a cult member, sequester them in the desert against their will for days, weeks, sometimes longer. The depositions stated that many of the victims were sleep- and food-deprived, and some were beaten and sexually assaulted. Their methods were terrifying.

The Kenny incident happened right after 1989, when actress Rebecca Schaeffer was killed in cold blood by a man described as a "deranged fan." Her murder inspired the stalking law to be enacted in California. I took Kenny to court and finally, after the District Attorney and the judge read the letters he'd written, they put him in jail. But the DA said they could only hold him for three months and suggested we get out of town. I recommended that Michel (his name at the time) change his name, because Ken would be angry when he got out of jail and would come looking for him. I was talking to Michel about this on the phone that day, with the music of Andreas Vollenweider playing in the background. "Andreas is a nice name," I said. He agreed, and that's how he got that name.

A group of us left LA and traveled for several months; and Jaime's mental state rapidly declined. This, I believe, was the major turning point for a lot of the older members, myself included. Jaime's mounting paranoia eventually became so extreme that even his most devoted inner circle questioned his "enlightened state." At one point his paranoia was so out of control and obsessive that one older disciple suggested we have an intervention, like they do in AA.

When we finally landed in Austin, I bought a 100-year-old farmhouse. My friend and I used the downstairs as a clinic and the upstairs as a residence. She was a bodyworker massage therapist and ran the business side of the clinic. Life was great for about ten years after the Kenny incident, but then my friend and partner started to act strange. Although we were very close and seemingly happy, I did not know what was going on with her and her relationship with Jaime. Everyone has their own way of dealing with things. Unfortunately, she was looking for an escape, and her exit strategy was drugs and alcohol. She had gotten herself in trouble with substance abuse off and on throughout the twenty years, but she had been clean and sober for about ten. Or so I thought. Everything was a deception; I seriously do not know the whole truth.

A young client of hers pursued her and seduced her back into a life of sex, drugs, and alcohol. As many alcoholic/drug addicts can be, she was also adept at lying and deception. As the situation unfolded, I soon knew she was using drugs again. And although I loved her and still do, I told her to move out. She moved about a half a block away, to a little apartment over a garage.

While all this was going on, anonymous threatening letters were being left on Jaime's car. I suspected a guy who lived just down the street from the little garage apartment. He was annoyed because, despite his many requests, he had not been invited to the group. Having had experience with the last stalker-nut-job, I thought this guy was showing all the signs for concern.

I received a phone call one afternoon. I was told that my friend was out of her mind and attempting to commit suicide. I went to the apartment and found her violent and hallucinating. In those days there was no internet communication. The best I had was a flip phone and a choice: either call 9-1-1 or Jaime. I was in a precarious position. The owner of the apartment was a sheriff. If I called 9-1-1, my friend might be arrested, committed, or evicted, and the troublemaker down the street would see emergency vehicles and might create more trouble. But I couldn't restrain her without help. So I called Jaime.

He was in his car, on the way to the lake with his entourage. I apprised him of the situation. In his sickening little accent, he said, "Rrradhia, juuusst meditate!" Rage swelled in me like a volcano. "That's it?" I said. "Just meditate? Never mind … I'll handle it. We're done," and I hung up. Well, I handled it. I got her calmed down and stayed with her for a couple of days until she was okay. At that point I hated Jaime, but I didn't leave the Buddha-field for another few years. My life was upside down, my clinic and businesses were collapsing, my relationship was in chaos, and my community was all I had in the world.

Later that week I saw Jaime in "cleansing." I sat in the chair in front of him and said, "Who are you, and where is the man I followed? We have turned you into a monster. You need to go away…without your entourage and learn to tie your own shoes again. You are no longer someone I can look up to or take guidance from. I don't understand what has happened to you. One of your oldest disciples has been at your feet, serving you since she was a child, and now in her greatest time of need you abandon her?" I went on like this for about an hour. Chiding and rebuking him. He was surprisingly contrite—for him. I now realize it was all an act to appease me. He said he was clumsy sometimes, but he loved her and would not abandon her. Then he had me go "down the long flight of stairs," which is how he always started his hypnosis, and showed me how I was just upset because her situation reminded me of my childhood experience with drug users. I left that day feeling somewhat satisfied that I had really gotten through to him. What a joke!

I didn't find out till years after I left that he got his entourage together that day for an emergency meeting. He told them that I was a danger to the community. He said I had gone crazy due to my distress over my friend and they had to be very careful around me. One by one, he turned my friends against me. Even my closest friend and business partner in real estate distanced herself from me, although we had serious real estate investments together.

Of course I *was* a potential danger. I was Jaime's fixer. I knew a lot about Señor Gomez. That name alone, very few people knew. I had his birth certificate and other legal papers, as well as boxes that we stored for him in our attic. Turns out those boxes held nude photos and videos of porn movies in which he'd appeared in his past.

In the months following that encounter, I started looking outside the Buddha-field for other friends and spiritual connections. I regularly frequented the Church of Conscious Harmony, a well-established church in Austin. I secretly went on ten-day silent retreats and studied Christian Mysticism on Sundays and Wednesday nights at the church services. Although I liked the things that were being shared, it was a bit too churchy and steeped in Catholicism for me to fully embrace.

Meanwhile, I was still taking part in the Buddha-field activities. At this point, Jaime's deep paranoia was peaking, which made it almost impossible for a newbie to get into our formal events. For some, it took two to three years to even meet him or be invited to take part in any of the functions. A handful of elders who had the "Knowing" were assigned to give newbies Săt Săng on Saturdays. Unbeknownst to us, Jaime sent his spies to attend the sharing and report to him who was staying on message and who wasn't. In other words, who were his loyal toadies, very similar to Trump; and I definitely wasn't. I talked about life and meditation, but rarely mentioned the "master" and certainly not in the sycophantic way he wanted. Like most of Trump's cabinet members who don't feed the narcissist's ego, I was slowly moved off the schedule and replaced by Jaime's most ardent bootlickers. I didn't even realize what was happening behind my back at the time.

The final straw happened the night I had just driven in from a ten-day silent retreat. Silent retreats are profound, and experiences like that were what I had missed about the early Buddha-field days, when it was more about communing with God than worshiping this bizarre clown. It was Thursday night class. I walked in and noticed a very dear friend of mine on the floor in the corner. She had thrown her back out and couldn't move. I went over to her and asked her what had happened. She pulled me down and whispered in my ear, "Rama!"

I instantly knew she was referring to something of a sexual abuse nature. This girl had been in a cult before the Buddha-field with an evil leader by the name of Rama. Rama had sexually abused her and emotionally tormented many of the girls in that group. She was traumatized by that experience, but because Jaime was gay, she felt safe. When she said

"Rama," I knew it involved a sexual scandal of some sort, but she wouldn't give me the details till the next day, when I went to her house to check on her. When I entered her bedroom, she was lying down with two guys standing by her bedside. One was her business partner and a member of Jaime's inner circle, and the other was an aspirant. She told me the story of this aspirant, who was sexually propositioned by Jaime in "cleansing."

Narcissists are convincing, practiced liars and when called to account, will make up anything to spontaneously fit their needs at that moment. They are highly manipulative, especially of people's perceptions and emotions. They are evasive and have a Houdini-like ability to escape accountability. They undermine and destroy anyone who they perceive to be an adversary, a potential threat, or who can see through their mask.

The aspirant was a very good-looking heterosexual man in his thirties. During several of this man's cleansing sessions, Jaime had brought up sex, inquiring about his sexual interests. He asked him if he'd ever had sex with a man. He had the aspirant work on getting over any inhibitions regarding that while under hypnosis. Like with many others, he suggested in the session that this man take his clothes off, to get over his shyness. The young man told me he knew what Jaime was trying to do and wasn't having any part of it. After he left the session, Jaime called all of his friends and told them to be careful. He said, "This guy tried to come on to me, and although I refused, everyone should know he will lie about it and say I, your 'master,' tried to seduce him." Your innocent, pious, celibate master. Sounds just like Trump. I looked at my friends and knew the story was true.

Then the older disciple started opening up and telling us horror stories about years of his own sexual and emotional abuses by Jaime. This was the guy Jaime had committed to a mental hospital, then had sent to India. It disgusted me. Not so much about the sex. That young man was obviously capable of handling himself and the situation. I was disgusted at the coercion, the lies, and the cover-up. We all looked at each other in that room that day and knew this was the beginning of the end.

That same day was the last day for me in the Buddhafield. Although I had decided to leave, I wanted to attend one more meeting to mentally say goodbye to my spiritual family. I knew that making this decision would blow up the life that I had known for so many years. This was not a decision I made lightly. I knew that I would be ostracized, branded, by the very friends and family I loved and had shared an extraordinary twenty-two years of my life with. I would go back to the world of the dead, misunderstood, despised by my spiritual family, lost, and alone. Jaime would make sure of that.

Manufacturing fear and division by flat-out lying is a strategic psychological manipulation. How many people have been alienated from their family and friends since Trump took office? If there's one thing that Donald understands, it's how to benefit politically from creating enemies, division, and chaos. This narcissistic sociopath has pushed this country to the brink of civil war. Yet his cult members will not acknowledge that it is his fault. They cheer him on and support his vicious bullying and divisive deceit, like aroused spectators at a street-fight.

The Senate has acquitted Trump for his crimes, although some have admitted he committed impeachable offenses. They are too scared to go against him. I get it! I can imagine what they are going through. At least with the Buddha-field, it was a private affair. It was a lot harder back then to publicly destroy someone. There was no social media, although Jaime would destroy you with whatever means possible. Trump, however, with millions of followers and Fox News, OAN, Newsmax, Twitter, and other alt-right media at his disposal, can viciously annihilate anyone who criticizes or defies him. While he often used bribery and extortion of other leaders or heads of state to do the dirty work for him, his favorite method is to get out there in the public and flat-out lie, belittle, and slander. He incites as many media minions as he can to repeat his fallacious narrative, over and over until it becomes engrained in his followers' psyche.

Yet even when he has beaten a lie to death, he won't ever be satisfied. Like a rabid dog with a bone, he will never let go of his obsession to destroy Obama's legacy, torment Hillary Clinton and Biden or any of his enemies, claim the election was stolen and the Impeachments were a witch-hunt. He continues to crush people's careers, their lives and reputations. He arouses hatred in millions of his sheep, encouraging them to threaten anyone who doesn't worship their God-King.

And now there's a pandemic. Over a half a million Americans are dead. But he was too obsessed with himself and his delusions to care.

They undermine and destroy anyone who they perceive to be an adversary, a potential threat, or who can see through their mask.

Trump said that COVID-19 tests were "overrated" and made us (him) look bad. He maligned Dr. Anthony Fauci, the nation's top infectious disease expert. He ordered hospitals to bypass the Centers for Disease Control and Prevention (CDC) and instead send their COVID-19 data directly to the Department of Health and Human Services, where he could control its dissemination. To conceal any data that would make him look bad, he was willing to literally kill thousands of Americans. And he succeeded.

On August 20, 2020, Trump retweeted a message urging the abandonment of cities. "Leave Democrat cities," the message read. "Let them rot." Cuz he cares so much! By the way, there are millions of Republicans and Trump supporters in all of those cities, but that didn't matter, his revenge was worth killing them, if he could get satisfaction.

The moment I decided to leave the Buddha-field was that day after hearing the story of the aspirant. It was a Friday-movie night in the summer. Usually on Fridays, we would go to the theater, but sometimes we would watch a video at someone's house. Jaime charged us the same amount as if we were at a theater. That night we crammed 150 people into a living room in the heat of the Texas summer and watched some stupid nature video. Always after a movie, Jaime would "share." His disciples would follow, rhapsodizing their syco-phantic devotion to him—often tear-filled expressions of exaggerated affection and gratitude for his very existence.

Sound crazy? Was it really? It was not unlike Trump's first cabinet meeting in June 2017, when he went around the room, lapping up the praise from his groveling toadies. Don't believe me? Take a few swigs of Pepto-Bismol and look it up. After the Donald commended the achievements of his young administration, he turned the focus right back to himself, asserting that he had accomplished more than any president in his first six months—with "few exceptions," like Franklin Delano Roosevelt.

In an ass-kissing frenzy, his Cabinet then went around the room adding on more adorations, starting with that dollop of curdled mayonnaise, Vice President Pence, who declared in a worshipful tone, "It is the greatest privilege of my life to be your Vice President." (I wonder how Pence feels about his dear leader provoking his angry mob to hang him on January 6.) And then there was his classic bootlicking house-ferret, Chief of Staff Reince Priebus, who said, "On behalf of the entire senior staff around you, Mr. President, we thank you for the opportunity and the blessing that you've given us to serve your agenda." Yeah, he was fired a few months later. Oh, and let's not leave out Alexander Acosta, the Secretary of Labor. You know, the Florida prosecuting attorney who let Trump's convicted pedophile buddy, Jeffrey Epstein, off with a slap on the wrist? Yeah, that guy. Hmmm, wonder how he got that job? He chimed in, "I am privileged to be here—deeply honored—and I want to thank you for your commitment to the American workers" and wealthy, elite pedophiles like you (okay I added that). That guy resigned shortly after. The Epstein case was a bit too awkward, even for Trump.

Uncle Ben Carson, the Housing Secretary, called it "a great honor to work for Mr. Trump." Where is the good old token black guy—the former neurosurgeon who became "desperately ill" with COVID-19? Probably stuffed in a closet somewhere and they forgot to get him out when they left. And then there's Trump's pet fruit bat, Stephen Mnuchin, the Treasury Secretary; you know—the demon who proudly presented pornlike photos of himself and his wife at the Treasury, molesting the new money they were printing. He said, "It was a great honor traveling with you around the country for the last year, and an even greater honor to be serving on your cabinet."

All of that was very similar to the adoration bestowed on Jaime. There is nothing wrong with humbly thanking your boss. But historians have said that no one had ever witnessed such a display of brown-nosing in the history of American presidents. And can we forget the 2020 RNC Trump salad-tossing convention? No policy, no plan, just an incestuous circus of Daddy's progeny licking Trump rump. What do you think that much adulation does to a malignant narcissist? I'll tell you—it creates a monster, and that's how Trump's sycophants contribute to his illness.

On this Friday-movie-night Jaime started a new ritual, where he would have people line up, one by one, and kneel in front of him. He had "open-eye-meditation" with the person, then would give them "Shakti," but that night he did something strange. He pulled his arm, with open hand, way back; hurled it towards the person's face; and just before he slapped them, he stopped suddenly and stroked their cheek. Was he testing to see if they would flinch? Nobody did. My mouth dropped open in horror. I saw nothing but contempt in his eyes. He was dark, with an evil expression on his face. If he could have gotten away with slapping them, he would have, and some would have let him.

"People are toys to the sociopath; to the sociopathic narcissist, they are trash."

At that moment I saw how he really hated us. To this sociopathic narcissist, we were trash. That's all I needed to see. My bubble had finally popped. I got up, walked out, and never looked back.

Donald Trump slapped the face of America and Democracy. He took a constitutional oath to "preserve, protect, and defend the Constitution of the United States." But his lack of self-control, disdain for the rule of law, and reflexive dishonesty showed time and again his woeful abuse of power and his danger to our constitutional liberties. Never in US history was a president so ignorant about the nature of his office, so openly deceitful, so brazen in his vilifying the courts, the press, Congress (including members of his own party), and even senior officials he had appointed himself within his own administration.

His use of the bully pulpit incited thuggery at his rallies. His influence over federal law enforcement and the national security was a threat to the citizens of this Nation and our democratic society. His attitudes toward freedom of speech, religion, and the press; his attacks on immigrants and minorities; his alienation of our allies; and his overall bizarre behavior corroded politics and induced harmful norm-breaking by the institutions he attacked.

The damage he did to this democracy will take years to repair. He and his followers have set precedents for generations to come. His cult members are imitating his reckless behavior. For example, even though all fifty states had officially certified the results of the 2020 presidential election, reaffirming what had been known for months—that Joe Biden was the victor and about to be confirmed as president of the United States—one hundred and six cowardly, sycophantic Republican members of Congress were willing to go so far as commit an act of sedition, and some scholars argue possibly treason. To this sociopathic narcissist, anyone who doesn't bow to him is trash. This country was here to be used for his own personal profit and self-aggrandizement, and his sycophantic followers foolishly—with cowardice—let him get away with it and fed his delusions.

News of me and other elders leaving spread like wildfire through the Buddha-field. When word got out, our own little MeToo movement started; I got phone calls from many guys coming to me with similar stories of abuse. Unlike the one aspirant, many of them, some heterosexual, did not refuse Jaime's seduction. And they had been carrying this shame and secret for years. Another elder called me and tried to get me to come back. She said, "I know you're in your mind..." That's what we said when anyone seemed to stray. I said, "I'm not in my mind. I'm leaving." She said, "Why?" "Do you really want to know?" I asked. "Yes," she said. I told her the story. She was furious. She worked for a guy in the Buddha-field who was very wealthy and had a company where several other members worked. She passed the story on, and one of her workmates who was also an elder told her of his own nightmare of sexual abuse by Jaime.

The owner of the company was a big, macho kind of guy with a vicious temper. He called me and bombarded me with questions. I filled him in with details that very few people knew. He released a scathing email to the members of the group. I didn't write the infamous email, but I unwittingly supplied or verified much of the information in it. He told me he was headed to Jaime's house to talk to him. I said, "Do you think we haven't tried?" He answered, "I have a special way of communicating with him." This guy had always been arrogant and braggadocious, so I thought he was just gloating as usual.

A few hours later he called and told me he had gone to Jaime's house with a baseball bat and smashed up his room in front of him. He got up in his face and threatened: "I will follow you for the rest of your life, and if I hear that you ever do this again, there will be blood." He said, "And I am wealthy enough to get out of jail in twenty-four hours and I will spread this story to every news outlet in the country." Within days, Jaime gathered the entourage and fled to Corpus Christi.

The Buddha-field was fracturing, and Jaime scrambled to keep as many followers as possible by announcing there would be a "Knowing session" in Corpus Christi. "Knowing sessions" in the past were huge ceremonies that went on for days. There was celebration and food and flowers and music. After eighteen years of keeping these people on the hook, hoping one day they would have their own Knowing session, like they had seen their brothers and sisters had in the past, he had the audacity to perform this half-assed—I won't even call it a ceremony. I heard he made them all wait while he finished watching *Family Guy* in the living room of his cheap Corpus Christi rental. He walked in and quickly gave them the four techniques (basically poked them in the eyes; I mean that literally), and that was it. That was it!

Will's sister Amy, who had watched her brother's four-day initiation take place in the forest in Mammoth Mountain eighteen years prior, had been denied the Knowing at the time and made to feel like she wasn't worthy. After two decades of service and devotion—that was it? It was as though Will had a four-day wedding celebration and an extended honeymoon, and she was raped. I can't imagine the broken heart and devastation she must have felt.

Jaime gathered what was left of the entourage and fled to Hawaii shortly thereafter. He is still there with some original Buddha-field members and new recruits.

Narcissists are quick to discredit and neutralize anyone who can talk knowledgeably about antisocial or sociopathic behaviors and are adept at creating conflict between those who would otherwise collate incriminating information about them.

After he fled Austin the website for former members was created, and I shared *Memoirs from Fellini*. I was so desperate to understand how this had happened. I did a lot of research on narcissistic leaders. In my section of the website, I took many quotes out of the *Diagnostic and Statistical Manual of Mental Disorders*, 5th Edition, like I'm doing here, and compared Jaime's behavior with the descriptions of a narcissistic sociopath. Several years after I left the Buddha-field, Will began producing his film, *Holy Hell*, and it was during that filming that I found out that Jaime had attempted to conspire with three different members (one of them was my dearest friend, business partner, and Will's sister Amy), to have me and the baseball-bat guy "taken out" or our lives destroyed somehow. It is my understanding that Jaime believed that I wrote or at least had something to do with the infamous email. But I think it was more than that. I think he read *Memoirs from Fellini*, and to portray one as a narcissistic sociopath is the most dangerous thing a person can do to someone with that pathology.

Fortunately for me the members Jaime tried to recruit still had a moral compass and…well, I'm still here. Although I confronted one of the three when I heard she went so far as to interview a hitman. Where does one even find such a person—Craig's List? Anyway, she was wealthy and fairly new to the Buddha-field. At that point, most of the elders had left, so I'm sure she was competing for Jaime's favor. When I asked her about it, she laughed and admitted she had talked to a real hitman. When I said, "I'm still here, so why didn't you go through with it?" she looked me in the eyes and replied, "It was too expensive." Seriously? Thank God I didn't loan her money. She laughed the whole thing off and later denied she ever said that.

A discussion about someone hiring a hitman to have you killed was probably the most noteworthy conversation I will ever have in my lifetime. Does she really think I forgot or misunderstood?

SECTION 3

REFLECTIONS

CHAPTER 16

WHAT IS A CULT?
IT'S COMPLICATED!

THE BIG "C." SOME people, when they hear that, think of cancer. To some, cancer is so scary, so threatening, that they can't even bring themselves to say the word. But to someone in a spiritual community, they have the same reaction to the word "cult." Thanks, Charles Manson and Jim Jones. In LA in the late seventies and early eighties, cults were everywhere. You couldn't go to the airport without being commandeered by ochre-robed, shaved-headed Hare Krishnas dancing in their bare feet, playing their tambourines and chanting. If you walked down Hollywood Boulevard, it was impossible to avoid the Dianetics Center, where Scientology followers would shove a pamphlet in your face and try to lure you in for a "free" audit. We frequently ate at Govinda's, a Hare Krishna restaurant, or at the Golden Temple restaurant, owned and operated by the Sikhs. Even the famous Source restaurant on Sunset Boulevard was run by a cult.

In a 2018 *Paris Review* article by Kirstin Allio, entitled "Why Are We So Fascinated with Cults?" she talks about *Wild Wild Country*, a Netflix documentary series that follows the guru Bhagwan Shree Rajneesh (aka Osho), a popular cult leader at that time. Allio says:

> America has always been fascinated by the fools—one born every minute, as Barnum (may have) crowed—and like any good culture, we relish the cautionary tale. At some level, perhaps we are tempted by that abdication. But surely none of us would be so easily duped, right? And so, we savor the inevitable fall and shiver with the catharsis.

It's interesting how we think we are immune to such abdication.

> A human trait: We can't look away from the antics of power or the circus of self-destruction, or the flagrant, the decadent, the grotesque. A terrarium is made to be viewed. A cult is already world built and glassed in like a snow globe, a fishbowl. Or a TV show. We can't look away from a train wreck (and could it be ours)?

Allio begs the question:

> Are we fascinated by cults because we want to watch folks just like us get smitten, overtaken, ensorcelled,

Stockholm syndromed without even having to be kidnapped? To watch them expose themselves?

I think so many people are fascinated with cults because they believe if they can watch from afar and take note of what to look out for, they can feel safe from being ensnared and content with themselves that they are not that gullible. I remember being approached by a Moonie in a parking lot, for example. She tried to sell me a flower and invite me to a meeting. She was so obvious; I could see her coming a mile away. How could anyone be fooled by that? Ha! Everything is relative. Twenty-five years later—wow! Did not see that coming—who knew?

"'Tis but thy name that is my Enemy," as Romeo would say. The word "cult" is so pejorative, so slanderous that if you're in a community that you like, you will find any excuse, any way, to avoid considering that you're in one. We see this in the fierce resistance of Trump devotees to consider that they and their "Chosen One" exhibit all the characteristics of a cult leader and his followers.

In the movie *Holy Hell,* one person being interviewed, after years of being out, could barely cough up the word. I get it! Another interviewee said, "Well, if it's a cult, at least it's a good one!" I've come to a place in my life where I'm ready to look at this four-letter word right in its vowel and consonance. I was in a cuh, cul, CULT! There, I said it. Here is what Webster's has to say about it:

**Cult noun, often attributive \ 'kəlt **
Definition of cult
1: a religion regarded as unorthodox or spurious (see SPURIOUS) also: its body of adherents, the voodoo cult, a satanic cult.

Definition of SPURIOUS.
1: of illegitimate birth: BASTARD.

Wow! Harsh. I didn't capitalize that—Webster's did. But yeah, that about sums up Jaime.

"also: its body of adherents."

Okay, that would be us. But here is where we automatically get thrown into the *"voodoo, satanic cult"* category and the very reason the word "cult" is so unsavory and understandably avoided at all costs. This is not a judgment on voodoo or Satan worshipers, who also claim to be widely misunderstood. I'm sure they're a lovely group of people. But while we're on the subject, who is to say that voodoo or satanic religions are "unorthodox"? Unorthodox according to whom? Someone else's religious or cult beliefs? Is there an orthodox version of vodun or Satanism, as opposed to a reformed or conservative version?

We must also note that often it is the very "unorthodox" nature of "cults" that attracts followers. Many groups who practice Eastern or Western esoteric spirituality are filled with those who found the orthodox religions in which they were raised unsatisfying.

And I would be remiss not to mention that Trump's unorthodox political persona is the very quality that attracts so many of his followers. They *love* that he is an "outsider," not like a "regular" politician. No experience? Doesn't read or value expertise? Lacks diplomacy? Ignorant of world affairs? Rejects science? Bring 'im on!

2: outwardly similar or corresponding to something without having its genuine qualities: FALSE.

Again, with the capital letters! FALSE BASTARD. Merriam-Webster really seems to take this personally. But yeah, I couldn't have described Jaime better. Or Donald Trump.

2a: of falsified or erroneously attributed origin: FORGED.

I came to find out that pretty much everything Jaime told us was a lie. Donald Trump is famed for his multitude of lies. Jaime plagiarized everything from the start. Unlike Trump, he was an avid reader and did adopt the expertise of others— without proper credit, of course. He would write notes and underline great quotes from many Indian masters and saints, write a script, memorize it (even the jokes), and use them in his Săt Săngs, as though they just blossomed from his eminent wisdom.

2b: of a deceitful nature or quality.

Deceitful? The only enlightenment we attained from this guy was when his story unraveled like the rubber threads in a broken golf ball. In hindsight, I don't think there was a truthful word or story that came out of this FALSE BASTARD'S mouth. Oh—did you think I meant Jaime? Yes, and Trump as well.

2c: great devotion to a person, idea, object, movement, or work (such as a film or book), especially such devotion regarded as a literary or intellectual fad.

d: the object of such devotion.

Now Webster has reduced the word "cult" down to a book club. So which is it? You're somewhere between Charlie Manson and a Trekkie at a Comic-Con convention? By this definition, everyone who has a deep interest in something is in a cult. But we can only hope that the cult of Trump is a short-lived fad; if only it were confined to a small group.

e: the object of such devotion.

Sooo, would that be like *Star Trek or Lord of the Rings*?

f: a usually small group of people characterized by such devotion: the singer's cult of fans, the film has a cult following.

What *is* the deal with Beyoncé, anyway? And if you're only defining it as a "small group," I guess that would make her a full-blown religion.

3: a system of religious beliefs and ritual also: its body of adherents.

Okay, that would also be us, but the techniques of the "Knowledge" were not Jaime's idea. Hindus passed these techniques down from generation to generation, and they go back thousands of years. Hey, we saw the posters of Lord Shiva sitting cross-legged, using a barragon (also spelled beragon, baragon)—a carved stick that supports your arms while doing these techniques.

I would be hard pressed to describe the beliefs of Trump's followers as a religion. His rallies, though, differ little from the performances put on by mega-churches to pump up the emotions of followers into an ecstatic frenzy, complete with thundering music, warm-up acts, and finally the appearance of the venerated one himself. Trump's sermons are filled with familiar call-and-response imprecations and the message that it's "Us against Them"—"Us against the rest of the world." We have the Knowledge; everyone else is just a loser chump. When we Make America Great Again, we're headed for heaven, folks. The others? Lock 'em up.

What do you think? Sounds like a religion to me.

4: formal religious veneration: WORSHIP

I think the word *worship* was in the eyes of the beholder, specifically Jaime's and Trump's. Some members of the Buddha-field did at some point "worship" Jaime, I guess. But not all of us. I never worshiped Jaime, but I was definitely in awe of his talent and dedication. In hindsight, perhaps his talent was his art of deception; whatever he was pretending to be, I wanted to be that. I have no doubt that many of Trump's followers would say they worship him, since some believe he was chosen by God and/or that he is the Antichrist and presages the Second Coming.

5. "No informed consent."

Well, Jaime didn't inform us he was lying through his teeth about everything from the master he never had to, well—everything. He neglected to mention that he had spies and informants who facilitated his magical, psychic predictions and public disclosures of people's secrets that made him look omniscient. Or that he used cheap parlor tricks to make you believe you were seeing the light of God or miracles.

It wasn't possible for Trump supporters to have informed consent when they voted to elect or re-elect him if they were only watching Fox News or following right-wing social media. They, too, were fed a steady diet of lies.

What about children raised in an ideological community, be it religious, racial, political, or otherwise? Do they or did I have informed consent? After all, it was the inspiration of Catholic indoctrination that led me to the Buddha-field. Some argue that I had the freedom to leave Catholicism; therefore I had a choice. Really? Would that be pre- or post-brainwashing of a child to believe that the saints had transcendental experiences of direct communion with the Almighty? Or that God the Father sacrificed his only beloved son, because of my evil sins, and this bread and wine are his body and blood? That sounds ridiculous to most rational thinkers. It must be symbolic, right? No, not to a devout Catholic. They believe that literally. And if you challenge them, you're in for a fight.

Once, I said to the wife of the master of the hunt club, a Catholic named Betty, that my friend's daughter was struggling with whether she should have her child baptized Catholic. I thought that was weird, because the mother wasn't even a Catholic, but she had the notion that her child would go to hell if he wasn't baptized. Betty said, "Well, that's true." "Oh, Betty," I said, "you don't really believe that, do you?" She said, "Well, it's true!" She then argued with me for about twenty minutes and finally delivered the knockout punch by sputtering, "You—YOU PROTESTANT!" Following that outburst, we both just stared at each other; you could hear crickets in the room. I realized at that point that that was her best shot. In her heart of hearts, she really believed that was the worst insult she could throw at me. Ah! Labels.

6: a system for the cure of disease based on dogma set forth by its promulgator: health cults.

Okay, now we're completely in the weeds with this definition. Just because a diet, product, or other health-related system is "based on dogma set forth by its promulgator" (promoter, one who makes widely known)—in other words, its PR and advertising—does not make said claim for a cure or benefit necessarily true or false, or a cult—it's just marketed better. Otherwise, Nike would be a cult. Wait, I never considered that, but come to think of it...

So there you go. Definitions of things are determined by who defines them and how successful they are in promulgating them. In my journey through the internet's definitions of "What is a cult?" I came across some doozies. Here is one of my favorites, from *The European American Evangelistic Crusades*, under the heading, "the definition of a cult."

A cult according to the Word of God is any group of people that worship anything or anyone other than Jesus Christ and believe anything contrary to His Word as found in the Bible.

Uh huh! Talk about projection! This one strongly resembles the Trump-cult believer's claim that anyone who "believes anything to the contrary" is a liberal cultist who is somehow missing the Truth.

As I scrolled down the web-search list, I came across an article in the *Atlantic* that defined a cult:

1. Opposing critical thinking.

Well, Jaime never was a fan of critical thinking. According to him, that was a sign that "You were in your mind/

WHAT IS A CULT? IT'S COMPLICATED

ego," and that was an impediment to union with the Alpha /
Omega, or Jaime/Michel/Andreas. Of course, when I questioned the nuns and priests in Catholic school, they expelled
me. But that's different, right? And Donald Trump assured us
frequently that he needed no information, briefings, or expertise to inform his decisions; he claimed "his gut could tell him
more than anyone else's brain." He wouldn't want any of us to
practice critical thinking, either, or we would soon see him as
the dangerous fool he is.

2. Isolating members and penalizing them for leaving.

Whenever someone left the Buddha-field—poor souls—it
became a topic of public discussion in Săt Săng and class. Jaime
said that they just "missed" in this life and would be subject
to a perilous demise and endless reincarnations. You know,
sort of like going to a place called limbo, if you're not baptized
Catholic. Or if you're not Muslim, good luck. "The Qur'an
takes away the freedom of belief from all humanity and rele-
gates those who disbelieve in Islam to hell (Qur'an 5:10), calls
them *najis* (filthy, untouchable, impure) (Qur'an 9:28), and
orders its followers to fight the unbelievers until there is no
other religion except Islam (Qur'an 2:193)." Wow; talk about
harsh! Or how 'bout as a Christian, if you don't take Jesus as
your personal Lord and savior, you won't get Raptured and
you'll fry like the rest of us poor sinners, on the fast train to hell
on Earth?

I don't need to repeat what Donald Trump does to people
he expels for perceived disloyalty (otherwise known as
expressing an expert opinion), or to those who rejected him
from the start.

3. Emphasizing special doctrines outside scripture.

Jaime had a knack for twisting "scripture" to suit his needs. Donald Trump used a Bible to demonstrate his piety and nod to his evangelical base, even though he was holding it upside-down. Jesus was crucified for throwing out the Old Testament and reducing the Ten Commandments to two ("Love the Lord Thy God, with all thy heart, soul, and mind; and love thy neighbor as thyself"—unless they're poor, black, gay, an immigrant, or any other non-white Christian, of course). But even though Jesus was explicit on this point, Christians love to use the Old Testament like Leviticus or Deuteronomy—a lot—if it suits their argument. Technically, according to Leviticus 24:16, they should have stoned me to death a dozen times already, just for writing this chapter.

4. Seeking inappropriate loyalty to their leaders.

I would say sucking the leader's dick was inappropriate loyalty. (Jaime here; we might think of others.) I would also say that demanding loyalty to oneself rather than to one's oath of office or the laws of the land is inappropriate (Trump).

The *Atlantic* article lists additional criteria defining a cult; but you get the picture. So, now that I have explored what a cult is, do I believe I was in one? Well, yeah! But at least it was a good one. Right?

In the book *Combating Cult Mind Control* by Steven Hassan, the author states:

> As for the philosophical position that everything is a
> form of mind control, it is certainly true that we are
> constantly being influenced by all kinds of people, ideas,

and forces. Yet there is actually a continuum of influence. At one end are benign or even helpful influences. At the other end are deeply destructive influences, such as indoctrinating people to kill themselves or harm others.

Hmmm, I wonder if he means—like—the military? I know... that will ruffle a lot of feathers, but by his definition, think about it. Where is one ideology considered heroic and another destructive? Cults are a relative term. I recently read a Vice.com article about the Buddha-field, entitled "This Buff, Speedo Wearing Guru Started a 1980s Sex Cult." Sex cult? Jaime had sex with about a dozen adult men. I'm not excusing him by any means, but if that is a "sex cult," then what in the hell is the Catholic Church or any other big religious organization? From Catholics to Christians, Mormons to Muslims, these organizations are fraught with thousands of victims of pedophilia, murder, and mayhem. Yet Hassan wants to make sure we don't confuse a "legitimate religion" with a destructive cult. Hassan is trying not to ruffle feathers.

Seriously, are cults just defined by the number of followers? If it involves enough people, that makes it legitimate? I love what the American author Sam Harris said, and I paraphrase: "One guy cutting off a girl's clitoris is a monster; hundreds of men doing the same is a culture."

CHAPTER 17

THAT LINE IN THE SAND: THE THREE BASIC TYPES OF PEOPLE WHO JOIN CULTS

EXCEPT FOR SOCIOPATHS, I believe most human beings have a conscience that dictates a line in the sand that they will not cross. A place in their soul where their moral compass finally takes the wheel and says, Stop—no more. But that line is usually preceded by little gray lines that we step over before we reach that point. From my observations, I've identified three basic types of people who join a cult: the hummingbirds, soldiers on a mission, and the kamikazes.

Type 1: The Hummingbirds of Religions

Hummingbirds are browsers. They are like looky-loos, fluttering through the fanciful world of spiritual communities. They circle around the perimeter, not ready to commit fully but if it looks interesting, they will hang around for a time. They don't know what they want, exactly, but they are not satisfied with what they have. They are searching for a place to belong. During the early eighties, the New Age movement was in full bloom. All kinds of oddballs and spiritual seekers were hunting for like-minded people they could find a home with. When you looked at the Buddha-field, especially in the early days, what was not to like? We were beautiful free spirits, healthy, happy, gentle-natured meditators. We sang and danced, and looked as if we were experiencing something extraordinary. So hummingbirds would mingle amongst us, hoping to find kindred spirits.

Come one, come all was our original motto, until eventually too many strangers forced Jaime to be more discriminating. Like the time someone brought a deranged homeless woman to Săt Săng. I suppose the thinking was that Jaime would give her Shakti or something and she would instantly be healed of her poverty and mental illness. Sort of a West Hollywood version of Sermon on the Mount. That miracle would have taken Jaime's little act to the next level. But then someone sat down next to the lady, and she bit them. Jaime immediately leapt from "Everyone gather around your master" to exclusive printed invitations to join the group with his approval, plus the installation of a bulletproof front window.

Before that event and the new rules they put in place, we had a rather broad assortment of hummingbirds. My Knowledge session (that was before he changed the name to "the Knowing"), for example, was quite the circus. Word got out of an impending initiation, and a parade of characters showed up from God knows where. Many we had never seen before. The newcomers looked like people right out of the New Age Expo. There were tarot readers and I Ching throwers. One person came wearing beads and bangles from head to toe, and a turban. She sat on the floor cross-legged and laid out an assortment of crystals in front of her.

Another guy showed up dressed in loose white kaftan pants, shirtless, with mala beads around his neck and long, nappy blond dreadlocks. This was a free spirit who believed bathing was optional. Soak your armpit hair in enough patchouli oil and you're good to go. I think he thought it would impress Jaime if he displayed his yogic prowess by sitting so upright it looked like he had a stick up his kundalini, in perfect lotus position, with the proper mudra (hands resting on the knees with thumbs touching middle finger). While rolling his eyes so far back in his head he could see his own brain, he quietly chanted OM. Apparently this Swami Showoffananda did not get the in-office memo. The "Knowledge" did not involve chanting. And as we now know—never try to upstage a narcissistic guru. I don't think this guy even got in the private room where Jaime was holding court. But if he had, it wouldn't have been pretty.

We all sat meditating for what seemed like an eternity in the Săt Săng room, waiting for Jaime to weed out the riffraff and call us one by one into the private interviewing chamber, normally used as the altar room. When you entered, he would be sitting on his little throne we made for him. Out of a deeeep state of pretend ecstasy, he would slowly open his glassy eyes and ask, "What do you want?" The correct answer would be, "I want to know God."

For those of us who were not blowjob material, he enjoyed a sadistic little test just to fuck with you and establish dominance. He would tell you "You're not ready yet, not fully cooked." "You're not surrendered enough." Once you had accepted the idea that you were just an unworthy piece of shit and you were about to crawl out of there in tears and complete despair, in a near inaudible voice he would say, "You will know God today." Then he'd slowly close his eyes, like the wooden fortuneteller in the box at Coney Island when your nickel runs out.

For me it was like...wait, what? Did he just say yes? I got the nod from his little flying-monkey assistant, and I burst with ecstatic emotional relief from the old trauma of the initiation rejection from Malila back in the little white house in Florida. I've described the painful, confusing, psychedelic experience that ensued in Chapter 7. That emotional rollercoaster was very deliberate, so the reaction when you returned to the Săt Săng room added to the heightened drama. The crowd waited in suspense, wondering—did you get it? Were you turned down? The terror of anticipation behind that closed door was agonizing. The only thing he could have added to the suspense would have been nail-biting music from a Hitchcock film. I don't recall whether crystal lady or dreadlocks ever made it to the inner sanctum. But we never saw those hummingbirds again.

Then there are your weekend and retreat hummingbirds. Every year Jaime would go to Hawaii, attended by a small band of minions. He would walk around the Island, wearing his Ray Bans and flaunting his package neatly tucked in his little Speedos. I heard tell he fashioned a type of home-made prosthetic penis to stuff in his bathing suit to enhance his display. His gopis carried his throne and his chiropractic adjustment table (swear to God), his boogie board, his towels, and his bags with snacks and water bottles. They looked like African safari baggage handlers, silently trailing behind him. And he was on a safari of sort. Hawaii is riddled with all kinds of New Agers, and he was hunting for fresh recruits. He meant to look just curious enough to attract hummingbirds.

He would sashay up and down the beach or on the boardwalks until he drew curious onlookers to investigate. One time, he and the entourage went to a secluded nude beach. They weren't nude themselves, but I'm sure the sight of weenies roasting in the hot Hawaiian sun were a feast for Jaime's perverted entertainment. They all went for a swim, and when he got out of the water, his gopis gathered around him and dried him off with their towels. He just stood there silently as they sprinkled his face with bottled water to get the salt off, brushed the sand off his body, rubbed sunscreen on his shoulders, helped him into a dry tee shirt, and held towels around his lower half so he could change from his wet Speedo into his shorts. You know, everything a mother would do to her wet toddler. They set up his throne, laid towels and blankets beneath his chair, handed him his Ray Bans and a small bottle of water (a large one would have been too heavy). He would take a squirt into his mouth, swish and spit, then hand the bottle back to his attending gopi.

A man named David, upon observing this doting display, walked right up to Jaime, who was sitting on his throne, chewing on a piece of pineapple. David dropped to his knees, prostrated himself on the towel in front of Jaime's feet and asked,

"Are you my master?" At that point, knowing Jaime, I'm sure with a slight grin of delight, he said something like "Humph" and commenced with the open eye meditation. They invited David and his girlfriend to dinner that night, and Jaime shared the auspicious occasion of recognizing your master for the first time. "There is nothing more natural than when a disciple recognizes his master," Jaime said. "When I met my master..." he continued—and on through the night with tales of so much bullshit you could have fertilized a golf course with it.

So, did David and his girlfriend drop everything and follow their master back to the mainland to join the other disciples in the Hollywood ashram? Oh, hell no. These little hummingbirds prefer to keep his picture and worship him from a distance. About 3500 miles of distance. And then, when it was convenient, David and his girlfriend were invited to our annual retreats, where they would show up and give another stellar performance of devotion to their master, until it got a little too weird and they would flitter off again. Their lines in the sand were short hops.

Then there was the boy in Arcada one summer. We were all on a retreat in Northern California. We had settled on a secluded beach (not a nude beach, just secluded), where we swam, did our exercises, and meditated, when this lone hummingbird drifted over to our group to check us out. Because we were a curiosity wherever we went, we always seemed to attract the most interesting characters. This little man-boy walked up to our group buck naked and plopped himself down next to us. He was a practicing Pagan, and he instantly felt right at home. We spent the afternoon sharing our prăsăd and Săt Săng. He felt so at home, in fact, that when we started singing, he began humping the ground. Apparently we were inspiring him to fornicate with Gaia, right there in the sand. That was too much even for the guru of porn, so Jaime politely requested that the kid take his impious ritual to another part of the beach. No doubt, Jaime figured he didn't stand a chance competing with the Goddess Earth.

Hummingbirds have a short path with very few gray lines between themselves and their final line in the sand. There are usually hummingbirds flitting through every religious organization. My parents, for example, were Catholic hummingbirds. They would go to Mass on Easter Sunday and sometimes to Catholic functions just to make an appearance, but Christmas Midnight mass? Well, let's not get carried away. After all, Mom had a huge Christmas Eve party to host. And Yuletide to a Swede (or whatever we were) was much more important than the birth of Christ. Similarly, many Jews identify as "Jewish" but refer to themselves as non-practicing Jews. They may dig their yarmulke out of a drawer to go to the son of Cousin Caleb's Bar Mitzvah, but they draw the line at refusing a good BLT.

New Age hummingbirds practice what can be called "cult-hopping" or "guru-hopping," visiting one group or teacher after another—Buddhist temples, Kabbalah centers, yoga retreats, Quaker meetings, Sufi communities, Ram Nam chanting circles—the list is long, but you get the idea.

These are examples of religious or spiritual hummingbirds. But who are the hummingbirds of politics?

CHAPTER 18

THE HUMMINGBIRDS OF POLITICS

POLITICAL HUMMINGBIRDS REALLY DON'T take the entire thing seriously. They flutter around the conversation, blurting out comments on Twitter, posting clever memes on Facebook, reposting their family's or friend's trendy opinions, but rarely bothering to read further than the titles of articles, much less fact-check or question the source. Even at the January 6, 2021 insurrection at the Capitol, many of the rioters admitted that they don't vote.

There are several varieties of political hummingbirds. You have your noncommittals; you'll find a lot of them registered as Independent, if registered at all. I often hear them refer to themselves as socially liberal and fiscally conservative. The dilemma in today's political climate is we have become so divisive and partisan that if they don't have the stomach to pick a lane, their strategy is to vote for a third party, just to muddy the waters, or not vote at all. As if that is some effective form of rebellion. It's about as effective as a child threatening to hold their breath if they don't get their way.

Here's a typical statement. "They're all bad." I can understand why they would say that. If they're not interested in putting in the time and effort to know the facts—a daunting task, I grant you—then it's much easier to say that politicians are all corrupt, grab a seat in the bleachers, and throw spitballs, or in some cases take a shit in the Capitol rotunda.

Take Mike, for example, a registered Independent (but hasn't voted since the nineties), who says that although he doesn't like Trump's personality, he thinks he has done some good things. When I questioned what those were, he gave a vague answer regarding Trump's executive order forbidding Twitter from fact-checking his tweets. Logical! Who wants those pesky facts, anyway? The guy's reasoning was that he didn't trust the fact checkers. Yet he trusts Fox News, so there's that. When I pushed him on this, he said, "It's really not about Trump; the Liberals are just as bad or even more dangerous." "Uh huh!" I said. Then he tossed around the usual misconstrued epithets, such as Socialism, extremism, radical left, the Green New Deal, and the dangerous AOC. Notice a pattern here? Had he ever read the Green New Deal Resolution? No! But that doesn't matter. For hummingbirds, facts and details take the fun out of spitball throwing. Ironically, this guy has been living off the taxpayer's tit his whole adult life. He had free college, free healthcare, and a pension that gives him a sizable income for the rest of his life. All because he had a desk job in the US military, during peacetime, thirty years ago.

Is their core argument true? Are they all bad? Or is the system itself corrupt to the core, which makes anyone involved automatically dirty? One of my favorite books is *Republic Lost* by Lawrence Lessig. Lessig describes the problem as "dependency corruption," meaning the problem isn't the illegal, quid pro quo type of bribery of yesteryear (although Trump brought that back into fashion), but that members of Congress and various interested parties—usually represented by lobbyists— have a constant interchange of political actions and campaign cash, or threats of contributions to opposing candidates. Politicians adjust their views in advance. The system features no overt trade of financial contributions for a vote, so the process is legal and has become so ubiquitous that those who wish to stay in the game see no other way out.

Once upon a time, lobbying was regarded as deceitful and treacherous; it was even a felony in California; and the Supreme Court regarded contracts to lobby as nothing less than diabolical. Our early fathers knew all too well the inherent problems with lobbying and predicted the fate of our Democracy today. Here is a statement from a justice in the year 1854, delivering the court's decision in a case concerning lobbyists and lobbying contracts:

> The use of such means and such agents will subject the state governments to the combined capital of wealthy corporations, and produce universal corruption, commencing with the representative and ending with the elector. Speculators in legislation, public and private, a compact corps of venal solicitors, vending their secret

influences, will infest the capital of the Union and of every state, till corruption shall become the normal condition of the body politic, and it will be said of us as of Rome—*Omnia romae venalia sunt.* Everything in Rome is up for sale!

For those American hummingbirds who say, "They are all corrupt, so what's the point?" I would say to them: Instead of voting for the candidate who promises to save every fetus the size of a lima bean or the candidate who promises to give everyone a livable wage (God forbid), here's a novel idea. Why not make it a priority to vote for the candidate whose mission it is to change this corrupt and broken system, regardless of party? Trump thought he could run on a fascist platform of "law and order"—of *We the People*—by suppressing the *people's* voice. Why not vote for a politician who vows to take up the fight for law and order in our government institutions that have become lawless and unethical? And to implement a strategy to enforce those laws?

Vote for leaders who will clean up the loopholes in the system and bring the 250-year-old Constitution up to date to meet the challenges of today. Reinstate the fairness doctrine. The First Amendment should not be abused by being allowed to include outright lies, deception, and propaganda. *Define* the Second Amendment: "A well-regulated Militia...?" as it applies to the twenty-first century, not musket-bearing farmers. Figure out a failsafe approach to the equal power of three branches of government. If Congress holds the purse, then use it. Don't just threaten with it, like a negligent parent who gives in to a spoiled child.

Stop financially funding criminal behavior, or letting presidents move Congress's appropriated money to wherever they please. And clean up the role of the president. We have given that position *way too much power*. They should be treated like presidents of corporations. If they fail to do their duty or they break the law, they should be fired by the House, by the people who voted for them. We are the investors, the shareholders of the government. They work for us. They don't get to be saved in some partisan impeachment process by a cabal of sycophantic cronies who are in on the take. The cabinet should be screened more closely and appointments offered to qualified candidates in their respected field only. And nepotism should be prohibited or at least be controlled based on qualification only, not blood relations. I wouldn't object to Dr. Biden being Secretary of Education. Why? Because Jill Biden is qualified, not because she's Joe Biden's wife!

So far, however, I'm not seeing the Trumpublicans prominently promulgating the promise to clean up the corruption. I get it; cheating is so much more profitable. But one can always dream.

Why not vote for the candidate who will replace Supreme Court judges who make corruption legal? In two cases—*Citizens United* and *McCutcheon v. FEC*—Supreme Court justices Anthony Kennedy and John Roberts wrote that "campaign contributions—gifts—given with intent to influence policy are not corrupting." Really? As they explained it, "Corruption requires more than intent on the part of the gift giver; it requires something like an explicit deal between the giver and receiver." After all, they said, "they are merely following precedent."

Now there is an example where cognitive dissonance reaches a Herculean level of mental gymnastics. But let's stop kidding ourselves. This is a war between the haves and the have-nots, and the haves will win every time. Because money has become king in America—not heart, not soul—money is power. And the bully Republicans smugly laugh at our platitudes while they kneel on the throat of Democracy.

Then there are the feelies. These hummingbirds just go with their gut, and in 'Merica that's usually massive. They are the type, as my mother used to say, who "are not encumbered by the facts!" They are the emotional voters. They don't care about the details; they care whether they like the candidate. Is he or she a person they would want to have a beer with? How many times in 2016 did I hear, "I don't know, I just don't like Hillary?" Cuz ya just don't like her...face, or the way she wears her hair or her pantsuits? Or "Joe Biden is too old" and "Kamala Harris is a bitch." Yeah, it makes sense—choose an incompetent, bloviating bully with six bankruptcies and twelve failed businesses, and zero expertise in politics or foreign policy, instead of a former Senator/Secretary of State, or a former Senator/Vice President and a Senator/State Attorney General with years of experience in law and governing. Yeah, I get it, little hummingbird, you do you. By the way, Trump doesn't drink beer, and if he did, he wouldn't drink it with you.

And finally, the duped! Putin loves these guys. These are the hummingbirds, a feisty little batch, who believe whatever they want, regardless of the truth. These are the angry-birds who run around with their hair on fire, screaming expletive-laden tirades. They prefer to use "alternative facts," as Kellyanne Conway suggests. Some don't need information of any kind; they just wish to "express themselves"—proclaim some sort of mob identity. Giant flags, red hats, and assorted paraphernalia the puppeteers are all too happy to capitalize on.

In true angry mob fashion, back in 2016 these hummingbirds hollered "Hillary Clinton is a lying, manipulative, nasty woman who deserves nothing except to be put in jail for life." In jail for life? Hmm. And for what cause would that sentence apply? Let's break that down, shall we? Starting with lying. Politicians have always had a whimsical relationship with the truth. By the sheer nature of a politician, their entire job is to win. And popularity is the only way to do that, in this superficial, irresponsible society of non-critical thinkers. It is also the job of the opposition to trap the politician. So they constantly must dodge topics that will make them look bad. A skilled candidate will do a pivot by dangling a shiny object and saying, "Oh, look over there." If they are lucky, they can distract the interrogator, like kittens with a feather on a string, long enough to move to a winning topic. Sometimes they can't pivot and out of desperation they fib, or twist the facts into a multi-dimensional Rubik's cube till the time runs out, or hope to exhaust the questioner into changing the subject themselves.

But the Donald took the idea of political pivoting to an Olympic-sized quadruple axel while teaching his loyal followers that anything contradictory to his word is "Fake News!" Here's the thing about facts, though—they are checkable. Oh yeah, these hummingbirds aren't encumbered by facts either.

The whole relentless blitz about Bengazi or Hillary's emails, or Hunter Biden, or the "stolen" 2020 election was about one thing and one thing only. These were well-conceived propaganda schemes that spit out media gristle so that angry-birds, who have a desperate need for a villain, peck at it, then fly around shitting out seeds of deceit. They are easy to dupe and useful marks—facts, truth, or common sense is irrelevant to them.

The worst thing about these hummingbirds is they don't really care about the tremendous damage they do before they reach their line in the sand. It has become a sport. They flutter about, self-indulgent and blind, not in the least bit concerned with facts, unwittingly causing chaos in their wake. They don't realize they are being duped and used as pawns. They are manipulated into annihilating some pretty decent people who have some remarkable accomplishments to their credit. Yet these hummingbirds irrationally support a malignant, narcissistic madman who makes Hillary's or Biden's indiscretions look about as evil as Count Chocula.

This doesn't matter to them, as long as they belong to a tribe, in this case a cult of haters. They will remain blind and addicted to "likes" on their social network, gluttonously stuffing themselves with unchecked loathing. The problem is that their seeds of deceit—wittingly or otherwise—fertilize dangerous soldiers on a mission, such as the "Proud Boys," a self-described fraternal group of "western chauvinists" spreading an anti-feminism, "anti-political correctness" and "anti-white guilt" agenda. Or the Boogaloo Bois, a loosely organized far-right, anti-government, extremist political movement. Boogaloo adherents say they are preparing for, or seek to incite, a second American Civil War that they call the *boogaloo*.

What is their final line in the sand? Civil war? The demolition of democracy? That remains to be seen.

CHAPTER 19

SOLDIERS ON A MISSION

THE SECOND CATEGORY OF people who join cults, after hummingbirds, is a little more complex. I call these people "soldiers on a mission." I admit I fit more into this box than the others. This group is for those who know what they're looking for and they are willing to step over a lot of gray lines to get it. For fourteen years prior to meeting Malila and eventually Jaime, I was on a mission to experience God Realization, Nirvana. And when I found someone who claimed he experienced that and could show me the way—I was all in. I had accepted the razor's-edge concept of enlightenment. And I was willing to step over as many gray lines as my conscience would endure to do what it took. I have referred to us in the Buddha-field as the Navy SEALS of spirituality. I do not mean to diminish the incredible endurance and sacrifice of the exceptional men of the SEALS by comparing them to our little hippie community. That would be ridiculous. But like the motto of the SEALS, many of us would never give up. I am one of them. So let's say it was more like being an Olympian. I was closer to being that, anyway. The following story may help to illustrate my drive.

As I described in Chapter 6, I was an equestrian—a steeple chase champion. The first race I ever entered was the most prestigious race on the West Coast, the Pebble Beach Gold Cup. Well, for women it was the Silver Cup, or silver plate, as the case was. Even though it was the same goddamn race on the same goddamn track, and it was just as fast and just as dangerous.

Although there were several riders, the competition was really between me and a very experienced rider who had won many steeplechases. I had trained hard for this race with the best steeplechase titleholder, David and I had the advantage of riding his preeminent champion horse, Dragoon. The spectators had bet heavily on me the night before.

The track was on the Pebble Beach golf course, next to the roaring surf of the wild California coast. It had rained for four days prior to the race. The air was crisp and fresh, but the ground was sopping wet and slick as a buttered eel on a marble floor. The crowd was gathering along the sides of the track. Dressed in red and white jockey silks, I represented the West Hills Hunt Club. As I carried my saddle to be weighed in by the stewards, my heart was pounding so hard, I could hear it throbbing in my helmet. My mouth was already dry, and my hands trembled as I picked up the reins and hoisted myself up onto this seventeen-and-half-hand thoroughbred. Foam

frothed from his mouth as he champed at his bit. He knew—
better than I did—what we were about to do. Back then steeplechase was considered the fourth most dangerous sport in
the world.

Before we lined up at the starting line, David raised my
stirrups and tightened the girth. He instructed me to weave
my hand in Dragoon's mane, hold on, and brace myself for the
bolt. When the bell went off, our horses leapt onto the wet turf
as if we'd been shot from a cannon. Forty miles per hour in a
car doesn't seem that fast, but on the back of an animal it's a
whole different thing.

Once I withstood the launch, something took over. There
was no time, no thought, no fear—just a weird tunnel of silence.
I relied strictly on my experience as a rider and my trust in the
beast beneath me. This was not a time to learn something new
or question if you're skilled enough to do this.

The difference between a horse race and a car race is there
are two consciousnesses racing. It's not all about you. Horses
are just as competitive. You either become one with the horse
and he with you, or you both could die. David had walked the
course with me before the race, going over every turn, every
stride, every jump. But now, none of that mattered. At that
speed you don't have time to think. It has to be automatic.

As I pulled into the first hairpin turn on the slick sod, with
ice plants on both sides, I was aware of everything and nothing at the same time. People were on the sidelines yelling and
cheering, but I couldn't hear them or see them. I was aware
of them out of my peripheral vision, but my focus was in the
moment—so critically, so completely that a bomb could have
gone off and I wouldn't have noticed.

The jumps were about four feet high and at least ten feet wide of brush, but at that speed all you could do is hold on and sail over them. And on a seventeen-plus-hand horse, the height alone would have scared the hell out of you if you gave it a second thought. But that's the thing. You didn't. You didn't think at all. You just kept on going in this heightened, transcendent state until the end. This is no doubt why people get addicted to extreme sports. I crossed the finish line first, and the crowds were cheering and running up to grab Dragoon's reins. Champagne bottles were popping as I dismounted, and people were patting my back and speaking to me, but I still couldn't hear them. It didn't matter that I won. It was over as fast as it began, and I had a deep feeling of emptiness.

All these people around me seemed foreign to me. As much as they thought they knew, they could not relate to what I had just experienced, and I felt alone in the middle of the crowd. I looked up and saw my opponent walking slowly towards me. She was all I could see. She handed me a glass of champagne, smiled, and said, "Now you know." And I did know. It was as though she and I had just gone through the most intimate experience and we were the only ones who understood. The feeling of emptiness was because it didn't last. It was over, and I couldn't stay there. The anticlimax was unbearable.

Not long after that, David and I were accepted as mounted marshals for the 1984 Olympics. I was right there on the track with the greatest horses and riders in the world. It was my job as a marshal to comb the four-and-a-half-mile track of spectators before each rider passed my section. If an Olympic rider approached and you were in the lane, you were instructed to run with them in order not to distract their horse. As they rode against the clock and over the most dangerous and terrifying obstacles imaginable, I was right there with them. Right there on the same four miles, staring down the same frightening hurdles. I had a taste, and it was thrilling. After that, I thought about training for the 1988 Olympics. People I knew who were members of the hunt club had sponsored two-time Olympic Silver Medalist Anne Kursinski. I had the horses and access to the trainers and sponsors. It requires a certain type of person to do what it takes to reach that level of skill. I was willing to put in the work; but to what end?

I was in the Buddha-field at that time, and Jaime would never have let me even be a marshal if he'd known, let alone pursue the '88 Olympics. He considered it a waste of time and a frivolous fancy—a distraction from the greatest Olympics of all, God realization. Then I remembered the moment after the steeplechase. All that work for less than ten minutes. And then it's over. I know—some people may think it's not the race, it's the process leading up to it. That would be a remark by someone who has never done it. I wanted that transcendent experience of being totally there, totally in the moment, where nothing including your life matters. Being in the world so fully, so totally present, that you are out of this world.

Psychedelics can take you there for a little while, but then you come down and you've risked having a bad trip and paid a toll on your body and mind. I wanted something that didn't need drugs or thousands of dollars and hours of mastering a skill or sport just to have it end after a few minutes. I wanted that transcendent experience within me all the time. I wanted that "in the world but not of the world" feeling of deep, uncon-ditional, Divine never-ending love. I wanted the feeling of mastering the impossible. Buddha did it, Jesus did it, the saints did it, why couldn't I? What was I here for, if not for that? All else paled in comparison, and I was willing to do what it took to find it. So for twenty-five years I rode a different horse, the horse of illusion, of the mental gymnastics of cognitive dissonance. And when I got off—it was the most painful, anticlimactic moment of my life.

I heard someone on a podcast discussing *Holy Hell*. She said, "...and what's with that Radhia woman? She seems like she wouldn't take shit from anyone." I assume she was suggesting I wasn't stupid or anyone's fool. But like the spectators who think they know—you had to be there. The "shit" that I was taking from Jaime was part of the ride. The ego is the identity of self, and I believed you could not be one with God if there was a "you." If there is a you and God, by the very nature of that duality, there is a separation. That's why I never believed I was being coerced. I was a willing participant. I was willing to let someone challenge my ego in order to overcome that ego. Willing to override my instincts and the gray lines as part of the discipline. What a perfect scenario for a malignant narcissist to take advantage of.

I've watched videos and heard Admiral William McRaven's famous make-your-bed commencement speech—a description of the SEALs' training: "If you want to change the world, start off by making your bed.... [Y]ou will have accomplished the first task of the day." When you see those drill sergeants screaming in the soldiers' faces and pushing them to do superhuman things, one might ask, what makes a person want to take that much shit? I think I understand that drive: to challenge yourself; to do the impossible.

But my journey was not as a soldier of war in the world, who learns sophisticated skills to kill other human beings. My journey was a war within, my enemy was my ego, and the goal was to sacrifice the self for the reward of never-ending Divine love. A love that wouldn't betray me. A love that wouldn't end. The secure attachment I never knew.

CHAPTER 20

THE MYOPIC MISSION OF ME, MINE, AND MARY

ALL KINDS OF MISSIONS motivate people to step over those gray lines in the sand. This includes the "soldiers on a mission" in politics. Some reflect pure selfish interest; some are a combination of ignorance and selfish interest. I want to be clear: the word "ignorance" comes from the root word *to ignore*. It doesn't mean "ignorant" people are stupid or necessarily uneducated; it just means, like the angry-birds, they hear what they want and ignore the details or substitute them for "alternative facts." The epitome of cognitive dissonance.

ABC News made an interesting documentary called *Roberts County: A Year in the Most Pro-Trump Town*. It's about a small town in the Texas panhandle. The population is 900, and 95% voted for Trump in 2016. That was the highest county percentage in the entire country. Most families in Roberts County are cattle ranchers who own thousands of acres they inherited from their great-grandfathers. Despite the value of the land, most of them are financially struggling. They are older, whiter, and have zero diversity. No, I stand corrected. There's Sonia Lopez, her husband and children, and one other Mexican-American family.

Despite the myth — the "alternative facts" the Republicans were floating that thousands of illegal immigrants were coming over the border just to vote against Trump—fun fact: "Federal law explicitly prohibits noncitizens from voting in federal elections, and no state has allowed it since the 1920s." Although Sonia's husband and the members of the other family are legal, she is not. But she still supported Trump. I guess the image of their nieces and nephews in cages wasn't a deep enough line in the sand for them. After all, their family made it in, so shut the door behind, right? Thank God Stephen Miller didn't find out that Sonia's in the country. If he got his way, he would have yanked her away from her husband and children and tossed her back over the border like an underweight minnow.

The delicate distinction between a destructive cult versus a club or mere group is the lies, scare tactics, coercion, and deliberate manipulation of a person or group who share a common concern. But mostly—it's the lies. According to researchers at the Rand Corporation, the term "firehose of falsehoods," which was perfected by the Russians, is a deliberate and effective information warfare method marked by "high numbers of channels and messages and shameless willingness to disseminate partial truths or outright fiction." The natural response to a deluge of lies, half-truths, and conspiracy theories results in confusion and cynicism, and the general conclusion is no one can be trusted. This uncertainty makes us more receptive to someone who seems to be bigger than life—one who appears to be omnipotent, omniscient, such as an enlightened master. Or, as we see with Trump, the public becomes swayed by demagogues and authoritarian figures. And thus they create their army of "soldiers on a mission."

Trump was so successful in propagating his lies that Roberts County swallowed the bait, hook, line, and sinker, and apparently still did in 2020. This story of a small rural town being duped by a flimflam man reminds me of the famous musical *The Music Man*.

There's trouble in River City! *The Music Man* is a story about a smooth-talking con man who arrives in a small town in the Midwest. He expects to dupe its residents with his elaborate money-making scheme: Despite his complete lack of musical literacy (not unlike Trump's complete lack of government or diplomatic experience), he convinces everyone that he is a brilliant bandleader and recruits all the boys in town to form a band, intending to pocket the cash for instruments and uniforms.

Trump promised that he would build a wall (and Mexico would pay for it) to keep all those drug-dealing-rapist and criminals from stealing Roberts County's ...what? Land, cattle, jobs? Well...Sonia was the first sign of an immigrant takeover; so it must be only a matter of time. But she can stay, cuz she is not eligible for any government benefits and they like her tacos. Trump promised to lower their taxes, and most importantly abolish inheritance tax, or "the death tax," as Republicans like to call it. Wordsmithing is a powerful tool to indoctrinate the populace. Think tanks and focus groups craft the best words to perpetuate these fallacies. Then they repeat them until they become part of our lexicon. This is a classic propaganda technique that Trump and the Republicans have mastered.

The filmmakers interviewed several people from Roberts County, who all repeated the same disinformation. They sounded like they were trying out for a job as a Fox News pundit. For example, Hillary would increase their taxes so much it would force them to sell half their land. Oh my! Is that really what Clinton said? Uh, no! As noted in a Fox Business broadcast, "only the top 0.5 percent of taxpayers would be impacted by the [inheritance tax] plan." Even Fox couldn't up-chuck that lie.

Did Trump's new tax law—known as the Tax Cuts and Jobs Act (TCJA)—help the middle class? Nope! It helped Trump's buddies on Wall Street, though. And unless those cattle ranchers had big investments in the stock market, instead of livestock—they were screwed.

Here's what the Brookings Institute had to say about it:

> The benefits of the Tax law tilt toward the well-off both now and in the future, according to the distributional analysis of the Tax Policy Center. By 2027, benefits of the tax law flow entirely to the rich. (The Joint Committee on Taxation finds similar results using a different measure.)

Here's how the tax increase will look after it sunsets: a young married couple will pay a 54% increase from where it is now and a retired couple will have a 21% increase. Because we are so myopic, we can't see past our noses. This is why people think the economy recovered because of Trump, when it was

Obama who bailed us of out of the shit pile Bush and his Wall Street cronies created, and Trump took a victory lap on the back of Obama's eight years.

What has been the Republicans' defense of every grey-lined, reprehensible action of Trump's for the last four years? "The economy, stupid," that's what they say. That's another propaganda slogan embedded into the political psyche. Yet we know the Trump picture of a rosy economy was a fallacy on so many levels. Republicans have historically trashed our country's economy like drunken frat boys at a weekend kegger party, and the Trump administration was no exception.

In fact, a recent paper by economists Alan Blinder and Mark Watson states:

> The U.S. economy was in a recession for 1.1 quarters on average during Democratic terms, but for 4.6 quarters on average during Republican terms.... The superiority of economic performance under Democrats rather than Republicans is nearly ubiquitous; it holds almost regardless of how you define success. Fact-checking groups have investigated similar statements and have found time and time again that they are true.

But this is the classic Republican economic bait and switch. Lower taxes for the rich, crush the middle class, fuck the poor, and from Reagan to Bush to Trump these administrations loot the country like thieves who break into your house when the family is on vacation. Then Democrats come in to clean up the mess and get blamed for it by the uneducated voters. Then we do it all over again in eight years. Because most voters are myopic.

Definition of **myopia,** mī'ōpēə/ *noun*
1. nearsightedness. lack of imagination, foresight, or intellectual insight.

Even Trump himself agreed when he told Wolf Blitzer: "I've been around for a long time and it just seems that the economy does better under the Democrats than the Republicans." That was in 2004, before he became Putin's kompromat so he could get his hotel in Moscow.

So, just for the record, what was Hillary's tax plan? Well, she proposed the "Fairness Act," which restored basic fairness to our tax code. She would implement a "fair share surcharge" on multimillionaires and billionaires, and fight for measures like the Buffett Rule to ensure the wealthiest Americans do not pay a lower rate than hardworking middle-class families. She intended to close loopholes that create a private tax system for the wealthy, and she would ensure multimillion-dollar estates were paying their fair share of taxes.

That last sentence scared the hell out of Roberts County because they think they are in the same league as Jeff Bezos, Warren Buffett, and Bill Gates—who actually pay little or no taxes, especially estate taxes, cuz they are smart enough to put their assets in a trust. But by God, Roberts County will be damned if they are going to sell half of Grandpa's land to pay those Liberal government handouts to lazy immigrants.

Here's what Clinton proposed. "A 5% increase to estate and gift tax and a decrease in the exemption from $5.45 million to $3.5 million. Even with the lower threshold, only about four in 1,000 families would be subject to the estate tax. But "Hillary Clinton is a lying, manipulative, narcissistic woman who deserves nothing except to be put in jail for life." Yeah, Roberts

County was on that bandwagon. I don't know…something about Benghazi and pantsuits.

Remember I mentioned ignorance? Choosing to ignore? Well, I can understand that, following the daily carpet-bombing of news about Trump and his accomplices' crimes, fraud, and deceit; or the Donald and his progeny using the Constitution for a napkin after stuffing their face at the emolument buffet; or the numerous scandals, staff firings, and backdoor deals with his sycophantic cronies. The truth is way too overwhelming for anyone, let alone hard-working ranchers, to absorb. But overwhelming the voters, by the way, with a "firehose of falsehoods," is right out of the authoritarian playbook.

When the good folks in Roberts County were asked about the impeachment hearings or Russia's involvement with our elections, their answer was, "The Comey stuff, ugh, it really bores me. If Trump colluded with Russia, I couldn't care less. It doesn't affect me." Wow! Okay, fair enough. When your focus is getting cattle to market and feeding your family, it's understandable that you don't have the time or interest to care about a foreign enemy hijacking the most important element of our democracy. Of course, if Hillary were elected under the same circumstances, they would have had an aneurism. And then there's Hunter Biden and that whole red herring. But because they didn't have time to listen to the Impeachment trial, cuz it really bored them, they relied on well-edited snippets of the Republican propaganda. I get it. In that case do us all a favor, though, comrade: Please don't vote, or call yourself American, let alone have the audacity to call yourself a patriot, for God sakes.

Definition of **patriot**. pa·tri·ot, / ˈpātrēət / *noun*
1. a person who vigorously supports their country and is prepared to defend it against enemies or detractors.

"It doesn't involve me, so I'm not interested." I like that answer. Maybe I'll use that when they whine about not being able to afford health care or education for their kids (which persisted through Trump's administration) or need help because a pandemic and tariffs have drastically reduced beef sales, and they may lose the ranch anyway.

This example is just to show that people on a mission will step over many gray lines (and Trump offered a veritable Pantone assortment of grey), to get what they think they want, regardless of whether it is real. And like me, who was willing to cross a lot of lines for Jaime and his scam, the good folks in Roberts County openly admitted they don't like Trump, BUT…

And then there is Mary!

Mary is a woman from the same socioeconomic lifestyle as I came from. She went to private Catholic schools. Her father was a lawyer like mine. But unlike me, she married and had children. Her husband and she were both alcoholics, and as you might imagine, the days of wine and roses didn't end well. She went to AA, cleaned up her act, learned how to become independent, and raised her children as a single mother. She struggled, but she made it. Big time! She is smart, white, has a college education, and although she had to push and fight her way upward in a male-dominated industry—the oil business—she became top in her field as a regulatory consultant.

Mary is a Trump lover, still. Why? Taxes and regulations, plain and simple. She is a high roller on the myopic, me-mine mission. She's one of those people who loves Trump and the

Republican party out of pure self-interest. If Ayn Rand were alive today, no doubt Mary would be a devoted disciple of that cult, reciting from Rand's playbook, *The Virtues of Selfishness: A New Concept of Egoism*. She bounces over those gray lines like a kid playing hopscotch. She once made the cocky remark, "I'm a Republican; we don't care about the environment."

Mary's a person who, because she had to pull herself up by her bootstraps (no doubt boots from Neiman Marcus), believes that anyone who is poor or needs help is just a lazy moocher. The blindness and callous cognitive dissonance of these myopic, me-mine people are flabbergasting. Most of our white, older generation was raised on the fairytale that every US citizen has an equal opportunity to achieve success and prosperity if they work hard and follow the rules. Yeah, when you live in a bubble and do not see anyone but yourself, it's easy to be manipulated by clever phrases and narratives. Another example of engineered consent.

Mary's mental gymnastics may go something like: "People's hardships are not my problem. I'm not my brother's keeper." Another fun fact: "I'm not my brother's keeper" is what Cain said when God asked him where Abel was. Or, my favorite statement: "I will not give my hard-earned money to lazy people who want to live off the tit of the government," which implies that people who are experiencing hardships are lazy and infantile.

After I left the Buddha-field my life was in ruins. I lost everything. I have worked my entire adult life and have several college degrees. I am neither lazy nor stupid. But after my exodus from the group, I lost my house and was forced into bankruptcy. By the time the economy crashed in 2008, people couldn't afford basic nutrition, let alone the luxury of spending money on a nutritionist.

I ended up on food stamps, $50 a week. Ah, the lavishness of the government tit. Just to put that in perspective, the other night my roommate and I treated ourselves by splitting a pizza. Because of the pandemic, the restaurant was only providing home delivery. When it arrived, the bill, which included tax, tip, and travel, was $54. Fifty-four bucks for a pizza. I only had two slices. I guess if I was still on food stamps, two slices of pizza would have been half my ration for the week. Mary and others may say, "Why should we pay for you? That's what family is for." Hey, what a good idea! Instead of receiving help from the government, which I've been paying taxes to my whole adult life, and because Republicans cut the regulations on Wall Street, which got us into that mess in the first place—I should mooch off the relatives. Her comeback may be, "Well, I happen to know my friend's cousin Marvin is still claiming disability, and he's perfectly capable, he's just a pot smoker." Well, there ya go. All 328 million of us should be denied help because pothead cousin Marvin is gaming the system.

The only family I have left is my brother (a sketchy relationship at best), and because of the crash, he was in a financial crisis of his own. We went from riches to rags, and unless you have experienced that, you may not understand that it's a lot easier emotionally to rise than to fall. And when you fall at age fifty-five or older, it's a lot harder to get back up.

That was another reason to stay in the Buddha-field. If you lost your job, you would never go hungry, and you would always have a roof over your head. During the eighties, when the AIDS crisis was in full swing, we all took care of our brothers, some until their last breath. They never died alone. They never left this world hungry or uncared for.

Now, while an out-of-control plague is devastating the country, income loss to hardworking people is creating mass evictions, leaving thousands homeless. Oh, but I know you don't believe in wearing a mask, Mary, even though a half a million American ghosts would disagree with your master's proclamation that it was just a hoax. Sociopaths like Trump and McConnell make Marie Antoinette look like Mother Teresa. But that's okay, right, Mary? Fuck those children, elderly, disabled, and poor. Screw the healthcare workers who are putting their lives on the line for others. Who cares, as long as you get your tax breaks and annoying government regulations knocked out of the way, so oil companies can continue freely raping and pillaging the planet for profit? Or my favorite, thanks to Mary's help to control those chafing regulating laws, when cold weather arrived in Texas over Valentine's weekend, prices on the ERCOT market rose to $9,000 per megawatt-hour – smacking some residence with bills as high as $16,000 for the month. You're happy to step over enough gray lines to make an airstrip to support your God King as he bilked this country for all it's worth and hopes to do it again.

Sooo many gray lines to step over for soldiers on a mission. My journey was a war within; my enemy was my ego. Your enemy, Mary, is everyone else, but it's still the same fragile illusion.

CHAPTER 21

THE ZEALOTS

*"Before the truth can set you free you need
to recognize which false belief is holding you
hostage!" — Anonymous*

FACTS ARE RELATIVE; TRUTH is immutable. It was a fact two hundred years ago that humans could not fly, but is that true? Could we not fly, or had we not yet figured it out? With religion or philosophy, it's difficult to recognize or to prove false belief. A search for a general understanding of values and reality based on speculation, rather than observation, yields abstract theories—beliefs. The very nature of a belief, faith, or confidence in someone or something means you don't know for sure. I had confidence in Jaime till I came to find out he was a total fraud. I would have said with great conviction that what he was selling was the truth. But was it? No!

It is difficult for people to admit they were wrong; that they have been duped. I know it was for me. And the longer the duration of your commitment to the lie, the more that lie can shake the very foundation of your identity and reality. Yet despite the evidence that our beliefs can change over time and may prove to be false, many will die or kill for a belief they hold at present. These are the third type of cult followers, the self-styled militias, the zealots: the kamikazes.

Notice that those who will die or kill for their belief are usually men? That's a fact! Not immutably true, but a fact nonetheless. In other words, that assertion could change. I'm leaving a little margin here for humankind, in hopes we'll eventually catch on and stop killing for things we don't know for sure. But women are not off the hook. Because in most cases women condone those beliefs; support them; "believe" them to be righteous. And then there are those who just keep their mouths shut and let others do the harm. To me, those are either the smartest fools or the biggest cowards of all. Prime examples: the 147 cowards in Congress and 43 Senators who acquitted Trump in his second Impeachment, even if they believed he was guilty.

Although many do so, some may think that killing or dying for a belief is their line in the sand. But if killing or suicide is the bridge too far, how many gray lines will someone cross before they get to *that* point? A malignant, narcissistic sociopath does not think the way most of us think. They do not feel or empathize the way most with a conscience feel or empathize. They do not experience shame or remorse. They are not bound to any of those lines. And if they are clever enough, they can psychologically influence a vulnerable subject to the point of causing them to override their reason and empathy and push them to those extremes. Take, for example, the case of Patty Hearst.

In 1974, Patty Hearst, the nineteen-year-old granddaughter of the wealthy newspaper publisher William Randolph Hearst, was kidnapped by the Symbionese Liberation Army (SLA), a small, armed revolutionary group with an obscure ideology and unclear goals. In Jeffrey Toobin's book, *American Heiress: The Wild Saga of the Kidnapping, Crimes and Trial of Patty Hearst,* he revisits the famous case and the ongoing question of Hearst's motivations and loyalty in the nineteen months that followed her abduction. Toobin shows compelling evidence that Hearst was consciously acting out of her own newly adopted belief. In an interview on Fresh Air, Toobin says, "If you look at her actions... over the following year, you see the actions of a revolutionary, not a victim."

One may ask what would possess a young, intelligent woman of privilege to turn so quickly into a bank-robbing political zealot who didn't hesitate to use a semi-automatic weapon and riotously fire toward a store clerk who had detained her captors, Bill and Emily Harris. This begs the question: What is a victim under these circumstances? The argument that she was not, in fact, "brainwashed"—that she did those actions of her own volition—easily dismisses the nuances of victimhood and defines her as a revolutionary. But I think that assertion woefully ignores the power of psychological manipulation and the complexities of each situation.

We often misuse the word *brainwashed*. We are tempted to use it as a one-word catch-all to describe anyone who acts in an extreme behavior outside of the norm. It's important to define the word and distinguish the difference between brainwashing and conformity or groupthink. In the film *Holy Hell*, one interviewee mentions that we were "brainwashed." But this is a complex notion.

Definition of **brainwashing** / ˈbrānwôSHiNG/ *noun*
1. the process of pressuring someone into adopting radically different beliefs by using systematic and often forcible means. "victims of brainwashing."

By that strict definition, were we really brainwashed, as one member says? We didn't adopt radically different beliefs. Most of us were already on the path of beliefs Jaime "taught" (borrowed from more reputable sources) before we even came to Săt Săng. And we were not physically forced, like prisoners of war. Jaime just clarified our beliefs a bit, gave them context and structure, and formed them into a way of life. He took on the role as leader as we formally employed our preexisting beliefs.

This is the common mistake we make when we accuse Trump supporters of being "brainwashed." That implies that they didn't originally believe in what he espouses and that somehow, they were coerced or radicalized by the leader. This is an important distinction and the premise of this book. It's about the followers. The programing goes much deeper than one leader. One could argue that he, along with the disinformation from a well-constructed propaganda machine, certainly greased the wheels. Indeed providing community and buzzwords and red hats via Fox and Facebook and Twitter helped to define and stoke the fears, insecurities, and outrage of the followers. But Trump tapped into what his "base" already believed and simply capitalized on it. He has no real policy, conviction, or interest other than Donald Trump. He is as big a fraud as Jaime. Yet, he is merely a symbol—a golden calf—representing the idolatry of his worshipers preconceived beliefs. When we say that his base is "brainwashed," that takes the responsibility away from them as enablers.

Social influence is a form of persuasion. Do it because everyone around you is doing it, or do it because it'll make you feel good/happy/healthy/superior, or it's just what you believe is the right thing to do. When you're in a social community where everyone is basically on the same page, it's a safe and comfortable place to hang your beliefs. So how did this happy little scenario in the Buddha-field turn into a disgusting web of deceit? How did we conform?

Here's what Cialdini and Goldstein say in the *Annual Review of Psychology:*

> **Conformity** is the act of matching attitudes, beliefs, and behaviors to group norms, politics or being like-minded. Norms are implicit, specific rules, shared by a group of individuals, that guide their interactions with others. People often conform to society rather than to pursue personal desires because it is often easier to follow the path others have made already, rather than creating a new one. This tendency to conform occurs in small groups and/or society and may result from subtle unconscious influences (predisposed state of mind), or direct and overt social pressure.
>
> People often conform from a desire for security within a group—typically a group of a similar age, culture, religion, or educational status. It often refers to this as groupthink: a pattern of thought characterized by self-deception, forced manufacture of consent,

and conformity to group values and ethics, which ignores realistic appraisal of other courses of action. Unwillingness to conform carries the risk of social rejection.

As we were examining our beliefs and identities in the Buddha-field, the very process of stripping those away gave us a new and improved identity and set of beliefs. One powerful spiritual identity we adopted was the belief that we were special—exceptional. We were not in the category of "chosen;" we had to work for it, which made the identity even more tangible, but perhaps not as appealing as those who are taught from childhood that they are the "chosen people" or "the faithful." The more you had to work for it, the more you were invested in the identity and the beliefs surrounding it. And the more investment, the more you had to stay with a group that identifies, understands, and supports the belief and identities. Without that constant support, abstract theories can fade when confronted with reality.

A common denominator with most cults, whether religious, cultural, or political, is the notion of exceptionalism. And that idea can be the strongest tie that binds. The most dangerous combination of a belief in exceptionalism occurs when religion and politics unite. This state of affairs was anathema to our founders, who took every precaution to avoid it. We need look no further to see the dangers than to the zealotry of evangelical Christians, who would support a demagogue as president and our courts stacked with Bible-believing theocrats. This is the opposite of American patriotism.

Division of Church and State is built into the very foundation of America. Many Christians, however, refer to America as a "Christian Nation." Ideologues manipulate thinking by infusing their ideas into the lexicon of a society and repeating them until they become fact—and so they have done with the phrase "Christian nation." But this characterization could not be further from the truth.

Christians who think of America as founded upon Christianity usually present the Declaration of Independence as "proof" because the document mentions God. However, the Declaration does not describe Christianity's God—Jesus. It describes "the Laws of Nature and of Nature's God." This nature's view of God coincides with seventeenth- and eighteenth-century deist philosophy, which posits a noninterfering Creator. Any attempt to use the Declaration as a support for Christianity is a willful revision of recorded history—or at best, a misunderstanding. When you are initiated from birth into the idea that the only God is Jesus Christ, however, then it's like the adage: "When all you've got is a hammer, everything looks like a nail."

To offer just a few citations of evidence to the contrary:

- Historian Robert T. Handy tells us: "No more than 10 percent—probably less—of Americans in 1800 were members of congregations. The Founding Fathers, also, rarely practiced Christian orthodoxy. Although they supported the free exercise of any religion, they understood the dangers of religion."

- The majority of our Founding Fathers were Freemasons. John J. Robinson, best known as the author of *Born in Blood: The Lost Secrets of Freemasonry*, states: "Freemasonry had been a powerful force for religious freedom." He does not singularize Christianity.

- The historian Robert Middlekauff writes: "The idea that the Constitution expressed a moral view seems absurd. There were no genuine evangelicals in the Convention, and there were no heated declarations of Christian piety."

Today's Christians emphatically peddle the notion, however, that America and the Constitution were God-ordained. This is a glaring example of cult members not encumbered by the facts. Here's what John Adams (you know, one of the authors of the Constitution and a Unitarian), said in his "A Defense of the Constitutions of Government of the United States of America" [1787-1788]:

> It will never be pretended that any persons employed
> in that service [the forefathers in the service of writing
> the Constitution] had interviews with the gods, or
> were in any degree under the influence of Heaven,
> more than those at work upon ships or houses, or
> laboring in merchandise or agriculture; it will forever be
> acknowledged that these governments were contrived
> merely by the use of reason and the senses.

In other words, regular old non-secular guys wrote the Constitution—not Jesus. Not anyone channeling Jesus. And to call this country a "Christian Nation" could not be more un-American.

CHAPTER 22

THE MOTHER OF ALL CULTS

Beware of false prophets, who come to you in sheep's
clothing but inwardly are ravenous wolves.
—*Matthew 7:15*

IT'S NO SECRET THAT evangelicals were one of Trump's most loyal constituencies. But many amid this Trump phenomenon scratch our heads, mystified by Trump-supporting Christians in America today. Over and over, I've read comments from people, wondering in astonishment how the Christian Trump devotees and even otherwise upstanding members of the Senate could possibly support this racist braggart and bully who gloated about sexual assault, cheated on his pregnant wife with a porn star, and could not name a favorite Bible verse nor correctly pronounce Corinthians, let alone know what it said. He robbed from the poor to give to himself and the rich. He supported murderous dictators and assassins, indiscriminately bombed other countries, separated children and infants from their parents and locked them in cages.

Didn't he go against everything we thought Christians professed to consider good and righteous Christian values? Apparently not! Perhaps some Christians—not all, as you are about to see—would say Trump wasn't a model Christian, but he gave them the power they craved, so they were willing to overlook his unchristian-like behavior. And we mustn't discount his toxic masculinity, which aroused the white Christian male's flaccid societal identity.

In a VOX interview with Kristin Kobes Du Mez, a historian at Calvin University and author of the book *Jesus and John Wayne*, Kobes Du Mez makes the argument that evangelicals were not acting against their deeply held values when they elected Trump; they were affirming them.

> What I look to as a historian is this critical period in the post-World War II era when gender ideals fuse with anti-communist ideology and this overarching desire to defend Christian America. The idea that takes root during this period is that Christian masculinity, Christian men, are the only thing that can protect America from godless communism. Evangelicals have made heroes of people like John Wayne and Mel Gibson, people who project a more militant and more nationalist image.
>
> In that sense, Trump's strongman shtick was a near-perfect expression of their values. If you understand

what family values evangelicalism has always entailed—
and at the very heart of it is white patriarchy, and often
a militant white patriarchy—then suddenly, all sorts of
evangelical political positions and cultural positions fall
into place. Their actual views on immigration policy, on
torture, on gun control, on Black Lives Matter and police
brutality—they all line up pretty closely with Trump's.
These are their values, and Trump represented them.

In other words, they don't want gentle Jesus; they want
William Wallace or John Wayne.

While there is disagreement within churches, communities, and families, the solid majority of white evangelical Christians bought into this programing. And this indoctrination is
fueled by media and pop culture. While some Christians still
read their Bible every day, many don't and never have, or they
will do only selective Bible study.

Take the epic example of political, engineered consent
enshrouded in Christian belief regarding abortion, for example. Yes, I'm going to go there. Most pro-choice folks think
the Bible says nothing about abortion, but it turns out it does.
Behold the "Test for an Unfaithful Wife" (Numbers 5:11-31).
Besides numerous passages condoning killing infants and children in general, not to mention women, it says that if a man is
feeling jealous of his wife, as a consequence for her infidelity—
whether real or just his jealous psychosis—he can force her to
drink an abortion-causing bitter elixir that will trigger a spon-
taneous miscarriage.

Then there's the anti-choice claim that life begins at concep-
tion, and that fetuses and embryos are persons—full and separate human beings with rights. For religious anti-choicers, this

usually means a belief that fertilized eggs are infused with souls. But the Bible states in many places (I've counted eleven) that life and personhood begin with the "breath." For example, with the creation of "man" in Genesis 2:7, God: "...*breathed into his nostrils the breath of life, and man became a living being.*" Or how about Ezekiel 37:5? "*Behold, I will cause breath to enter you, and you shall live.*"

Now I know preachers have prepared anti-choicers with a convenient rebuttal to these scenarios. The flock relies on being spoon-fed like infants—many even call their preacher "father"—on a diet of filtered and selective scripture, doled out by religious leaders and talk radio, Christian storybooks, movies, television, and websites telling them what to think. They raise their children on the same fare. They don't call it television "programing" for nothing.

Illinois Republican Congressman Adam Kinzinger was one out of ten who voted to impeach Trump. Kinzinger has been censured by La Salle County Republicans. But he also received a (handwritten) letter signed by eleven members of his extended family. Excerpts:

> Oh my, what a disappointment you are to us and to God! We were once so proud of your accomplishments! Instead, you go against your Christian principals [sic] and join the "devil's army." (Democrats and the fake news media). How do you call yourself a Christian when you join the "devils army" believing in abortion! We thought you were "smart" enough to see how the left is brainwashing so many "so called good people" including yourself and many other GOP members. You have even fallen for their socialism ideals! So, so, sad!

President Trump is not perfect, but neither are you or any of us for that matter! It is not for us to judge or be judged! But he is a Christian! (If God can forgive and use <u>King David</u> in the Bible, [take note of that comment, I'll get to that] He can do the same with President Trump.) … Obviously, you did not hear President Trump's "Christmas Message" [neither did anyone else, cuz he didn't give one], to the American people (fake news media did not cover his message) where he actually gave the plan of salvation, instructing people how to repent and ask the Savior into their heart to be "Born Again"! (To believe in John 3:16). When was the last time you proclaimed your faith Adam? (Oh, we forgot you now belong to the "devils army."). You won't convince us otherwise with your horrible, rude accusations of President Trump! (To embrace a party that believes in abortion and socialism is the ultimate sin.) We should list even more grievances against you, but decided you ae [sic] not worth more of our time to list them. We have said enough! … You should be very proud that you have lost the respect of Lou Dobbs, Tucker Carlson, Sean Hannity, Laura Ingraham, Greg Kelly, etc. and most importantly in our book, Mark Levin and Rush Limbaugh and us! [I would be proud]

It is now most embarrassing to us that we are related to you. You have embarrassed the Kinzinger family name. We are not judging you. [Wow, I'd hate to see it if they were.] This letter is our opinion of you! …

This is a perfect example of the kind of pressuring, shaming, and ostracizing a cult does to their members who reject any aspect of their beliefs. How hurtful and upsetting for Adam. He is very courageous to stand up for what is right against this kind of vicious attack, especially from his own family members. But I would have defended Jaime with just as much vitriol and self-righteous fervor as these befuddled and bamboozled cult members.

Just to be clear, Christians and everyone else have a right to believe that camels shit gold bricks for all I care. Just don't force your beliefs, faith, or confidence—which means you don't know for sure—into the non-secular laws of my government. It's un-American!

For such men are false apostles, deceitful workmen, disguising themselves as apostles of Christ.
2 Corinthians 11:14

(You know, the book Trump couldn't pronounce.)

I'm about to take you on a journey into the bowels of American evangelical history and show you who is pulling the puppet strings of the "Christian" right. Looking for a "Deep State"? Turns out there is a secret cult of evangelicals on steroids. They represent consciously amassed pre-Trump power that will permeate this post-Trump world. Its connections reach to the highest levels of the US government and include ties to the CIA and to numerous current and past dictators around the globe. They are so powerful and so enmeshed in the political structure of our country, its existence is the most frightening revelation I have ever heard. They may even have been mentioned in Revelations...something about the false prophets working as agents of the Beast. Welcome to The Family, also known as The Fellowship. I know this sounds like something out of a conspiracy theorist's wet dream, but fasten your seatbelts, because it is not only disturbing, it's downright bizarre.

Just as Will and I are able to give you a glimpse into the cult of the Buddha-field from the inside, distinguished journalist Jeff Sharlet was a member of this powerful Christian Fundamentalist cult. Among his many writings, Sharlet published two important books: *The Family: The Secret Fundamentalism at the Heart of American Power* and *C Street: The Fundamentalist Threat to American Democracy*. In this chapter I will summarize the highlights of these books, but if you are really interested in the origin of the evangelical movement in America, I recommend reading *The Family*, where Sharlet describes the early history of evangelical Christianity in America. Then he moves to the history of a sect of evangelicals who call themselves The Family, dating from 1935, when Abraham Vereide, an immigrant preacher, organized a small group of businessmen sympathetic to European fascism and integrated the far right with his own brand of authoritarian faith. Sharlet writes:

> *The Family* is about the other half of American fundamentalist power—not its angry masses, but its sophisticated elites. From that core, Vereide built an international network of fundamentalists who spoke the language of establishment power, a "family" that thrives to this day. In public, they host the Annual Prayer Breakfast and other prayer breakfasts or cells around the country throughout the year; in private, they preach a gospel of "biblical capitalism," military might, and American empire.

Sharlet tells the story of Vereide's legacy, perpetuated by his successor, Douglas Coe, known as "the stealth Billy Graham"—a gentle, unassuming man who went on to direct the Fellowship. Sharlet documents the Family's deep roots and influence in American politics on both sides of the aisle, and in international governments. Regardless of cultural or religious affiliation, these influences are secretive, insidious, powerful, and dangerous.

The question Sharlet believes we must ask is not "What do fundamentalists want?" but "What have they already done?" I would add, "And what do they intend to keep right on doing?"

The Family is all about power, control, and wealth. The goal is an "invisible" world organization led by their version of Christ. They justify their actions through stories in the Bible—though not the Bible most of us know. They have selected excerpts from the King James Bible and assembled a mishmash of Old and New Testament (whatever works) into their own version. Their un-Holy Bible version is not about the loving words and deeds of Jesus. Although their motto is "Jesus + nothing," they don't believe in the Lamb of God they openly admire and instead emulate the Big Bad Wolf.

Beware of false prophets, who come to you in sheep's clothing but inwardly are ravenous wolves.
Matthew 7:15

The Family models itself after the murderous homewrecker King David. Remember I noted that in Adam Kenzinger's letter? And do you remember David and the object of his lust, the married Bathsheba? He sends her husband off to fight in a war that he created, then knocks her up. So as not to be discovered, the king brings hubby back on furlough to have sex with

Bathsheba, so everyone thinks the child is his. But the guy is so loyal to his buddies on the front line, he doesn't want to leave, so David has him killed during a battle.

Sharlet describes the Fellowship's depiction of David as a sort of original alpha male, lending legitimacy to men who believe they have been chosen to be in charge. They use David as proof that strong men in power, like Hitler, Lenin, and Mao (their acknowledged role models, I kid you not), as well as Trump and other male political leaders, are like David, who have that manly characteristic of being an adulterer and murderer. The Family's faith and devotion are token, a means to an end, a justification for their actions. Their actual goal is power and control—in the name of their Jesus, of course.

Although I do not subscribe to the Bible, or Christianity per se, I am a fan of Jesus' teachings—at least the ones I and most people are familiar with. However, if you were ever to define the Antichrist, literally meaning anti Christ's teaching, that would be the Family.

Let's take some of Jesus' famous teachings and match them up with the Family's interpretation. Starting with:

"Blessed are the poor in spirit."

My understanding of this passage is that it's about being humble. Humility is the realization that all your gifts and blessings come from the grace of God. Well, that's tricky for the Family. They would agree that all gifts and blessings come from the grace of God or Jesus, as the case may be—only with a twist.

A fundamental danger of a spiritual identity is considering yourself to be exceptional. These guys take exceptionalism to a whole new level. Their belief allows them to pretty much do whatever is needed to gain power and wealth to control the populace. And they can justify their actions because Jesus chooses them. Their reasoning is if they are rich, powerful, and successful in their deeds, it is because Jesus ordained it, regardless of what they had to do to get there. So corruption, infidelity, even murder and mayhem are not necessarily off the table. As long as they repent and invoke Jesus' name (like a talisman), all is forgiven, and they expect to receive a "Get Out of Jail Free" card. And now—with the secret Family members embedded in all three branches of government, regardless of party affiliation, including the courts—that free card is accessible. Their rationale for their impunity is always their righteous exceptionalism. Because Jesus + nothing. If they are successful then Jesus allowed it, so it's cool.

"Blessed are the meek, for they shall inherit the earth."

This one has another crafty little twist for the Family. St. Augustine advises us to be meek in the face of the Lord and not resist but be obedient to him. The Fellowship preaches "Obedience is freedom." Sounds like a contradiction in terms to me, but they believe in doing whatever the bidding of macho-man Jesus the Wolf demands. Jesus is not here to say what he wants, though, so it's easy to claim his "bidding" is whatever they want to do. Many of them convince themselves that they are hearing the voice of Jesus. How is that done exactly? Apparently, they literally just sit there and let Christ give them instructions. How convenient!

At past "Prayer Breakfasts" (and I use the term "Prayer" loosely), the Family has facilitated meetings between a mind-boggling number of foreign dictators and the US president and members of Congress, outside the reach of the

Department of State and traditional US diplomatic protocol. These so-called Prayer Breakfasts are where all the wheeling and dealing goes on, with attendees of any authoritarian regime welcomed, regardless of their religious affiliation.

The Family, led by Doug Coe, formed relationships with some of the most cold-blooded dictators of the last half-century, including totalitarian despot "Papa Doc" Duvalier of Haiti, who kept Haiti in illiteracy and dire poverty. And get this—Duvalier even went so far as to indoctrinate Haitian children with a political catechism that included his own parody of The Lord's Prayer:

> "Our Doc, who art in the National Palace for life,
> Hallowed be Thy name by present and future
> generations. Thy will be done at Port-au-Prince and in
> the provinces. Give us this day our new Haiti and never
> forgive the trespasses of the anti-patriots who spit every
> day on our country; let them succumb to temptation,
> and under the weight of their venom, deliver them not
> from any evil... "

The way Republican members of Congress are acting towards Trump even after losing the election, I would not put it past them to recite a similar prayer with Trump's name on it at the "Prayer Breakfast." Or even as they kneel in front of the golden calf, I mean the statue of Trump in gaudy gold leaf, wearing American flag shorts at the CPAC conference. And you thought Kapernick was dishonoring the flag.

Now the Republican party is splintering away from conservative toward radical extremist. Besides being Republican, what do Ted Cruz (R-TX), Josh Hawley (R-MO), Cindy Hyde-Smith (R-MS), Cynthia Lummis (R-WY), Roger Marshall

(R-KS), John Kennedy (R-LA), Tommy Tuberville (R-AL), Ben Sasse (R-NE), Tim Scott (R-SC), John Thune (R-SD), Marco Rubio (R-FL), Jim Lankford (R-OK), Bill Hagerty (R-TN), and Marsha Blackburn (R-TN), have in common? They're all Christian extremists, and all objected to Biden's election. Tommy Tubervile (spelling intentional) made the statement that "Trump was sent here by God." And of course, Senators Ted Cruz and Josh Hawley were some of the inspiration for the January 6, 2021, insurrection. All Hail Trump! Their modern-day King David.

To give you just a few other examples of the types of leaders these evangelical radical extremists endorse: Vereide and Coe organized junkets for congressmen and oilmen, who became champions in Washington for Indonesia's ruthless dictator, <u>General Suharto</u>. They considered Suharto's genocide of an estimated one million people a "spiritual revolution." Suharto did, however, say, "I am sorry for my mistakes," after killing 500 student protesters. So there ya go, all is forgiven.

Then there was Jonas Savimbi of Angola. Savimbi was long considered the darling of the American right wing; conservative politicians; and the CIA. Fellowship member President Ronald Reagan invited Savimbi to the White House, hailed him a "freedom fighter," and gave him $15 million of taxpayer money to fund covert military aid in the late 1980s; the Bush Sr. administration kicked in another $15 million. I wonder if their Jesus likes to wear "blood diamonds"? Asking for a friend.

The butcher Siad Barre of Somalia was considered a "brother" to the Family. And another favorite of the Fellowship and the right wing Republican regime was President-elect Arthur Costa e Silva of Brazil. The Family inspired a US-sanctioned coup that ushered in two decades of military rule. The military regime probably gave Coe an erection when it promised swift action to bring "order" back to a country it perceived as slipping towards communism. You know, the popular epithet that Republicans use to smear Liberals. Five hundred people were disappeared or killed, and many more detained and tortured by Costa e Silva's authoritarianism. Thy will be done!

Members of the Family have been behind efforts to pass Draconian anti-gay legislation in countries like Uganda and Romania that includes life imprisonment—and in some cases the death penalty—for anyone convicted of having gay sex. An LGBTQ activist in Romania puts it: "They have a purpose in their life now. To hate you." I would say that's a rather grotesque view of Jesus' teachings.

I could offer more examples, and the Family's efforts are ongoing. But you get the idea. The agenda of the Fellowship explains a lot about how the Republican Party became the cult of hate. We can also see how the pernicious actions of this shadow theocracy have made America hated around the world.

When interviewed on NPR, Jeff Sharlet was asked which members of the Senate and Congress were involved in the Family. This was his answer:

> Every US President on both sides of the aisle, from Eisenhower to Trump, attended the Annual Prayer Breakfast, including President Obama. Rep. Newt Gingrich (R), Col. Oliver North, Sen Jeff Sessions (R-AL), VP Mike Pence, Rep Steve Largent (R-OK), Senator John Ensign (R-NV), Senator Sam Brownback, United States Ambassador at Large for International Religious

Freedom (R-KS). Senator Jim Inhofe of Oklahoma boasts of traveling around the world, doing The Family's political business. Senator Tom Coburn (R-OK) did the same thing. Senator Chuck Grassley (R-IA) has been very involved in African affairs on behalf of the Family. Senator Mike Enzi (R-WY) of Wyoming is a part of it. John Carter (R-TX), Rep. Robert Aderholt (R-AL), and Gen. Claud "Mick" Kicklighter served on the board of the Family. Maj. Gen. Robert Caslen bragged, "We are the aroma of Jesus Christ.", [more like the stench of the antichrist], Rep. Frank Wolf (R-VA), Rep Pete Hoekstra (R-MI), Rep Mike Doyle (R-PA), Rep. Joe Pitts (R-PA).

Over in the House, you have guys like Representative Zach Wamp of Tennessee, a very conservative Republican. You have Representative Frank Wolf (R-VA) of Virginia. You have Democrats as well, and I think that's—part of what distinguishes them from a lot of other Christian-right groups. They survived for seventy years by not locking themselves in with any one faction. So you see Democrats like Rep. Mike McIntyre (D-NC), a very conservative Democrat from North Carolina; Rep. Heath Shuler (D-NC); Rep. Bart Stupak (D-MI); Former Senator Mark Pryor (D-AK), who is pro-war, anti-labor, anti-gay, and a creationist, but he is a Democrat. And he's a guy who explained that through the Family, he had learned that the meaning of bipartisanship was that, "Jesus didn't come to take sides; he came to take over."

In 2012, Amy Coney Barrett—raised as a "handmaid" in the Christian cult People of Praise" and later confirmed as one of Trump's Supreme Court Justices—told a class at the University of Notre Dame that it is always good to remember that a "legal career is but a means to an end…and that end is building the Kingdom of God." That must have made Family members happy as a tornado in a trailer park.

Trump was an easy mark for authoritarian dictators like Vladimir Putin. But he was no less susceptible to the flattery and funding of The Family. Donald was a pathetic pawn who was playing the card game *Go Fish* (in his case go fish for compliments and money) against a sophisticated game of 3-D chess with a cult of powerful men who have been on a mission to control America and the world for eighty years.

And now, with a stunning number of Family members ensconced in the halls of power and Ruth Bader Ginsberg replaced by elite cult loyalist Barrett, they are poised for a ruthless and unscrupulous power-grab that will have repercussions for generations to come.

We have lost our Queen, and they may have just put Democracy in check!

CHAPTER 23

THE KAMIKAZES

MUCH LIKE MEMBERS OF The Family, whose gray lines and final line in the sand are sketchy at best—I guess they give those lines up to Jesus—the third type of people who join cults, the kamikazes, also don't seem to have a final line in the sand. They come to the abyss of reality and jump off. They can range from benign people who will follow their leader to the bitter end, regardless of facts or morals, to dangerous, destructive, blindly obedient devotees who will kill. Examples of the latter include the followers of Charles Manson; Timothy McVeigh and other domestic terrorists; or those willing to commit suicide at the behest of the leader, such as followers of Jim Jones or the Heaven's Gate UFO cult; ISIS suicide bombers; or Japanese kamikazes.

When the Buddha-field broke up in Austin, most members had seen or at least heard the details of the infamous email that exposed Jaime's sexual assaults, fraud, and manipulations. Yet many followed him to Corpus Christi because he announced he would have another "Knowing Session." I can understand, even though they had the information about his deeds. His lies and subterfuge can be convincing, especially when he tells followers what they want to hear, similar to another tax cut. After all, they had invested eighteen years waiting for a "Knowing Session," so what the hell. They decided to step over that giant gray line, maybe even for the last time, but were willing to gamble for the prize. To the dismay of many disciples, Jaime's shoddy performance of poking them in the eyes, while the cartoon *Family Guy* was playing in the background, just didn't imbue the anointing of the Holy Spirit with the same pageantry as they had witnessed in the past. For some, that pathetic dog-and-pony show was their final line in the sand.

But despite that abysmal disappointment, lo and behold, some still followed him to Hawaii, and some are still with him. Those are your kamikazes. To them, even when faced with irrefutable facts and evidence, nothing matters. They will believe what they want to believe. They close their eyes and ears to truth, and their mental-gymnastic cognitive dissonance is so strong that it drowns out all doubt. HE'S A FRAUD PEOPLE, STOP BEING DUPED! I just needed to get that off my chest. Not that the kamikazes will read this; they wouldn't even go see *Holy Hell*. Jaime will just chalk me up as another unfaithful disciple who "missed in this life" and hang a Medal of Freedom on those who remain the faithful devotees who serve him.

Someone asked me if I was worried about retaliation, given that he did conspire to have me "taken out" or hurt in some way before. As I think about it, I'm not as worried about that old queen, as much as I am about his flying monkeys, because I was one of his flying monkeys. I know what he is capable of when he thinks his identity, or his messiah gig, may be threatened.

Back in those days, it was a lot more challenging to damage someone's reputation. There was no internet, so if you wanted to write a public exposé about anything, you had to have it published as an article in a newspaper or magazine. Then the person so exposed or maligned would have to rebut the article in a letter to the editor. Ah! Those were the days of civility and restraint. When I was still among his followers, Jaime chose me as one of his elite writers, who he assigned to contest anything having to do with cults, using an assumed name. He was big on anonymity. In 1993, for example, after the lengthy standoff between the armed Branch Davidian sect and federal agents in Waco, TX, Jaime's paranoid mind was as much on fire as David Koresh's compound. Citing "religious freedom" and other useful arguments, he would have me and a select few skilled disputants publish fierce defenses of the group.

Of course, such letters were nothing, compared to what social media can do to someone today, in a matter of hours. I had a friend and colleague hate-bombed on Twitter and Facebook once. I don't remember the exact reason, but it had something to do with her being a homeopathic practitioner. Within a matter of days, she had 130,000 hate-bomb comments. Between the death threats and the viciousness of the remarks, she was so badly frightened and traumatized that she gave up her practice for a period and moved.

Creating campaigns of public smearing, shaming, and hate-bombing is just one of many extreme techniques a kamikaze may embark on when their beliefs are challenged. I—no doubt— expect some scathing comments on social media and other online venues from "anonymous" sources, you could trace back to Hawaii. Don't forget who you're dealing with Jaime. They can be terribly hurtful at best. At worst, they can be dangerous and violent. And when they are anonymous, the beast in them is even more tempted.

We have already seen right-wing militias and hate groups take up arms when they believe their cult leader Trump—and thus their own "manly" or white way of life—requires defending. Kamikazes become so attuned to their idol's most subtle gestures and "dog whistles" that they often do not even need to be ordered to take action. They take it upon themselves to attack their imagined enemies. As Michael Cohen, Donald Trump's former lawyer, testified before Congress, Trump operated "like a mobster." "He doesn't give you questions, he doesn't give you orders. He speaks in a code, and I understand the code because I've been around him for a decade."

Jaime, on the other hand, will gather his loyalist flying monkeys to sit at his feet and strategize for hours on how to extinguish the bad press. His brightest and most anxious-to-please will offer a variety of scathing and conniving scenarios to hurt and avenge his enemies. Deep down they believe that by appealing to his sadistic little mind with fantasies of revenge they will gain his favor, making them feel more important. Don't be fooled by that. Like Trump, he couldn't care less about you, and one day you'll find his knife in your own back.

CHAPTER 24

IT'S A MAD, MAD, MAD, MAD WORLD: FROM PIZZAGATE TO WAYFAIRGATE

CONSPIRACY THEORIES ARE HARD to fight because they're about what we want to believe. Today's world is so complex, diverse, and an imminent threat to old identities, that conspiracy theories, ironically, serve to create the perception of order in chaos; they attempt to make sense of events that don't make sense. People would rather believe that there are criminal masterminds out there pulling the strings than accept the occurrence of arbitrary incidents. Like the hummingbirds who are not encumbered by the facts, believers in conspiracy theories aren't burdened by facts either. People's desire to believe that there must be something more to the events that shape our lives, culture, and politics than accident or happenstance is so strong that they forgo rational thought.

But now there is a new form of conspiracy floating around the cybersphere. Harvard political scientist Nancy Rosenblum, coauthor with Russell Muirhead of *A Lot of People Are Saying: The New Conspiracism and the Assault on Democracy*, argues that conspiracies such as QAnon represent a hybrid between traditional conspiracy theories and a new kind of thinking, what she calls "conspiracy without the theory." Unlike traditional conspiracy theories, which seek to uncover evidence of secret machinations by the powerful—cover-ups of information relating to the Kennedy assassination or UFOs, for example—the new form relies on patently false or evidence-free assertions, repetition, and attacks on sources of actual knowledge. "It's a prophetic prediction." And it's one that is promulgating a paranoid right-wing political agenda.

Conspiracy theories are essentially a collection of creative mental gymnastics run amok. At least with the Buddha-field, we shared a somewhat tangible reality in the form of a centralized community, based on unified ideology, with limited access to global information and communication. So the metamorphosis of our happy spiritual co-op was a very slow, gradual descent into a deviant cult of deceit over twenty-plus years. But with the internet and social media today, you or an anonymous troll can reach hundreds of thousands of strangers in a matter of hours.

As the hummingbird "feelies" I talked about in Chapter 18 can tell you, lies that are frequently repeated and retweeted will soon be "felt" as if they are true. Or, as is ascribed to Joseph

Goebbels, Hitler's Minister of Propaganda, "If you tell a lie big enough and keep repeating it, people will eventually come to believe it." Trump—a master of lies big and small—knows all too well that instead of an honest, nuanced, and thorough engagement with an ever more complex and contradictory world, it's easier and more effective to release emotionally charged, simplistic messages that feed into people's fears and racial stereotypes, which in turn garners millions of followers.

The media knows this too, and their business model is about sponsors and ratings, rather than straight journalism that presents boring factual news. They wrap information in partisan pundit opinions and shovel a mixture of selected facts and biased appraisals into a mini horror series in order to scare the bejesus out of us, because—that's what sells. On the liberal-leaning cable news shows, the message was: Trump bad, we were all gonna die. And on the conservative cable media shows, it was: Trump good, we're all gonna lie. On the internet it's about "likes" and "click-bait."

The amount of traffic to mainstream social networking sites like Facebook, Twitter, Reddit, and YouTube has exploded since 2017. Conspirators analyze social media conversations, including popular hashtags, to decide where and how to interject their latest toxins. Social network platforms do not judge your beliefs. They use algorithms designed to target your interests; so if you're posting or commenting on a topic, the platform's algorithm will gladly send you more and connect you to other like-minded users. Here is the latest toxic conspiracy that is bringing our country to the brink of destruction:

"There is a secret cabal that is taking over the world. They kidnap children, slaughter and eat them to get power from their blood. They control high positions in government, banks, international finance, the news media and the church. They want to disarm the police. They promote homosexuality and pedophilia. They plan to mongrelize the white race so it will lose its essential power."

If you haven't been hiding under a rock, you probably have heard about this conspiracy by now. QAnon, right? Oh wait—no, my bad. The above paragraph was taken from a fabricated document referred to as *The Protocols of the Elders of Zion.* Yes, that's right! It was written by a Russian anti-Jewish propagandist in 1902. Hitler used this "protocol" as his argument against the Jews in his Nazi manifesto, *Mein Kampf.* One would hope these QAnon boneheads would at least be more original.

The QAnon movement began in 2017, but it really started back in 2013, pre-Q, when a movement known as #SavetheChildren first became a rallying cry among conspiracy theorists attempting to root out a deep state pedophile ring. So the cybersphere was primed and ready for the "big lie." By 2017, someone known only as Q claimed to have a level of US security approval known as "Q clearance." Q clearance or Q access authorization is the Department of Energy (DOE) security clearance required to access Top Secret Restricted Data, Formerly Restricted Data, and National Security Information.

Q posted a series of conspiracy theories (obviously plagiarized) about Donald Trump on the internet forum 4chan. Participants on 4chan can say and do virtually anything they want with only the faintest threat of culpability. 4chan and later 8chan, and now another called Endchan, are responsible for some of the largest hoaxes, cyberbullying, and internet pranks.

Despite the site's insistence that minors are not allowed on the site, the participants—usually teenage boys, many out of Japan, Vietnam, Eastern Europe, and Asia—spread hoaxes, often for the simple pleasure of laughing at someone else's stupidity/expense.

4chan's "politically incorrect" message board—an obscure political forum—seems more like that of the dark web and has served as a general assembly for all manner of extremists. The QAnon conspiracy theory appeared on a section of the 4chan site trending with Trump supporters from the radical White Nationalist Alt-Right. It started as a conspiracy theory about a "deep state" satanic cabal of global elites involved in pedophilia and sex trafficking that is supposedly responsible for all the evil in the world. Sound familiar?

All kinds of conspiracy theories, including "Pizzagate" (I'll get to that), bubbled up from 4chan onto the mainstream internet when a Reddit user conveniently posted an extensive document with all of the "evidence" of said evil, coincidently just days before the 2016 presidential election. Gird your loins, Hillary; the hummingbirds are about to be spoon-fed a pile of chocolate-covered cow dung. But, but, Benghazi…and what about the emails…and now pizza and pedophilia, oh my?

At its heart, QAnon is a wide-ranging, baseless conspiracy theory that says that Donald Trump was—and to many, still is—waging a secret war against elite Satan-worshipping pedophiles in government, business, the mainstream media, and Hollywood. Oh yeah, and apparently, like in Germany in the 1900s, they eat babies. It's a German dish; I've heard it's good with schnitzel. Yes, that's right. Evidently liberal "global elites" torture children to harvest the chemical adrenochrome from their blood, which they then inject to stay healthy and young.

What? Oh, yeah! These kamikazes came to the abyss, and without hesitation—they jumped off. By the way, adrenochrome does not appear to be working for Hillary or Nancy Pelosi. And George Soros looks like a dried turd. But evidence—even for their own theories—is considered unnecessary.

QAnon is a cult of salvationists: like members of The Family, the righteous few will liberate the world from the spell of evil. Under the guise of labels such as "Save the Children," this mission is appealing to the white suburban soccer moms (so called mama bears), who fill their time seeking out pedophiles and their protectors or sending tips to hotlines—which has a participatory aspect. It makes disenfranchised suburbanites feel like a detective on a massive online hunt, consumed with the thrill of the chase. It fuses together strangers in an illusory sense of shared identity, as they barrel full speed ahead on an unprecedented historic mission to save the world from Satan's grip. Why are they willing to fall for this fantasy? People join cults such as QAnon because in this anonymous, lonely, alienating world of competition, isolation, and loss of identities, they crave belonging. And not only belonging—a membership in a tribe that touts its own exceptionalism. They belong... and they are special. They possess secret knowledge not available to the rest of us poor schlubs.

CHAPTER 25

BINARY CONSPIRACY NARRATIVES OF GOOD VS. EVIL

QANON FANS FALL FOR the classic "superhero versus the villain" scenario. And when Trump is Batman, to go any lower the villain would have to be nothing less than a Satan-worshiping, baby-eating pedophile. In my search for answers as to why and how this conspiracy phenomenon has gripped our country and is now bleeding into a global network of political upheaval, I found a great article entitled "6 Reasons so Many Spiritual People Have Been Fooled by Qanon," by Martin Winiecki, writer and activist at the Tamera Peace Research & Education Center. Winiecki observes that totalitarian regimes have always employed "simplistic and dualistic spiritual narratives" to incite people "to suppress and external-ize their shadow... by projecting it onto others." He writes:

> Implicit racial bias, i.e. racist prejudice that people carry within themselves unknowingly... makes people fall for far-right conspiracy theories. In a world in which Black, Indigenous and People of Color are rising for equal rights, many white people socialized to feel entitled to their privilege of racial superiority, currently feel (subconsciously) threatened and so victimize themselves.

> Though people who spread those narratives might not be willing to admit it (or intend to perpetuate racism), the infinitely repeated stories of "George Soros is controlling all the social movements" or "Black Lives Matter is a tool of the liberal elites to stage a race war" are clearly reflections of well-known racist tropes.

> The Soros narrative is just another version of the classic antisemitic fairytale of "the powerful shady Jews who pull the strings from behind closed doors... The equation of BLM with "riots" and "looting" is just another testimony to the anti-black sentiment of white people who associate black equity and liberation with danger, threat and violence.

To add insult to injury, the progressive left is disrupting the dominant White, Christian Conservative identity. So for that group, it can be easier to accept that a malevolent power must be at work rather than to accept societal change. The four years of the Trump administration have inflamed the country and doused it with the gasoline of confusion and chaos. QAnon provides a soothing salve. Believers are assured that the only people who really know what's going on are the believers— and Trump, of course. Which must be true because the *stable genius* passed his "cognitive test"—a test given to people if they are showing signs of dementia. So there ya go.

The QAnon conspiracy theory is generally pro-Trump and anti-"deep state." Here is where Christianity and QAnon collide. QAnon is a poisonous stew where batshit-crazy conspiracy meets Dominionism. Dominionists hold the theocratic idea, based on their interpretations of biblical law (so there's that), that God calls Christians to exercise dominion over every aspect of society by taking control of political and cultural institutions. Their goal is to attain sociopolitical and economic transformation through the gospel of Jesus in what they call the seven mountains or spheres of society: religion, family, education, government, media, entertainment, and business. So basically, they preach the Western equivalent of Sharia Law. Their purpose is to establish a fundamentalist Christian nation with no separation of church and state.

QAnon's apocalyptic desire to destroy the deep-state-controlled society blends well with the Dominionist vision of the kingdom of God on Earth. The combination is The Family's wet dream. A large percentage of QAnon devotees are Trump-supporting evangelicals. So they are already drinking from the pro-Trump, anti-liberal Kool-Aid punchbowl. Some followers even believe that Trump is Q—though others think Q is John F. Kennedy, Jr, who they believe faked his 1999 death. Which is curious; has no one told them that JFK, Jr. and the whole Kennedy family are the archetypical liberals? Regardless, QAnon enthusiasts subscribe to the narrative that global elites (only not JFK, Jr.?) were seeking to bring down Trump, whom they see as the world's only hope to defeat the "deep state."

I want to take a moment to address the term "deep state." Does it exist? Apparently! Is it what Trump or the Q clan are referring to? No! The term was first used in a 2007 book, *The Road to 9/11: Wealth, Empire, and the Future of America* by Peter Dale Scott, who was one of the first to refer to the "deep state" in the context of the US Government. In a VOX interview with David Rohde, author of *In Deep: the FBI, the CIA, and the Truth about America's "Deep State,"* Rohde interviewed many people from both sides of the political spectrum, including Peter Dale Scott. Rohde explains:

> Scott used the term "deep state" to describe what liberals typically fear, which is the military-industrial complex. Scott wrote about a sense that the military and defense contractors had driven the country repeatedly into wars and maybe helped fuel 9/11 and the wars that followed. For Scott, it also applied to large financial interests, like Wall Street banks.

Here is a comment from Martin Winiecki on that subject:

> ... [T]rying to cast blame for systemic problems on particular individuals or groups without addressing the system itself is just another way for the system to protect itself. And ... QAnon is ... an extremely smart "divide and rule" wedge that channels the disillusionment with a broken and structurally unjust system, which could lead ... to identification with a proto-fascist government by, for and of the billionaire class, Wall St, oil companies and the Military-Industrial Complex.

Rohde eventually ended up doing interviews with people on the right, like conspiracy theorist Alex Jones, and the term "deep state" was recruited and vulgarized into what it is today, which is a shorthand for a conspiracy against Donald Trump. "The problem is that the term has become an effective way of signaling a conspiracy for which there just isn't any evidence."

One popular QAnon theory is that the COVID-19 pandemic was planned, so the public would be sequestered and out of the way in order for Trump to round up the liberal evildoers and put them in prison, specifically Guantanamo. Yet another QAnon conspiracy theory is that the coronavirus crisis is a liberal hoax being deployed to cover for a shadowy take-over of the government. Although there is no evidence of this, I'd like to personally thank the rest of the world population who sacrificed their lives in order to take Trump down. But this may explain the horde of mask-hating right-wing nut jobs who refuse to succumb to the liberal plot to prevent the populace from going bowling or getting their hair done.

New Christian-QAnon online churches are popping up on the internet. They use selective Bible studies to verify and sanctify QAnon propaganda. Scammers are leveraging religious beliefs to indoctrinate attendees into the QAnon church. Q narratives are explained through the lens of the Bible. One QAnon theory, called Project Looking Glass, claims that the US military has secretly developed or is hiding a form of alien time-travel technology, which can be explained by certain passages in the Bible. Remember our QAnon aficionado Daniel Divine from Chapter 11? Here's what he has to say about it:

> This in [I'm not makin' up these typos] not a battle of liberal or republicans, left/right, or even black/white

inequalities. It is historic Biblical battle of Fact/Fiction, moral/immoral, freedom/captivity but more along the lines of Good vs Evil On a global scale.

In the coming days/weeks people are going to enter into a dark period where everything they thought they knew or believed is opposite of the relative truth and will discover that everything ever shown on msm [I love that] was a lie.

The Great Awakening is a monumental Event ending history and beliefs in which the truth and nature of this techno-matrix ["matrix,"see what you've done, Warner Bros?] world is exposed to the people enslaved within it, on every level imaginable.

We can only [wait, shouldn't that be "not"] proceed in peace and prosperity until we Acknowledge the darkness behind the madness. Here are the facts:

Give it your best shot, Danny boy!

The United States of America, since the Act of 1871 was not a Country, but a Corporation with a long list of dark secrets that most will not be able to conceptualize. It's is a global power structure in which has for the most part of its history, been controlled by the [wait for it] (V)Atican and London, England, Global Banking Aristocrats.

On Nov. 2, 2020 US Inc. under the Act of 1871, owned and controlled by the [V]@tican was Bankrupt and ceased to exist. In 2017 Trump essentially Forced [P]ope Francis to resign and hand the Country back to the people.

Is that a fact? Okay, let me stop your deranged ranting for a moment to interject some reality. The Act of 1871, also known as the Ku Klux Klan Act, was passed in response to a wave of terrorist violence sweeping the South. It was an Act of the United States Congress that empowered the President to suspend the writ of habeas corpus to combat the Ku Klux Klan (KKK) and other white supremacy organizations. It was designed to protect the civil rights of African-Americans, prevent and remedy conspiracies to violate civil rights, and reestablish the supremacy of federal law. Okay go on, I'm enraptured.

> The Earth Alliance (EA) took control of the NSA, an entity which monitors every single person and everything they do on Earth's surface, [so, only on Earth's surface…I guess that doesn't include undersea or underground] Everything! To sum it up brief, DJT dropped 3 stacks of paper on the table, 3000 docs, photos, and Accounts incriminating [P]ope Frances of Crimes against Humanity at the worst levels imaginable. PF [Pope Francis] complied and signed back control of USA into hands of DJT. US Inc. no longer exists as of Nov 2, 2020, so an election on the following day for a US Pres. for US Inc. is meaningless!

Uh huh!

Now, if this mass psychosis hadn't metastasized into the body politic of America and the world, I would bust a gut laughing; but it has, and we'd better take it seriously. Nut jobs like Daniel Divine use just enough poly-sci jargon to make their rants sound feasible to the lazy, non-critical thinkers who are looking for answers to their miserable lives. But when 199 lawmakers back Congresswoman Marjorie Taylor Greene (R-GA) and her QAnon conspiracies rhetoric—including comments on social media suggesting that some mass shootings, such as the Parkland school shooting and the 2017 Vegas massacre, were staged by supporters of gun control, and that a Jewish cabal had sparked the deadly wildfires in California with a space beam—it's no laughing matter.

And if that weren't enough, Greene "liked" a comment advocating "a bullet to the head" of House Speaker Nancy Pelosi (D-CA). And in another post, from April 2018, a commenter asked, "Now do we get to hang them ??" referring to former president Barack Obama and Hillary Clinton. In response, Greene did not denounce the suggestion of assassination and instead wrote, "Stage is being set. Players are being put in place. We must be patient. This must be done perfectly or liberal judges would let them off." In 2019, she led a group of Trump supporters into the Speaker's office, where she accused Pelosi of "treason" and suggested she "shall suffer death or shall be imprisoned." Classic QAnon rhetoric!

And then there was January 6, 2021, when a gallows was erected to hang Vice President Pence and Speaker of the House Nancy Pelosi and other lawmakers.

This madness is becoming as dangerous as the rise of any totalitarian regime in world history, and just because they failed does not mean they will not continue to try, regardless of Trump being out of office. Remember Daniel Divine's assessment: Trump is still their leader and Biden is illegitimate.

Like the QAnon conspirators, who tap into the vulnerable psyche of the believers, Jaime did this all the time. He would often take stories and teachings out of Indian or Buddhist sacred texts and twist them into a distorted portrait to validate his scam. For example, after the Branch Davidian incident in Waco, persecution was a hot topic for him. Especially because he was trying to convince us that he was the equivalent of the Buddha or Christ. Jaime wove historical events into a false narrative, in this case implying that non-believers—or those we called "the unconscious"—would try to destroy the *Holy Ones*—that would be us.

He told the story of the mass persecution of Siddhartha Gautama, the Buddha. Not familiar with that story? That's because it didn't really happen that way. The Buddha's adversary, Davadatta, his own cousin, became a follower of the Buddha; turned out to be responsible for a schism of the Sangha (Buddhist community); and he even tried to kill the Buddha. But to my knowledge there was never a mass persecution of Siddhartha. That's not how Jaime would spin it, though. If he could convince us that they—whoever "they" were—were coming to snuff out the God King, RayJi (Jaime) and his Holy Company, it would prove that he was important enough for anyone to care about, let alone kill.

The funny thing was, by that time many of the elders, including myself, were doubting his holiness and could not understand his anxiety. One time he was seeking solace from his fixer—that would be me—regarding his delusion that it was only a matter of time before the authorities would be at our door. I was trying to console him on the phone while he was on this obsessive paranoid rant when I asked him straight out why he thought anyone wanted to come after him. "You never told me you were the way, the truth, and the light," I said. There was an awkward silence. He did not want to hear that. But what was he going to say at that point? "Yes, I am!"

like a childish retort. Yet I continued to humor him—I still couldn't walk away from this nutbag.

One QAnon conspiracy theory holds that the Russia investigation was really a ruse, designed to cover for Special Counsel Robert Mueller and Donald Trump working together to expose thousands of pedophiles hidden in plain sight—including the usual suspects: Hillary and Bill Clinton, Barack and Michelle Obama, Nancy Pelosi, Chuck Schumer, Adam Schiff, oh, and of course Oprah, and Tom Hanks (he always struck me as a baby-eating-pedophile), and many, many, more who will soon be under arrest. Or perhaps already have been arrested and are on their way to Guantanamo Bay. Some believe the claim that military personnel rescued 35,000 "malnourished" and "caged" children from tunnels running under Central Park in New York City and other US cities, (which apparently led right into the Clinton's Manhattan apartment). 35,000, wow, they must have been hungry that day. Notice the common denominator? All liberals—not a conservative cannibal in the bunch. *Quelle surprise!*

At a dinner event one evening in 2017, Trump was heard making the comment, "Maybe the calm before the storm." When a reporter asked, "What storm, Mr. President?" Trump responded, "You'll find out." It amazes me at this point that his followers have not yet figured out that comments like "You'll find out," "People are saying," "We're looking very closely into that," or "You'll see very, very soon" are standard Trump retorts when he is pulling baloney out of his ass. "The storm" soon became the most important "movement" of the QAnon/Trump era.

Another popular saying among Q buffs is "Everything is fine;" believers must only "Trust the plan." I would take this with more tongue in cheek—even more than my normal stance—if it weren't so terrifyingly infectious. More and more people I know—smart, well-educated professional people— are coming down with this mass psychosis faster than the spread of the common cold. Friends, clients, and colleagues; even myopic Mary from Chapter 20 are falling for this prank and spreading it on social media. Daniel Divine's little psychotic screed was sent to my Facebook page by a good friend. And they have this "in the know" arrogance as they recite things like, "Everything is fine, soon you will see we were right all along"—a confidence that is impossible to penetrate. I get it! We had the same arrogant attitude. We—"holy company"—were just placating you poor "unconscious" souls.

Another friend of mine, a dyed-in-the-wool gay liberal— go figure—whom I've known for over thirty years from the Buddha-field started shoveling this crap on Facebook. "You can take the man out of the cult, but ya can't take the cult out of the man," was my response. He was offended.

CHAPTER 26

DELIVER US FROM EVIL

ET'S BE CLEAR, HUMAN trafficking is a real thing and a heinous problem. But the issue is shamelessly being used as a psychological weapon. It's a natural reaction for most humans to respond very strongly to the threat of sexual violence against children. The hysteria regarding satanic sex abuse rings in the late 1980s led to many criminal convictions, with some of the accused only being exonerated after serving years in prison. An example of this hysteria was the case of Fran Keller and her husband Dan, proprietors of a small daycare in Austin, Texas. Accused of satanic ritual sex abuse of the children, they spent twenty-one years in prison, before evidence proved them innocent.

I had a friend back then whose therapist was trying to convince her, through hypnotherapy, that she was a victim of ritualistic sexual abuse by both her parents in satanic ceremonies in their basement. Such abuse always seems to take place in the basement—ever notice that? Needless to say, she was more traumatized by the therapy. But Satan-worship and pedophilia make a formidable recipe for sensational news that most people can't ignore. We universally consider pedophilia a horrific atrocity, and accusations of it are the easiest way to damage someone's reputation with no proof necessary.

The QAnon conspiracists target purported enemies far and wide with their indictments, using satanic child-sex-trafficking as a potent weapon. All they need is a fraction of similarity to their enemies' deeds and they gotcha. Take Timothy Larson, a QAnon follower who vandalized the landmark Chapel of the Holy Cross Church in Sedona, Arizona. This kamikaze accepts without question the QAnon allegation that the Catholic Church—as a whole—is a sex-trafficking syndicate run by Satan. I suspect a deeper look into Timothy's history might reveal that he was sexually molested as a child. As Bill Maher like's to say: "I don't know it for a fact, I just know it's true".

We know this about Jaime, whom we believe was molested by the men on his family's ranch. "That's how you learn," he used to say. Whoa! We also saw his extreme post-traumatic reaction to Catholic choir music. Every year at Christmas some of the singers in the group would gather to perform at our Christmas dinner. Jaime made it explicitly clear to me and the choir director that we could sing any adoring song—directed to him of course—*as long as it wasn't choir music!* He was either jealous of baby Jesus; or my guess is that probably the choir-director-priest of his childhood, who always referred to Jaime's little behind as "manzanas pequeños" ("little apples"), had more going on in the choir than Gregorian chants. Really, Father? Why would a priest be interested enough in a little boy's butt to give it a nickname? Just sayin'!

But this is where conspiracy theorists only need a smattering of similar details to make their accusations seem plausible to the emotionally vulnerable. Is the Catholic Church riddled with cases of pedophilia and sex abuse scandals? Absolutely! But that does not mean that the priests who committed those acts were minions of Satan or selling children for their blood. For the fanatics looking for what they want to hear, however, the pieces fit comfortably into the conspiracy puzzle.

QAnon is popular among Protestant evangelicals, and the antipathy between Protestants and Catholics has been going on since the sixteenth century. If you recall my conversation in Chapter 16 with a devout Catholic: the worst insult she could throw at me was to accuse me of being a Protestant. QAnon incendiaries only need to use minor connections to factual occurrences to twist their narrative just enough to capture the gullible. And the more the captured hate the targeted enemy, the easier it is to make the puzzle pieces fit.

The mythical figure of Satan is the perfect villain. Much of Western culture is beguiled and obsessed by him. Why? Because most of us, and certainly Christians, grew up with that fairytale. Back in 2017 a good number of Christians became convinced that Satan even made an appearance at the Grammy Awards. It is not a novel idea for Christians to detect Satan's influence on rock 'n' roll lyrics, but the fact that Satan showed up right smack in the middle of a performance by Katy Perry and Juicy J caused this particular sighting to be more noteworthy than most. Some evangelicals even surmised that Perry, while singing "Dark Horse," had evoked an ancient satanic ritual, one that had actually summoned the Prince of Darkness to join her on the Grammy stage. One religious broadcaster, Kevin Swanson, called the performance "a satanic, twerking orgy" and then blamed the Beatles. Huh? Jesus-loving conspiracy theorist Mark Dice called Perry a "Babylonian bimbo" and then went on to declare her a "slithering servant of Satan." Funny, that's how I refer to Mitch McConnell.

I remember going to a Rolling Stones concert when I was young, and when I saw how mesmerized the crowd was and witnessed women taking off their tops and underwear and throwing them at Mick Jagger, I was fascinated by his power over the crowd. I needed to understand his power. He certainly didn't fit into my constructs of Jesus, so he had to be the opposite—right? I even illustrated a poster depicting him as Satan. In my underdeveloped and Catholic-indoctrinated mind, I consented to the subconscious belief that no one could have that much power without the help of some metaphysical force.

In 2013, a poll conducted by YouGov found that nearly 60 percent of Americans believe in a literal Devil. It's no surprise that, of those surveyed, believing in Satan was most popular among those who identified as Protestant, Catholic, or Christian.

In a study in *Scientific American*, researchers found support for the hypothesis that 1) evil people cannot be rehabilitated, and 2) the eradication of evil requires the eradication of all the evil people. Belief in pure evil (BPE) predicts such effects as advocacy for harsher punishments for crimes (e.g., murder, assault, theft); stronger support for the death penalty; and decreased support for criminal rehabilitation. Follow-up studies corroborate these findings, showing that BPE also predicts the degree to which participants perceive the world to be dangerous and vile, the perceived need for preemptive military aggression to solve conflicts, and reported support for torture. This is all right out of the Christian-Right Republican playbook.

Those who have accepted the identity of being "Christian" must have a Satan; otherwise Jesus would have no purpose. Who would Jesus save them from, if not from Satan? They cannot conceive of the idea of goodness, absent evil. The idea that Satan exists reinforces the idea that God or Jesus exists. Like Jaime was to the Buddha-field, Satan is the glue that holds the evangelical/QAnon/Trump-cult community together. Hmmm, I didn't intend to equate Jaime with Satan, but if the shoe fits.

And if not Christian, what would their identity be? If a member of a Christian community wants to renounce their Christian identity, no doubt their community would chalk that up to Satan's work. In order to hold on to the ideology of the community, the family or ministers either try to bring them back into the fold, or the community may ostracize them, branding them, like Adam Kenzinger, as a member of the "Devil's Army." It's a vicious trap. I get it! For those of us in the Buddha-field, the players may have been different, but the structure was the same.

Like Sherlock Holmes about to finally capture the phantom arch villain Moriarty, some might be thrilled to be closing in on the architect of evil. By following the most heinous of crimes, such as pedophilia and baby-harvesting, to its source, QAnon's devotees can imagine themselves as Batman's Robin—attaché to Jesus—the righteous against the unholy. QAnon provides followers with the desired identity of being God's emissaries, thus giving them a sense of safety in this chaotic and dangerous world. But only someone as powerful as the president of the United States has the ability to do what is needed to take down the evildoers. So by supporting Trump you are supporting Jesus' mission, and therefore shall be in God's favor and saved from his wrath. Ya know, the "all-loving, all-knowing, all-powerful—wrathful God, who apparently can't do the work himself.

This is our "simplistic and dualistic spiritual narrative" that Martin Winiecki talks about. This is why Satan is close, but not quite human-looking. We make sure he doesn't resemble us or our tribe. Satan represents the shadow side of us that is too scary or painful to look at; it is so much more appealing to project it onto our enemies. At the same time, such phantom enemies glorify our own identity and purpose. Carl Jung put it succinctly, in *Fight with the Shadow* (1946), and it applies quite aptly to Trump:

> Like the rest of the world, [the Germans] did not
> understand wherein Hitler's significance lay, that he
> symbolized something in every individual. He was
> the most prodigious personification of all human
> inferiorities. He was an utterly incapable, unadapted,
> irresponsible, psychopathic personality, full of empty,
> infantile fantasies, but cursed with the keen intuition
> of a rat or a guttersnipe. He represented the shadow,
> the inferior part of everybody's personality, in an
> overwhelming degree, and this was another reason why
> they fell for him.

On the other hand, it's just as easy for liberals to see the vile behavior of Donald Trump and identify him as the Prince of Darkness. They point to his sexual misconduct, alleged pedophilia and rapes, harassment, and bullying; his racism, homophobia, and xenophobia; his character assassination of people he hates; his nasty tweets; his alignment with brutal dictators, collusion with foreign adversaries, and obstruction of justice; his condoning of murder and assassinations of American soldiers and journalists; his silence and mixed messages regarding the dangers of the pandemic; his endless corruption with his abuse of power and in family business dealings; his cheating and lies; his dismantling of fragile environmental protections; kidnapping and locking children in cages; his incitement of a violent insurrection; and on and on... His efforts mirror so many characteristics of Beelzebub it's almost cartoonish. And it's much easier to define his actions as pure evil, rather than acknowledge that he is sick. Liberals, too, can unwittingly take on the mask of righteousness. Anyone can!

After reading Mary Trump's book, *Too Much and Never Enough*, I feel more compassion for Donald Trump than I ever did. I identify with the era and the type of father we both had. His mother was just as bad. I think my mother was my saving grace. Mary Trump describes her uncle Donald as having such a fragile ego and complex set of psychoses, compounded by a family of enablers and now an entire population of sycophants, he is basically unfixable. If it wasn't for him having been the president of the United States and thus able to engineer so much long-lasting damage to so many people, I'd be more understanding.

I also have compassion for Jaime. I don't believe he is evil. He had a terribly traumatic childhood. He was abandoned by his father for most of his life; his mother died when he was two years old; and his brother drowned at age twelve, for which he somehow feels responsible. Come to think of it—he is a sociopath, so maybe he was; who really knows? I do believe he is sick and a victim of sexual abuse as a child. When I left the Buddha-field and even today, I was angry, disappointed, and sad, but I had no desire to hurt him. I still don't. This book is not about him. It's about me and followers in general who are targets of the mind-control traps set by narcissistic sociopaths.

CHAPTER 27

THE KAMIKAZES' AUXILIARY CRUSADERS

MEDIA AND TABLOIDS LOVE titillating tales, but mostly for fun and profit. Former Chicago gossip columnist Liz Crokin, who worked for the publishing company that owned the *Star* and the *National Enquirer* (just to name a few tawdry rags she was involved with), used tabloid platforms for sensational QAnon propaganda and is now a celebrity crusader among far-right conspiracy theorists. Liz Crokin accuses the mainstream media of "ignoring Trump's sex trafficking busts." In Crokin's reality, "authorities have arrested an unprecedented number of sexual predators involved in child sex trafficking rings in the United States" since Donald Trump took office.

Here is what Ryan Smith, social media editor of the *Reader* who did an extensive investigation into Crokin's allegations, had to say:

> This is, as Trump would put it, "fake news." Every part. For starters, the 2014 data she links to is *far* from a complete account of U.S. sex-trafficking arrests that year. "The idea that there has been "an unprecedented number" of sex traffickers arrested since Trump took office has similarly little basis in reality, and there's zero truth to the claim of law-enforcement busting up child sex-trafficking *rings*.

Conspiracy theorists spin tales with just enough truth in the details to make them sound plausible, regardless of how irrational the conclusions really are. And for those who can't muster enough fanciful thoughts, Hollywood has helped to spark our otherwise dormant imagination beyond our own limited whims.

Television cop shows like *Law and Order: SVU* and Hollywood films and documentaries portray a plague of sex traffickers. Examples include *Tricked* (2013), a documentary that follows a Denver vice squad as they rescue survivors and track down traffickers; *The Storm Makers* (2014), a documentary that follows the lives of two recruiters who force young girls into labor or sex work in countries like Taiwan and Malaysia; and *The Whistleblower* (2010), a biopic about the fate of a UN peacekeeper when she tries to educate the viewer on how corruption affects attempts to deal with human trafficking. *Sex Trafficking in America* (2019), a documentary that aired as part of PBS *Frontline*, follows a Phoenix-based police unit dedicated to stopping sex trafficking and relates a survivor's story.

The Abolitionists (2016) is a documentary about Special Agent Tim Ballard, who resigned from Homeland Security, believing he could do more to fight child sex trafficking victims apart from the agency. The Netflix documentary *I am Jane Doe* (2017) focuses on the lawsuits brought against Backpage.com, a classified ad website notorious for sex trafficking. Others include *Priceless; Girl Model; Born into Brothels; The Chosen One;* etc., etc.

Be it prurient fantasy or gritty reality, consumers are fascinated by this subject, and it sells. This is not to say we shouldn't be aware of this issue; but the media loves to titillate our imagination, and the more we are exposed to these stories, the easier it is for a conspiracy provocateur to put these puzzle pieces together to create any picture they want.

In addition to sucking attention away from the very real problem of sexual exploitation, another problem with widespread false reports of sex trafficking is the creation of hysteria. We have seen a similar issue with the alarmist "Karen" phenomena, where Trumped-up (pun intended) social network partisans peddle more cow dung that all black and brown people are out to rape and kill them, so they call the police anytime they see such a person, even if said person is merely barbecuing in their backyard or jogging or bird-watching—cuz that's suspicious right there. Similar incidents are being reported regarding sex trafficking.

Take the story of Oklahoma housewife Emily Stringer. While shopping at her local Hobby Lobby, she noticed a middle-aged white lady following her around the store. With a keen eye, she immediately recognized a dangerous middle-aged white woman with obvious nefarious intent, so she immediately left the store and called the cops. When the officer arrived, he said, "This is unfortunately a common thing;

they are abducting people for sex trafficking." Stringer posted a subsequent Facebook warning about sex trafficking out of Hobby Lobbies and the story got 147,000 shares.

Sigh! There have been no cases of anyone, of any age, being stalked and abducted by sex traffickers at Hobby Lobby in Oklahoma or any of its franchises in any other city in America. The police rebuttal to Emily's warning, however, was shared less than 500 times. This is, unfortunately, the kind of thing that fuels public perception of the sex trafficking "epidemic" in America. Which gives teenage boys in Eastern Europe and Asia a big laugh. It also provokes Draconian laws regarding prostitution.

And then there's the radical, psychotic, kamikaze wackadoodles jumping the fence to crazy town by violently acting out. Meet Edgar Maddison Welch. In 2016, Welch was a frequent flyer on 4chan, which began posting about an alleged pedophile ring operating out of the basement of a Washington, DC neighborhood pizza restaurant known as Comet Ping Pong. The misinformation campaigns on 4chan about Comet began when the email account of John Podesta, an aide to Hillary Clinton, was hacked and his emails were published by WikiLeaks during the 2016 presidential campaign. Days before the election, users on 4chan's online message board noticed that one of Mr. Podesta's leaked emails contained communications with one James Alefantis, owner of Comet Ping Pong Pizza, discussing a fundraiser for Mrs. Clinton. Sounds suspicious to me.

Edgar, age twenty-eight, drove from Salisbury, N.C. to Washington, DC, with the intention, no doubt, of killing Hillary Clinton and the other Satan-worshiping, baby-eating pedophiles and heroically freeing the captive children who were about to sacrifice their adrenals. He told the police he had come to the restaurant to "self-investigate." Here's a suggestion, Edgar: the next time you feel the need to drive 350 miles to "self-investigate" a pedophile ring in a neighborhood family pizza parlor basement, I suggest you leave your AR15 and your various other assault rifles in the car, go in, order yourself a large pepperoni with cheese, and then see if the restaurant even has a goddamn basement. Cuz Comet Ping Pong doesn't.

You may have noticed, unless you've been living under a rock, that alarming numbers of armed, primarily white vigilante kamikazes have come out in recent days to defend small towns from Antifa "invasions" that haven't happened. White supremacists, right-wing extremists, provocateurs, and no doubt Russian trolls have a hand in it (Putin loves to stir our American stew) and are salivating to start a civil war. These would-be vigilante groups have been duped by another far-right hoax on social media, which warns that busloads (I guess the word caravan was taken) of antifascist activists are being sent to small towns to destroy their white-owned farms and businesses. There is zero evidence to support that fear-mongering assertion, according to media reports and statements by multiple police departments across the United States. But disinformation claiming the George Floyd protests were being inflamed by Antifa quickly spread up the conspiracy chain, via impostor Twitter accounts and throughout the right-wing media ecosystem, where it still circulates among calls for an armed response. Like for our hummingbirds—facts for kamikazes are no fun. Mommy, get me my flak-jacket, I'm off to Idaho.

Among other social media platforms, Twitter admitted the presence of influence operations calling for violence and information on antifascists, and confirmed that a fake "Antifa" account, running for three years, was tied to a now-defunct white nationalist organization that had helped plan the 2017 Unite the Right rally that killed Heather Heyer and injured hundreds more in Charlottesville.

In *Data and Society*, researchers published a study called *Source Hacking, Media Manipulation in Practice*. They found that disinformation campaigns tend to proceed cyclically as media manipulators learn to adapt to new conditions, but the old tactics still work—such as impostor accounts, fake calls to action, and grifters looking for a quick buck.

CHAPTER 28

SATAN'S OWN E-COMMERCE SITE

AND FINALLY—WAYFAIRGATE! The mischief-makers who first started the unfounded claims regarding the Wayfair home décor company originated in the QAnon community. Of course they did! They pointed out that certain cabinets sold via the Wayfair online e-commerce site were "all listed with girls' names," which understandably prompted followers to allege that the pieces of furniture actually had children hidden in them as part of a supposed Satan-worshiping, baby-eating, sex-trafficking ring. Apparently, the purchaser received a child who was ripe and available to impregnate in order to harvest their own babies. The initial tweet gained little traction until discussion about it was reignited on a Reddit discussion group called "r/conspiracy." By that point, QAnon followers were making supposed links between the fact that some expensive pieces of Wayfair furniture are named after girls, and actual cases of missing children in the US with the same names.

As soon as I heard about this, I couldn't help but take a moment to ponder certain obvious questions like, for example: Wayfair uses only Fed Ex and UPS to ship their merchandise—soooo...? Well, I'm sure that the cannibal-buyer would want to pay extra for overnight shipping to assure freshness. There's also the issue of weight; a "ripe" girl would have to have reached puberty, so we are talking a rather large cabinet.

This also begs the question, what if a buyer isn't a Satan-worshipping, baby-eating, pedophile and he just wants an expensive cabinet to go in his den? Perhaps he was painting the room, so he wasn't in a hurry, so he ordered the cabinet to be shipped regular ground—seven to ten days. Does the girl stay quietly in the cabinet in a crate in the UPS warehouse for at least a week, or how does that work? And what happens when the cabinet finally arrives at the buyer's house? He drags it into his den and opens the doors to find extra merchandise? Upon discovering the item, does he just close the cabinet and return it? And what do they use to protect the product from injury or bruising—bubble-wrap? That could be problematic.

I realize that I am being terribly flippant about a gruesome and dangerous yarn. But just given the sheer lack of critical thinking, if for nothing more than logistics, the Wayfair conspiracy is so absolutely ridiculous that it warrants mockery.

Some of the children are no longer missing, by the way, and one woman, who was mentioned when a cabinet with her first name was linked to her alleged disappearance, did a Facebook live commentary refuting the claims. She said she "never went missing in the first place."

It wasn't long before QAnon activists put forward a new theory. Some said that after they put stock-keeping unit (SKU) numbers of specific Wayfair products into Yandex—a major Russian search engine—images of young women would appear in the search results. Let me stop you right there. *Anything involving Russia should be your first clue.* That claim was true, but the problem was caused by a malfunction in the search engine. Newsweek reported that a Yandex search for "any random string of numbers" would return the same results. Yandex seems to have corrected the issue now, as they found similar searches no longer return images of young women. But I'm sure with the "self-sealing" phenomenon of conspiracy theories, that explanation will only provoke believers to claim that it's all part of the cover-up.

I spoke with someone the other day who was wearing her version of a mask. It was the equivalent of a clear plastic sneeze-guard protruding from her chin. She asked me what I thought of masks. I told her it was not that big an inconvenience to err on the side of caution. She then launched into some insinuations about government conspiracies and said, matter-of-factly, "Some people aren't even aware of Wayfair." I asked her if she was referring to Wayfairgate? She murmured "Yes" in an "I'm in the know, are you?" tone of voice, her eyes wide in shock, as if she feared that not enough people know the "truth." This woman is an educated, intelligent professional with a psychology degree. Another young friend of mine started posting pedophile-sex-trafficking and Wayfair connections on Facebook. When I cautioned her not to spread bogus conspiracies, she became defensive and scolded me for being dismissive and unaware of the epidemic of child-sex-trafficking.

Every Sunday I have a Zoom meeting in which I read a chapter of this book-in-progress and discuss it with some close friends. Some are from the Buddha-field; some are not. In our post-reading discussion of this chapter, we questioned whether we would have believed these types of outrageous conspiracy theories. Unfortunately, we came to the unanimous conclusion that yes, if Jaime had told them, at least at some stage of our discipleship, many of us would have accepted them as truth. Even if we had some niggling doubts, we would have certainly gone along with it.

One member of the group stated that because she lives in Ft. Worth, a veritable hive of right-wing Christian Republicans, she hears these conspiracy stories everywhere, but she would never dare even question them with her neighbors, let alone have a rational discussion, for fear of being ostracized at best—or annihilated at worst. Another member of the group, from California, said he hears conservatives express the same fear of extreme reactions from liberals. The groupthink from both camps is so thick you could cut it with a knife.

Once, I met a woman who had seen the movie *Holy Hell*. She told me she loved the film and congratulated me for my courage. I told her I was writing a book. She said, "Oh, about your story?" I said yes, but I'm correlating my experience in a cult with the cult of Trump and other narcissistic, authoritarian dictators. Her eyes glazed over; then she made a sudden excuse and ran out of there like her hair was on fire. Obviously, she—being a MAGA supporter—did not want to be confronted with the reality that she herself was, in fact, in a cult. That's just for those gullible people—right?

To most critical thinkers Wayfairgate or QAnon would be laughable if this mass psychosis weren't becoming ubiquitous in our society. But it is turning out to be very serious. The FBI warns that QAnon is domestic terrorism, and like Edgar Welch and Pizzagate, has inspired some emotionally unhinged individuals to commit all kinds of crimes, even murder. Blinded by QAnon, for example, twenty-four-year-old Anthony Comello thought President Trump wanted him to kill Francesco Cali— whom he believed was part of the deep state; so he did.

Jessica Prim, thirty-seven, was arrested after live-streaming on Facebook that Hillary Clinton and Joe Biden "need to be taken out." In her live post, Prim referenced "Frazzledrip," an alleged video that QAnon believers say depicts Clinton and former aide Huma Abedin attacking, sexually assaulting, and murdering a child. Ripping the baby's face off and wearing it like a mask as she drinks its blood. She believed Trump was speaking to her through his coronavirus press briefings.

Buckey Wolfe, who was twenty-six at the time, believed in QAnon and expressed interest in the far-right White Supremacist extremist group the Proud Boys. Buckey called 911 himself after stabbing his brother and told the dispatcher, "God told me he was a lizard."

Montana police arrested Cynthia Abcug, age fifty, who had been planning a kidnapping "raid" with other QAnon supporters. Police also said that Abcug had been giving weekly interviews to "libertarian media" tied to the QAnon movement. That doesn't surprise me. And recently, a Texas QAnon follower tried to attack two strangers with her car because she thought they were child predators.

Not to mention a deadly mob insurrection executed by thousands of red-eyed, rageful, rabble rousers flying Trump and Q flags on our Nation's Capitol, prompted by our very own former president and his cabal of sycophantic fruitloops.

Although it began in the US, QAnon and Wayfairgate soon became a global trend. According to data from CrowdTangle, a Facebook-owned social media analytics tool, the term Wayfairgate has generated 4.4 million engagements on Instagram. It also spread rapidly in public groups and on Facebook pages, resulting in more than 12,000 posts and nearly a million direct engagements. Analysis by BBC Monitoring shows the theory also gained huge traction in Turkey, with the second-highest amount of content after the US. And in Latin America, a YouTube post about the conspiracy by a popular Argentine YouTube personality had nearly 90,000 views over a weekend.

The most frightening thing about these kamikazes is that they have spread these conspiracy theories from the bowels of obscure online platforms into mainstream popular culture; now they are being pushed by some of the far right's biggest voices, including Alex Jones and Sean Hannity. Still others, like our own lawmakers, such as House Minority Leader Kevin McCarthy (R-CA), for example, claimed to not know what the QAnon conspiracy theory was (he even tried to mispronounce it at a press conference), despite his own disavowal of the theory (which he named correctly) last year. And other members of our own legislature are winking and nodding, retweeting #QAnon references while pretending to be none the wiser.

Researcher Alex Kaplan, of the US not-for-profit publication Media Matters, found sixty-two QAnon believers ran in congressional primaries in twenty-seven different states, and fifteen QAnon-linked candidates were on the November 2020 ballot. Almost all of them ran as Republicans, although a few were independents. Results from primaries showed nearly 600,000 people voted for candidates who support QAnon.

Marjorie Taylor Greene is the star QAnon candidate; she won the runoff for a safe Republican seat in Georgia. Trump congratulated Greene after she came in first in the party's primary and went on to be the elected official. Trump called her a "big winner." But again, it's not people like Marjorie Taylor Greene or Donald Trump who are as much the problem as it is the followers who put them in office. It wasn't Hitler, or Mussolini, or Jaime for that matter. It was us. It is the devotees of a cult of personality who enable a narcissistic authoritarian to have power. It is the followers who support them and do their bidding.

So we have to ask: Like Patty Hearst, are we victims or perpetrators? I think a little of both. We are definitely victims of disinformation and skewed reality. But it's complex. I know from experience that followers truly believe they are righteous in their actions—heroes—soldiers on a mission—"good guys with a gun." Which is why they are so dangerous. Those delusions of exceptionalism cause them to override their sense of morality and shame. They replace those psychological stopgaps with arrogance and pride. And that certainly feels better than guilt or remorse.

Social media platforms are programmed in ways that encourage binary thinking, reducing an idea to "good" or "bad" with nothing in between. This creates echo chambers in which like-minded people reinforce each other's beliefs, invoking groupthink without critical assessment of allegations. Just as Jaime did so well with us by insulating us from the outside world, conspiracy groups create an internal cyber community with an "us" versus "them" narrative.

With the Buddha-field it was the world of the "conscious" versus the "unconscious." With Cult 45 and QAnon it's the "woke" versus the "sheeple"—the righteous Right versus the evil Left.

CHAPTER 29

WORDS THAT BIND,
WORDS THAT BLIND

"THAT WHICH WE CALL a rose by any other name would smell as sweet!" Not necessarily!

I want to talk about words and labels, and how they are used to control our minds. Words, labels, slogans, and phrases can be humankind's simplest yet most powerful tool for mind control. Jaime always referred to us as the "conscious" versus the "unconscious"—"Holy Company" versus the "dead world." That right there evokes a feeling of elitism and would obviously make you want to be with the Holy Company rather than the dead.

One day I read a section of this book to someone, and the first thing she said was, "Do you have to use cuss words?"

It wasn't the content or the story she heard, it was the salty language. Really? This is a classic example of deep social programing. One four-letter word affected her so viscerally that she couldn't get beyond it without voicing her discomfort. Everybody knows the literal definition of *fuck* (fornication under the consent of the king), or just fornication. But unless you're sexting your partner, that word is less used for its literal meaning than for one of its many colorful slang meanings. In fact, a recent study found that the use of swear words correlates with high—not low—intelligence, and that they are used by "an articulate speaker...to communicate with maximum effectiveness." Despite the frequent occurrence of common "cuss" words, we are taught from an early age that using such words is vulgar and not sociably acceptable. It shows how powerfully just four letters can evoke deep emotion, prejudice, and resistance.

The other day a guy on Facebook defended the killing of George Floyd. I was so stunned I had no words for this racist Neanderthal. His comment was just beyond the effort it would require to argue so "Fuck you" was all I could muster. It's not that I couldn't expound on the disagreement; I just wrote a book on these topics, for Christ sakes. But "Fuck you" is simple, direct, and I had no time for this guy, so that was my easiest way to express that his opinion is not socially acceptable. His response was, "Do you talk to your mother with that mouth?" That's it? That's your clever comeback? First of all, my mother died over thirty years ago, and I learned that expletive from my father. And second of all, you just said it was perfectly acceptable for a cop to choke a black man to death because he tried to pass a fake twenty-dollar bill, but your beef is with my cuss word? Yet we have no problem with other four-letter words that I would consider more obscene. Like how about the word "hate," for example. Nowadays, that word trips off people's tongue like a benediction from a priest. And is far more powerful and meaningful.

Edward Bernays, the nephew of Sigmund Freud, is known as the father of public relations and Madison Avenue. He pioneered the scientific technique of shaping and manipulating public opinion. Joseph Goebbels, the Reich Minister of Nazi propaganda, used Bernays's writings on these techniques in World War II. One method focuses on the use of language and other forms of communication to influence brain behavior. Bernays wrote:

> The conscious and intelligent manipulation of the organized habits and opinions of the masses is an important element in democratic society. Those who manipulate this unseen mechanism of society constitute an invisible government which is the true ruling power of our country. We are governed, our minds are molded, our tastes formed, our ideas suggested, largely by men we have never heard of.

What about words like "libtard," "snowflake," or "cuck"? Here's where we get politically specific, and just one word can be emotionally provocative. More sophisticated trigger words or phrases, like pedophile, cannibal, sex trafficking, and Satan worshiper, I covered in the previous chapter, but words and phrases like Socialist, Communist, and now even the words Liberal or Progressive, have become damning epithets. How 'bout catchy phrases like "voter fraud" Or crowd-roiling chants like "Stop the steal" or "Send her back" or "Lock her up"? How about "Hang Mike Pence"? All easily evoke visceral emotions and violent reactions.

People use labels when convenient, which is another ruse. How many times have I heard the argument that Abraham Lincoln was a Republican? Sooo, does that mean that your racist position is now cancelled because 150 years ago the president who freed the slaves was a Republican? *It's not about the label;* it's about what it represents, *now*, in the present moment. And if the principles and policies of that label were in reverse, I'd call myself a *Republican*.

One of the essential books in a lawyer's office is the dictionary. A law student must study words and their definitions, because when defending the law, everyone has to agree on the same understanding of the words.

Here's how Wikipedia describes liberalism:

Liberalism is a political and moral philosophy based on liberty, consent of the governed and equality before the law. Liberals espouse a wide array of views depending on their understanding of these principles, but they generally support free markets, free trade, limited government, individual rights (including civil rights and human rights), capitalism, democracy, secularism, gender equality, racial equality, internationalism, freedom of speech, freedom of the press and freedom of religion.

If you subscribe to these principles, then I have news for you—you're a liberal. Oh, and just to be clear, "limited government" means government has no business deciding who you love, what you wear, what you do with your body, or your personal choices, as long as you do not hurt another. "Liberal" should not be confused with "Libertarian." That hornet's nest is a whole 'nother story that I'll touch on later. I have several friends who have been duped into thinking they are Libertarians. They have no clue. But if you really want to know the truth about the "Libertarian," read *Democracy in Chains: The Deep History of the Radical Right's Stealth Plan for America* by Nancy MacLean, followed by *Dark Money* by Jane Mayer. The Libertarians are actually the maleficent party that got us into this totalitarian Trump madness in the first place.

And by the way, in a Democratic Republic, "freedom of Religion" is not defined as obstructing the civil rights of others because of *your* religious beliefs. Stay in your lane.

This is not to say liberalism or any other political ideology is as pristine as the dictionary may suggest. But please don't use that as a false equivalency, such as my hummingbird friend who loves to say, "They're just as bad on both sides". The definition offers the model of a liberal in a perfect world—not that they always live up to their ideals. But they live up to them enough to be a threat to conservatives' identities. And the perceived threat gives the alt-right a motivation—a mission, if you will—to destroy such ideology by any means possible.

"Globalist" is another trigger word. The term "globalist"—those favoring economic policies that emphasize international cooperation, free trade, and the lowering of barriers—is the opposite of "nationalist" and a right-wing dog-whistle for antisemitism. Conservative media pundit Ann Coulter posted a string of tweets on the topic that "globalist equals Jew." And then there's good old George Soros, the right-wing's reviled boogeyman, who has become the poster child for globalism in far-right circles worldwide.

The technique—straight from Bernays, Goebbels, and Madison Avenue—is all about crafting the message with simple one- or two-word slogans or lines that our minds can grab and react to emotionally. We hear "Lock her up!" or "Socialist!" and begin to salivate like Pavlov's dog. The well-crafted right-wing narrative spooks the herd, stoking the flames of fear and confusion. Blame the government, blame the minorities, blame the liberals…and we in return blame the conservatives. Manipulate the people to feel that their livelihood and safety are in danger or difficult to attain because of outsiders—exactly what Germany did in the thirties.

Trump said at his rally, "No matter what label they use, a vote for any Democrat in 2020 is a vote for the rise of <u>radical socialism</u> and the destruction of the American Dream." At last year's RNC, Nikki Haley began with a propaganda windup pitch, spouting, "Their vision for America is <u>socialism</u>. And we know that <u>socialism</u> has failed everywhere." Lending a communist flair to her description, she continued, "They want to tell Americans <u>how to live</u>…and <u>what to think</u>. They want a government <u>takeover</u> of health care. They want to <u>ban</u> fracking and <u>kill</u> millions of jobs. They want <u>massive tax hikes</u> on working families." Oh my! Then Kimberly Guilfoyle, performed her interpretation of Kali, Hindu Goddess of Doomsday. With her blazing, cocaine-soaked red eyes and flailing arms, Guilfoyle looked like the multilimbed goddess, no doubt imagining a sword in one hand and the heads of Biden and Kamala in the others. Her extended wagging tongue screeched out, "Biden, Harris, and their <u>socialist</u> *comrades* [love the communist touch] will fundamentally change this nation." Aaaaaaah!

The term *socialism* is used a lot these days—thanks to Bernie! He may be a great guy with a lot of progressive ideas, but he's a real bonehead when it comes to being an American politician. Read the room, Bern. But Republicans linking Democrats and Democratic policy proposals to "socialism" or "communism" is nothing new. Republicans have used this old "red-baiting" device to discredit policies, including Social Security, the G.I. Bill, and Medicare, since the Great Depression. It's the oldest trick in the book, and voters fall for it like a faked ball toss to a labradoodle. And now that Trump has released the kraken of racism, dog whistles have turned into bullhorns, terrifying white rural voters and suburbanites that their tax money will be spent on all those "brown people" coming in caravans.

By the way, the word is "antifascists," not "antifa." "Antifa" is more deliberate wordsmithing, engineering of consent, to put a disparaging identity on those who are against fascism. I am antifascist, and I hope you are as well. The other day I heard a Republican congressman in an interview use the phrase "Antifa incorporated." Notice how subtle that is. There is no Antifa Inc. He deliberately slipped that into the conversation to project the illusion that there is a well-organized corporation behind the protests. He knew exactly what he was doing. The words "antifa" and "liberals" were also terms the Nazis used to describe anyone opposed to Hitler and Nazism. Today it would be anyone opposed to Trump and Trumpism. So I invite us all to think the next time we're inclined to use those words—cuz we're all being subtly manipulated!

And here's another interesting word exploitation—"Gate." Slap "gate" onto any root word and it instantly becomes a scandal. You could take a series of your favorite kitty videos, title it "kitten-gate," and that's all you would need to immediately invoke images of—probably Hillary Clinton—engaged in some sort of kitty porn before she held them by their tails, unhinged her jaw, dropped them into her mouth, and washed them down with a chalice of adrenochrome. Now, you may think that's funny, but I guarantee you, if I posted that on 4chan, I'd have 100,000 clicks in a matter of hours and the #savethekitties would have a whole new meaning.

History has shown us that great empires fall from within. Fear is another vulgar four-letter word, but it works every time. Keep the message confusing; polish and reinforce beliefs in the churches and media. Fear begets primal thinking. Blame the "other." Blame turns into violence and chaos, and eventually in order to control it, authoritarianism and oppression ensue. This has been happening to our country, while the rest of the world pities us, and Putin plays his fiddle and laughs at how easy it is to destroy the great United States of America, without getting out of bed.

Joining the bluster that rages from the far-right conspiracy theorists and the alt-right indoctrination that spews from talk radio hosts, the cable news pundits from entertainment media such as Fox News—faux news, masquerading as journalism— spoon-feed the ill-informed masses. Using classic engineered consent techniques to manipulate the uneducated public, Fox News uses audio/visuals of "commentators" blathering buzzwords while a running scroll displays little pernicious hyperbole like "Dem Socialist hits campaign trail" at the bottom of the screen. Do you really think this is by accident? It's all about slogans and catchy titles. "Big bad government is out to get you." "Drain the Swamp." "Make America Great Again." They need not define what that means; they just need to repeat it so it sticks in the psyche of enough people. The followers don't ask for a definition; they will fill in the blanks themselves. This is psychological warfare, and the right-wing consent engineers are winning.

CHAPTER 30

LEST WE REST ON OUR LAURELS

OVER SEVENTY-FOUR MILLION voters still ride on the Trump train. Wow! Seventy-four million cult members. While I danced in the streets with the other voters who celebrated Biden's bullet-dodging defeat of the Donald, we cannot plant this wilted wreath of greenery on our crown and call it a victory, when almost 44% of the voting population still refuse to see the bullets.

Consider our GIANT blue wave. Was it really a blue tsunami or more like a periwinkle ripple? Yes, we won the presidency; get over it, Republicans. But we owe that to anti-Trump sentiment rather than policy. That's evident by the fact that we actually lost house seats and the "wave" did not wash over the Senate, although it was certainly warranted, after years of blatant obstruction, corruption, and betrayal. As Rep. Abigail Spandberger (D-VA) said, "If we are classifying Tuesday [November 3, 2020] as a success, we will get fucking torn apart in 2022." So it begs the question: Why were over seventy-four million voters not on the same surfboard?

While Papa Joe and Mamala give us all our blankets and binkies, let us not fall asleep for the next four years. Cuz these Republican cult members don't sleep, and next time we may not have a mouth-frothing, rabid fascist lunatic in the White House scaring the hell out of lazy non-voters to get off their butts and save us.

It's one thing to have a malignant narcissist who is desperately attempting an authoritarian coup d'état on the United States. Not to mention, well…sigh! The list of his transgressions is endless. It's another thing, however, when over seventy-four million voters and a vast swath of our Senate and judicial branch are all in. I can understand the cowardly Republican Senate's effort to mollify the toddler-in-chief, in order to continue to confirm conservative judges and cut more taxes for the rich; that's always been their shtick. But the voters are still keeping them in office. Even after the second Senate Impeachment hearing proved without a doubt that Trump incited a violent insurrection to overthrow the government, they still acquitted him, and the meager few who opposed are being censured and may lose their seats. What gives?

The old adage "It's the economy, stupid" is wrong. "It's the messaging, stupid." Today's internet and media blitzkrieg of false and disinformation has so inundated the collective psyche, we are rapidly letting go of the wheel of reality. We are truly living in parallel universes. Folks seem to like it that way.

They are not interested in truth or facts; they are interested in securing their beliefs and identities by destroying anyone they perceive is taking them away.

The real ruling class, with the help of Russian oligarchs and right-wing Christian extremists, create a culture war and replace the fight against inequality and the public good with anti-intellectualism and anti-liberalism. They will stop at nothing.

How did America come to this?

A new breed of Republicans emerged in the mid-eighties and early nineties who adjusted their sense of fair play to a winner-takes-all attitude, no matter what. That includes bullying, cheating, stealing, slandering, ignoring the rules of law or the Democratic system, and most of all, lying. Just flat out lying to the American people.

As the title of the 2018 article in *The Atlantic* by McKay Coppins succinctly puts it, "The Man Who Broke Politics: Newt Gingrich turned partisan battles into bloodsport, wrecked Congress, and paved the way for Trump's rise." Coppins describes Gingrich's contention that "For their party to succeed . . . the next generation of Republicans would have to learn to 'raise hell,' to stop being so 'nice,' to realize that politics was, above all, a cutthroat 'war for power'—and to start acting like it." Newt's strategy was to demolish the bipartisan coalitions that were fundamental to legislating, and then use the resulting dysfunction to wage a populist crusade against the institution of Congress itself. Bravo, Mr. Gingrich, you have succeeded in devolving American consciousness into the Neanderthal swamp creatures you and your ilk have always been.

Gingrich kicked off the trend to gain maximum media attention by baiting Democratic leaders with all manner of epithets and insults: *pro-communist, un-American, tyrannical*—not only to provoke the Democrats, but also to scare the moderate Republicans. And the circus ringmasters of cable television were happy to put on a show, recklessly disregarding the consequences of their lucrative carnival acts. "The number one fact about the news media is they love fights…" Gingrich recounted. "When you give them confrontations, you get attention; when you get attention, you can educate." Would that be educate or obfuscate?

Folks like the Newt and others, like Carl Rove, Roger Ailes, and Chris Jankowski (the guy behind the Republican RedMap gerrymandering scheme), became the tools of the new Republicans, supported by a relatively small sect, including the Koch brothers, the Mercers, the Mellon family, the Heritage Foundation, John M. Olin, the De Voses, and the Coors family. This cabal of uber-wealthy elites has been financing the well-crafted messaging to divert attention away from the shenanigans of Wall Street fat-cats and propagate the idea that the United States is divided into two groups—the hardworking, industrious elite and the lazy masses who leech off their labor through government handouts and entitlement programs. Like a slow poison, the anti-government, anti-liberal message began to contaminate the minds and hearts of people who were already becoming disillusioned by the dismantling of the American dream.

Even though Charles Koch stated in his latest book, *Believe in People: Bottom-Up Solutions for a Top-Down World* (2020), that "he regrets dividing the country"—sorry, Charlie! Now that you've opened this Pandora's box, you can't wash America's blood off your hands by simply making some half-assed mea culpa while continuing to throw money at your right-winged Frankenstein monsters. The "top-down world," as you put it, is the world that you and your coterie of wealthy elites created.

How do they pull the wool over the eyes of the American people? It works like a card trick—a classic sleight of hand. Distract you over here and play the trick while you're not looking. The elite/neocons spend fortunes on focus groups and propaganda techniques. This isn't some half-baked conspiracy theory, it's a fact, and they are proud to admit it!

This clan of Conservatives has implemented a decades-long, calculated strategy to gain complete power and dominance over democracy and *We the People*. Their method? A slow and methodical campaign to dumb down America by manipulating groupthink, then dividing and conquering.

The political action group that melted down the Grand Old Party and poured it into a cauldron of molten racist, alt-right extremism was the Tea Party, mostly backed by Libertarian millionaires and billionaires, such as the Kochs. And their base doesn't even know they've been played by the very corporate power-hungry scoundrels who have much to do with their economic misery.

Many express curiosity as to why the base would vote against its own interests. Trump's comment in 2016 bears repeating: "I love the uneducated!" The corporate elite fabricated the Tea Party. As Jane Mayer said in her book *Dark Money*, like the Nazis, they created an "Astro-turf"—a fake grass-roots movement—and called it the Tea Party. Catchy, right? Why would they choose that name? Because it's a symbol of revolution—patriots wearing tri-cornered hats. And these redneck couch-jockeys fantasize themselves as patriots. The most ironic thing about the name is that the original Tea Party was the exact opposite of what these so-called patriots think it is. Revolution against tyranny, right? No taxation without representation? Well—yes and no!

That's what most people think the Boston Tea Party was about—the colonial Americans protesting high taxes on imported British tea, without having a say in the matter. This is a twisted myth. The truth is, it was a revolt against *tax exemptions*, specifically, one to give a monopoly to the East India Trading Company. This tax break allowed the East India Company to sell tea for half the old price and cheaper than the price of tea in England, so they could easily undercut the prices offered by the mom-and-pop tea merchants. Colonists resented this favored treatment of a major company. "Taxation without representation" meant hitting the average person and small business with taxes while letting the richest and most powerful corporation in the world off the hook. It was government sponsorship of one corporation over all competitors.

Sound familiar? Today it's called Amazon, Home Depot, Walmart, etc. There is nothing "free enterprise" (another misused term) about these huge corporations, and the little guy can never compete with these giants. The American dream of small family businesses and independent entrepreneurs is being sucked into the corporate vacuum, along with the middle class, creating a modern-day feudalism. And most Americans fight for this distorted form of capitalism because they are being duped.

The new Tea Party named themselves after a revolt against the very kind of government abuse they helped elect today. But they created the Tea Party a decade ago, when social networks were in their infancy. Today the powers-that-be can manipulate the minds of the populace exponentially, via slogans and groups like MAGA and QAnon, in a matter of days.

I'm still seeing pundits scratching their heads and wondering how the Donald could have pulled this off. But his blind followers accepted the loser-in-chief's repeated narrative that the election was rigged by nefarious forces like the Democratic Party, "big media," "big tech," oh, and Venezuelan communist dictator Hugo Chavez, dead since 2013—all engaged in a broad conspiracy to steal the election while simultaneously facing devastating Democratic losses down the ballot. Huh? Oh, and now they're spreading the rumor that the Dems and Antifa were behind the January 6, 2021 insurrection. That makes sense, attack the capitol to stop the count because we're angry that we ...won?

In classic malignant-narcissist style, Donald tweeted "This is a great and disgraceful miscarriage of justice." "The people of the United States were cheated, and our Country disgraced. Never even given our day in Court!" Wait what? First of all, elections don't get decided by the courts; they get decided by the voters. So, in the words from the *Big Lebowski*, "Shut the fuck up, Donnie." Let's start out with the sublime and end with the ridiculous. Trump lost two recounts his campaign requested in Georgia. An initial risk-limiting audit consisting of a hand recount of all the votes cast in Georgia's general election also confirmed Biden's victory. "It›s been 34 days since the election on November 3," Georgia's Republican secretary of state, Brad Raffensperger, said at a news conference. "We have now counted legally cast ballots three times, and the results remain unchanged." Then Donnie lost a recount in Wisconsin, after which Biden actually gained votes. The Trump campaign shelled out three million dollars—which I'm sure he didn't pay for—for recounts in Dane and Milwaukee counties. The whiner-in-chief received an additional 45 votes following the Dane recount, while Biden snagged 132 more votes after Milwaukee's recount, for a net gain of 87 votes for Biden. Much obliged, bubba!

The Trump campaign and Republican officials lost dozens of lawsuits challenging the election results since November third and won a grand total of one suit over a minor technicality. Otherwise, not-a-one, zero, nada, nichego, bupkus! Overall, according to the Washington Post, at least eighty-six judges across the country, from the state level all the way to the Supreme Court, have rejected every legal challenge filed by the president or his disciples. Many of the judges who threw out GOP requests to nullify the election results in different states were appointed by His Royal Heinie himself and previous *Republican* presidents, and they did not mince words when dismissing the lawsuits.

Trump's precious Supreme Court handed him his ass when he urged the justices to overturn the election, which is why he rushed to put them in their seats in the first place. Then they issued a blunt order declining to hear a case brought by the corrupt Texas AG, Ken Paxton, who is being investigated by the FBI and has an indictment on his back. Paxton, looking to buy the favor of a pardon, was backed by eighteen other GOP sycophantic attorneys general, as well as a majority of House Republicans who sought to throw out the election results in Michigan, Wisconsin, Pennsylvania, and Georgia over unsubstantiated allegations of widespread voter fraud. Trump repeatedly hyped the case as being "the big one." The "big one" fizzled out like a fart in a windstorm. But it wasn't just a criminal looking for a favor; it was the most brazen and far-fetched attempt yet by Cult45 to ignore the will of the voters, overturn the results of a free and fair election, and reinstall Donny the authoritarian-dictator wanna-be as president.

Bat-shit crazy lawyer and QAnon conspiracy theorist Sidney Powell pitched to the Donald a plan to seize voting machines as he continued to dispute the result of November's election. He even reportedly proposed naming her as special counsel to investigate alleged electoral fraud but then backed out. He seriously flirted with the pardoned former national security adviser and treasonous scumbag Michael Flynn's suggestion that the army might be used to rerun votes in battleground states. State Sen. Amanda Chase, who ran in the open Virginia governor's race in 2021, and House members including clowns like Matt Gaetz (R-FL), QAnon kook Marjorie Taylor Greene, and Barry Moore (R-AL), who shares the same gene pool as sexual predator Roy Moore, joined Alabama Rep. Mo Brooks (R-AZ) Paul Gosar (R-OH), Jim Jordan (R-OH), and Louie Gohmert (R-TX) in using an 1880s law that allows members of Congress to dispute a state's results and make the House and Senate vote on the challenge on January 6. This whole cadre of die-hard demented devotees supported Trump's scheme to institute martial law in order to keep him in office. But the wheels of justice slowly turned. And even Moscow Mitch finally yielded to reality, not because he cares about democracy or the rule of law but because he knows this was going to hurt Republicans. He may be a self-serving snapping turtle, but he's not stupid like his president was.

Even though Joe Biden won three hundred and six electoral college votes and set a new record with over eighty-one million votes total, Democrats and pundits are still asking the question WHYYYYYY????? Why are Trumpublicans willing to stoop so low—willing to risk their lives, their careers, their reputations—willing to go down in the history books as treasonous, scoundrels—to commit acts of insurrection for notably the worst president in American history? IT'S THE MESSAGING, STUPID!

Millions of deluded people think this man was not only the greatest president in history, but some believe he walks on water. Literally! They believe he was sent here by God. Meanwhile, the Democrats and left-leaning pundits still wring their hands and reiterate "This isn't normal." Yes, we were all saying that five years ago, and four years and three years and six months ago and two hours ago. When are the Dems and the pundits going to stop with the bombastic assertions and realize the grim reality that the Donald is a dangerous psychopath?

That statement is not meant to be hyperbole or slander. I am talking about a serious pathology, as serious as a heart attack. And as Martha Stout says in her book *The Sociopath Next Door*, "one out of twenty-five Americans are sociopaths," which would explain the aforementioned list of QAnon quacks and sycophants. It's time we follow good old Newt's advice and take the gloves off.

I understand why the Dems keep beating around the bush for political reasons. There's also the Goldwater rule, which states that it is unethical for psychiatrists to give a professional opinion about public figures they have not examined in person, and from whom they have not obtained consent to discuss their mental health in public statements. Regardless of the fact that the psychologists and the rest of us got to examine this sociopath 24/7 for 5 years, in his natural narcissistic habitat. More than any therapist would ever see in a professional evaluation. Nevertheless, in December 2019, three top psychiatrists sent an urgent letter to the Senate Judiciary Committee, accompanied by a petition to Congress signed by three hundred and fifty psychiatrists and other mental health professionals, warning that Donald Trump's mental health was deteriorating rapidly. So Congress is continuing to play risky politics. While seventy-four million people have been duped into this precarious cult, two hundred and fifty-four million more continue to be held hostage by this dangerous man and his blind devotees.

Then again Democrats have been known to eat their young by wasting time insulting and fracturing our own groups, instead of spending constructive time focusing on solutions to the problems at hand. Diversity is the hallmark of the Democratic party, but it can also be our biggest weakness. Even though Biden's cabinet is the most diverse in history, the Bernie Bros are pissed because Biden is too moderate; the minorities are mad because Biden hasn't put enough people of color in positions of power; women are pissed because, well…we just are. Perhaps it's because many of us could see this train wreck on November 8, 2016, and by January 21, 2017, 4.6 million of us marched in protest. But we have boobs, so we are pretty much left on the bench most of the time. Remember the Hummingbirds who want to say, "They're just as bad on both sides"? That's just to justify their inexcusable collaboration with a catastrophe. But the Dems love to blame themselves, to appear to be the bigger party. "When they go low, we go—whatever…" The bar couldn't get any lower.

Take former Senator Claire McCaskill (D-MO), for example, who stated on MSNBC's *The 11th Hour* that: "We're not listening to the Trump voters." Which ones should we be listening to, Senator? The ones who believe Trump was sent here by God to save us all from Satan-worshiping, baby-eating pedophiles?

There comes a time when we have to admit the bad guys are simply BAD GUYS. Dems remind me of victims of rape who feel guilty for how they dressed. McCaskill went on to say, "We have to stop thinking we're smarter than them, because we're not!" I would agree with Claire; we're not smarter than "them," but not for the same reason she's suggesting. We're not as cunning because, unlike our political counterparts, we haven't figured out how to effectively neutralize the engineered word schemes that create and reinforce public opinion. And as this out-of-control, internet and cable media disinformation vessel careens down this slippery slope, I'm not sure there will ever be a way back up the hill.

We need to put our educated heads together and figure out how to effectively counter the right's bundle of indoctrinating words and slogans and get Americans on all sides to wake up. We're being duped, people! Stop falling for it.

I realize this is just a pipe dream, because internet platforms have become echo chambers for people to hear only what they want to hear, even if they have to make it up. And if the powers-that-be, such as Facebook or Twitter, try to correct the unforeseen consequences of providing a platform for disinformation and propaganda, the provocateurs just create their own echo chambers, like Fox, AON, NewsMax, and now an out-of-control heap of online social network platforms popping up everywhere like a cyber cockroach infestation. And they're allowed to do it!

The First Amendment was designed to protect citizens' freedom of speech, not the freedom to lie. And that goes for all sides. But we don't seem to care about honesty, integrity, and quality in journalism anymore. Today we put profit and entertainment at the forefront, and the politicians are giving us what we seem to want. Bread and circus.

Not all Trump supporters are QAnon wackos, of course; but Trump and his manipulators have been spectacularly adept at nurturing an "America-First" brand of paranoia that was already stewing in many of his followers. They may not believe in left-wing cannibalism or space lasers; but they do believe that non-white people are not true Americans; are "stealing" jobs and draining the national coffers; and are erasing white Christian culture; and that white liberals are helping this to happen. They also believe that commerce is king; climate change is a hoax; expertise is not to be trusted; and probably that Putin is a great guy. They certainly believe that people on the left are their enemies.

So how do we meet and reverse this messaging? How do we reach the seemingly unreachable?

WITH **OUR** MESSAGING, FOLKS. We need to be smart; consistent; and relentless.

CHAPTER 31

HISTORY'S HAIR
OF THE DOG

*"Those who cannot remember the past are condemned
to repeat it."* —*George Santayana*

THE PHENOMENON OF TRUMPMANIA is nothing new to the world. But America is young; we're about at the level of a teenager. So it's a good idea, if we are willing, to look at the history of the countries of our older brothers and sisters to understand what is happening to this country today. Take the rise of Hitler and Nazi Germany, for example. Oh, here we go, I know, comparing Trump to Hitler—ridiculous, right? But indulge me here. There are many parallels to be drawn between Hitler, a charismatic cult leader who knew how to work a crowd, and the cult of Trump. And it wasn't one man—Hitler—who committed all those atrocities; it was his followers. That's the point of this book. It's not the leader, it's *the followers*.

I asked a German friend whose mother was a Hitler supporter how Hitler could have possibly gained so much popularity. She told me that the economy was really struggling, and Hitler was making sense to many Germans. The German people were in shock after losing World War I because they had been lied to. They'd been told throughout the war that they were winning. They faced food and coal shortages, and millions were killed and wounded by the end of the war. But the army told them these sacrifices were necessary because victory was close. That was the narrative for four years, and suddenly they were told that they'd lost the war.

Thus many factors led to Hitler's widespread endorsement in Germany, from economic depression to the country's hatred of the Treaty of Versailles, because they had not been allowed to take part in the Conference. And Germany had to pay £6 billion 600 million in "reparations," a huge sum the Germans felt had been designed to destroy their economy and starve their children. They also hated to give up their territories to Belgium, Czechoslovakia, and Poland; return Alsace and Lorraine to France; and cede all of their overseas colonies in China, the Pacific, and Africa to the Allied nations.

For the Germans to understand how such a thing could happen, many turned to conspiracy theories—sound familiar?—claiming that Jewish people on the Homefront had stabbed Germany in the back. Scholar Randall Bytwerk writes: "The Nazis justified their attempt to exterminate the Jews by claiming that they were only defending themselves against

Jewish plans to destroy Germany and its population." It started with a letter—today it would have been on 4chan—from the president of the World Zionist Organization, who wrote to British Prime Minister Neville Chamberlain stating: "Jews stand by Great Britain and will fight on the side of the democracies." In Nazi propaganda, the letter was presented as a "Jewish declaration of war" against Nazi Germany, and a threat of an actual attack by "the Jews." Throw in the Satan-worshiping, baby-eating pedophile part of the made-up protocol from the Elders of Zion and voila!

The Nazis perpetuated this theory in part via the mass media. Ah, the media; it can be the voice of a free people or the deputy of the devil. This is not at all far from what is being propagated today about liberals and Democrats. And the stress on the economy and the morale of the country due to the COVID19 crisis is fanning the flames. The Dems blame Trump, and the Trumpublicans blame the Dems. We're pitting ourselves against each other. Trump and his ring of enablers shouted from the giant public megaphone: "They're stealing our country!" "...We have to fight and fight hard," "...trial by combat" "...save America" "...you can be a hero or you can be a zero."

Hitler expanded his appeal from the beer-soaked halls of Munich, which shows how unprofessional the Nazis were in the beginning. They were only a few White Nationalist thugs, trying to gain support through public disturbances, not a serious political party. Similar to Trump's original base, the Tea Party crowd didn't exactly start from the wine-bars on Rodeo Drive. (Although knowing what we know about who created this Astroturf, they probably did.) The Tea Party has morphed into MAGA, and MAGA into QAnon. QAnon is like Nazis on psychedelics. These guys are chasing hallucinations.

See the list in the Appendix of the people who were allegedly rounded up and executed between June 13 to June 28, 2020, according to QAnon devotees—and including their misspellings—from the Pope to Brad Pitt, Beyoncé to Oprah, Hillary Clinton to Mike Pence. I counted 192, plus all members of royal families and all prime ministers, who have purportedly been removed, arrested, or executed around the world.

No—so far, those folks on that long list were not executed or imprisoned. It is my understanding that QAnon cult members think the ones we see walking around are clones. Okayyyy! There's QAnon logic for ya! So indulge me here. If the listed "enemies of Q" are all either locked up or dead, but the clones are walking around doing exactly what the originals were doing—WHAT DIFFERENCE DOES IT MAKE? One may look at this and think it's so ridiculous, it's laughable. So why include the list? Because this is the short list of the people they hate, the people they are demonizing. This is a list of the Satan-worshiping, baby-eating pedophiles that is circulating on social media, that the QAnon folks believe are inhuman—lizards.

That's a big problem. This is how Germany could exterminate eleven million people—people they considered subhuman—without batting an eye. Besides justifying that it was out of self-defense (like QAnon's case of "#save the children"), the conspiracists' propaganda convinced the Germans that the Jews were not human. And even today, with all the evidence of the Holocaust, many do not believe it even happened. That is cognitive dissonance on steroids.

One would have to be naïve to think it can't happen here. Look what Alex Jones did to the families of Sandy Hook Elementary School. Jones's story that the Sandy Hook massacre of twenty-seven children was a hoax spread from his vile *Infowars* show so fast, and enough people believed it, that the poor grieving parents—tormented with death threats, lies, and slander—were forced to move and hide in fear for their own lives.

On Dec. 12, 2020, during a rally in Washington, D.C. by Trump supporters protesting the results of the presidential election, Jones screamed into a microphone: "I don't know who's going to the White House in thirty-eight days, but I sure know this. Joe Biden is a globalist, and Joe Biden will be removed one way or another." Four people were stabbed and one person was shot during the weekend's protests. Dozens were arrested.

In America today, conspiracy theorists are turning the American liberal into the German Jew of the 1930s. Silly, right? Impossible, right? A Facebook group titled the "Alt-Reich," which refers to the German Third Reich, is chock-full of racist incitement directed at liberals, and ethnic and religious minorities, primarily black Americans. It is one of many cyber-sewers readily available for any sociopathic sicko seeking a home. Today the neo-Nazi movement is alive and growing. Consider the Proud Boys, a far-right, neo-fascist and male-only political organization that promotes and engages in political violence in the United States and Canada, which proudly displays Confederate and Nazi flags while wearing shirts with Nazi symbols and letters like 6MWE which means "6 million weren't enough." I would have thought it was ridiculous too. But this is no longer a fringe group—and there are plenty of similar groups. They are armed with assault weapons, and they can't wait to play with their toys.

The QAnon movement and the alt-right neo-Nazi movement, with its overt clashes with Black Lives Matter and antifascists, are now major discussion topics on mainstream media. QAnon followers are slithering into the legislature in frightening numbers. Remember, fifteen QAnon-linked candidates were on the November 2020 ballot, and the victories of Marjorie Taylor Greene and Lauren Boebert—both QAnon nut-jobs—put the delusional conspiracy in the halls of power. The camel has gotten its nose under the tent. It took over thirteen years before the Nazis became a serious political party in Germany. On January 6, 2021, one hundred and forty-seven members of Congress supported a conspiracy-fueled mob and violent insurrection, at the risk of their own lives. Even the design configuration of the stage at this year's CPAC was the shape of the "Othala Rune"—a Nazi symbol. We are well on our way.

In Germany in the late 1920s, Nazis were just a small group of White Nationalist extremists. They often deliberately held rallies in areas where the left lived, to agitate them. They provoked violent brawls that got them media attention. But what was far, far more important was how their actions fed an escalating spiral of street violence. That violence helped the fascists enormously. Violent confrontations with antifascists gave the Nazis a chance to paint themselves as the victims of a hostile, lawless left. They seized every opportunity for publicity and it worked.

Alex Jones and other alt-right extremists create rabble-rousing rumors that fan out from the bowels of the internet to spread across social media outlets and far-right news sites, blaming "Democrat terrorists" for all social woes. They claimed, for example, that antifascists deliberately lit the fires in California and Oregon, and that radical left protestors were going to "behead white people" and loot and burn businesses and homes. Police Departments in many Oregon towns had to assure concerned locals there "has been no Antifa in town."

But the hoaxes continue and fuel right-wing media and political leaders. Fox News used words like "Antifa apocalypse." An unfounded claim went viral in a Twitter post by failed Republican Senate candidate Paul Romero, that police had six antifascist activists in custody for supposedly setting fires in Portland. "This is not true," the sheriff's office said in a statement. "Unfortunately, people are spreading this rumor and it is causing problems." Congressman Matt Gaetz, a Republican from Florida, took to Twitter and called on the US government to "hunt down [Antifa] like we do those in the Middle East." The following day, Senator Ted Cruz accused antifascists of carrying out a "terrorist assault" on the country. Alex Jones and his followers have spread theories falsely claiming mass shooters were actually antifascist activists.

Despite having no evidence to support his claim, Trump's "now retired" bootlicking AG, Bill Barr, said, "Antifa was heavily represented in the recent [summer] riots." Senator Ted Cruz chaired a committee focused on "how Antifa and other anarchists are hijacking peaceful protests and engaging in political violence that is not only criminal but antithetical to the First Amendment"—when in fact, like in Germany, the truth is exactly the opposite. It is alt-right thugs hijacking peaceful protests. It was rhetoric and propaganda like this in Nazi Germany that provoked voters and opposition politicians alike to believe the government needed special police powers to stop violent "leftists." Dictatorship grew more attractive. One of Hitler's biggest steps to dictatorial power was to gain emergency police powers—just like what happened in Oregon and around the US; both Hitler and Trump claimed they needed to suppress "leftist" violence.

The fact that the Nazis themselves were inciting the violence didn't seem to matter. In 2020, I saw, over and over again, more comments on social media about a broken store window than a black man shot seven times in the back. I heard such false equivalence as the burning of a taco stand deemed just as bad as the destruction of our nation's Capitol. I heard more accusations about the phantom boogeyman antifa than the well-organized neo-Nazi groups that are coming into cities from other states and killing people or provoking violence, while our impeached president gleefully expressed approval from his Twitter vomitorium. They even had the nerve to blame antifascists for the Capitol Insurrection. As if all of us didn't see it with our own eyes—hear it with our own ears. But gaslighting is a distinct technique used by narcissistic sociopaths and authoritarian dictators. And this country has been gaslit on a daily basis for the last five years.

In an article in the *Conversation*, entitled: "How We Should Protest Neo-Nazis? Lessons from German History," author Laurie Marhoefer, assistant professor of history at the University of Washington, states: "In the court of public opinion, accusations of mayhem and chaos in the streets will, as a rule, tend to stick against the left, not the right."

Corporate oligarchs and religious extremists who wield the puppet strings of the Republican party spin a pernicious and erroneous narrative that intellectuals are "a privileged liberal elite" out of touch with "the real people." Uttered by Republicans, the word "liberal" becomes a sinister epithet, while the dark-money-funded far right promotes phrases like "free enterprise" vs socialism/communism, or "individual rights" vs government intrusion. They use words such as "patriots," Nationalists, and "the American way" to describe themselves as the opponents of liberalism—which in fact is a very American characteristic.

Historically, it has been American liberal thinking that has inspired innovation and paved the way to global progress in the modern era. But the right-wing covert clan of elites— yes, they are elites—pull off a clever yet devastating coup by diverting public anger away from corporate power, corruption, and abuse, turning it instead on experts, journalists, scientists, and intellectuals. Making them public enemy number one. Well played!

CHAPTER 32

WHAT'S IN A NAME?

TO RETURN TO OUR inquiry about followers: What about the word *cult*? I think the word itself carries such a scandalous stigma that it takes a lot to admit you could be so deceived, so duped as to have joined or still be a member of a cult. Whether it's the Buddha-field or the cult of Trump, you may ignore all the signs that you belong to a cult because the word is too scary to accept. It's too hard to face that you're in one—that you've been played, manipulated, used, and controlled. No one wants to believe that about themselves. On the other hand, people are enthralled by stories about cults and their members. There are books, films, television series, podcasts, and documentaries about cults. Why?

In a 2018 Salon article entitled "Why are we so fascinated with cults? They reveal the dirty cultural secrets all around us," author Gwenda Bond asked her podcast co-host, Cher Martinetti, this question. Here was Martinetti's answer:

> It's a very human thing to want to have this understanding of a higher power or a god or something else. If you look back since the beginning of time, humans have had these mythologies, ideologies and religions... When they go into that extreme area where it becomes classified as a cult... there's a definite type of personality that ends up being a cult leader. They're almost always men, almost always white men, which speaks a lot to power structure and dynamics in our society. Those cult dynamics often mirror abusive or toxic relationships in a way many of us can directly relate to, especially in the time of #MeToo and #TimesUp. As much as we all want to believe cult-think and behavior exists at the far edges of our society, we're living in a world where extremism is often presented as the norm.

Perhaps the fascination with cults is a form of voyeurism. There is a certain titillation in catching a glimpse into a society that falls into that extreme territory Martinetti talks about. There is nothing more arousing to humans than uncovering a mystery or an underground society. We hate to be left out of a juicy secret, and the more bizarre or salacious the better. Thus the attraction of the shadowy QAnon cult—voyeurs of dastardly crimes being done in secret basements, while leaving most of the details up to the imagination and keeping them collectively at a safe arm's length. Having inside knowledge of a secret makes you special—exceptional—and it's seductive.

While the same behavior may go on in established organizations, it's not the same, is it? Even though it may be just as bizarre. A Christian is proud to say they bathe in the blood of Christ, for example. But that's right out there in the open; it's not a secret, it's not clandestine. This is also what Trump did. He commits his crimes right out in the open, right in our face. He impertinently flaunts his corrupt behavior with no shame, which makes us question just how wrong can it be? He white-washes his crimes to make them less shocking—even laudable; so his base seems to accept them more readily. Although a narcissistic sociopath has no shame, he knows exactly what he is doing. And it works. How could it be a dangerous cult, when the leader was the president of the United States?

It is easy to excuse the victim of rape or robbery—incidents where the victim has little or no choice but to surrender to its perpetrator. But cults involve willing participants. One friend, after reading my first couple of chapters, was concerned that the things that went on in my childhood were traumatic to the point that readers might look at that and say, "Well, I can see why she ended up in a cult, but that's not me." By justifying another person's reasons, we can separate ourselves from those who fall for the cult leader's con and wrap ourselves in cognitive dissonance. Like the Donald said, "I could shoot someone in the middle of Fifth Avenue and they would still vote for me." And January 6, 2021, proved his point. He started a bloody insurrection and not one, but five people died, and yet, even while admitting his wrongdoing, his followers acquit him.

The word *con* is derived from the word *confidence*. And we are all being duped every day. As Bernays put it, "[W]e are governed, our minds are molded, our tastes formed, our ideas suggested, largely by men we have never heard of."

We are all duped from an early age. When we are born, in the hospital they immediately strap on our identities: "boy," "girl," "Caucasian," "Black," "Asian," "American," "Texan," etc. And we program society to respond accordingly to those identities, subcategories, and tribes. We are unnaturally defined as a "me" and a "you;" a "them" and an "us" society, and we compare our differences more often than our similarities.

I remember once Malila, the guru in Miami, asked me, "Who are you?" "I'm Linda," I said. "No, that's your name, who are you?' "I'm a woman." "No, that's your gender, who are you." "I'm an artist, I'm a writer, I'm a nutritionist," etc. "Yeah, yeah, that's what you do, not who you are…" and on and on till I had no answer. There they were—all my identities, from my first breath.

Ironically, a lot of the work we did in the Buddha-field was identifying and stripping away our assumed identities—our masks—to find our authentic selves. I say ironic because Jaime taught us to explore these masks while he was the biggest impostor of all. In hindsight, I can see that we replaced one identity for another. Using words like "aspirant," "initiate," "Holy Company," in the "Knowing"—as opposed to "outsiders," those of the "dead-world of the unconscious." We went from preprogrammed identities (labels)—the ego—and ran smack dab into a spiritual ego; a much more dangerous place to be because of its exceptionalism.

I am curious about those who think they are free from being deceived. Madison Avenue created an entire industry of deception and enchantment to capture our rabid consumer nature. They prey on our identity. "You've come a long way, baby!" was a famous advertisement slogan, created in 1968, when Philip Morris launched the very first cigarette brand marketed specifically to women. The slogan instantly caught on, and the "Women's Lib" theme perfectly tapped into the female consumer's mindset. The ads featured an old-fashioned photograph of repressed women smokers behind a vibrant, colorful "New Woman" who was free of oppression, smoking proudly. Smoking Virginia Slims represented women's freedom. It was liberation! And women fell for it, as though cigarettes were about image—about how we wanted society to perceive our identities, rather than the flavor and quality of the tobacco. Nothing has changed since then. A pair of Air Jordan Nike tennis shoes, for example, can range anywhere from $109.97 to $25,276. Twenty-five grand for sneakers! Now you may argue, well, I would never buy those; but people do. Why? To be identified as special, exceptional; to stand out in the herd. Actually, to claim the individuality we lost in the first place.

Politicians, especially partisan politicians, find it particularly helpful to cast the "other" as boogeymen to spook their constituents into electing them. It's simple, really; tap into their identities—i.e., proud, masculine, pro-gun, God fearing, law-abiding, hard-working, family values touting, conservative-type identities; or equal-justice-seeking, pro-feminine, open-minded, supportive of individual rights, human rights, gender and racial equality, secularism, democracy, intellectual, artistic, liberal-type identities. Like the Virginia Slims ad, load your campaign with images and slogans that match the type you're trying to lure, and you really need little else, other than to fine-tune the message.

Find out what people need, want, or are afraid of—and in most cases, they are afraid of losing their familiar identity. Promise to either fulfill their desires or dispel their fears. And if they don't know what they need, want, or are afraid of, then create it. The fastest and easiest way to do that is through fear, because humans are hard-wired to avoid danger. And in an "us" and "them" world, propaganda-meisters can easily cast the other as the enemy—the boogeyman.

And there we are—Duped!

CHAPTER 33

A NICE PLACE TO VISIT

I **DESCRIBED IN MY INTRODUCTION** a conversation I had with a Trump supporter. After she expounded upon the evils of Clinton the pedophile and racist Obama, she then added, "But I believe we both really want the same thing." I looked at her and said, "No—we don't!" But that's not exactly true. I believe we both want the same things, but the details are different. Sure, we both would say we want peace and harmony on Earth. Most people act as though they are averse to conflict—or at least we think we are. But human history does not reflect that. Human beings can be pretty malevolent creatures. We can be pretty benevolent creatures as well, and often the greatest tragedies bring forth our greatest attributes. So the heaven-and-hell duality we dwell in has some interesting side effects.

When the Buddha-field started it was beautiful, with high ideals and a utopia-like life of love and devotion to something higher—a group of supportive, healthy, creative young people. Many people who saw us in the beginning of *Holy Hell* said, "Yeah, I want to live that life." Be careful what you wish for!

One of my favorite *Twilight Zone* episodes is the 1960 "A Nice Place to Visit":

> Portrait of a man at work, the only work he's ever done, the only work he knows. His name is Henry Francis Valentine, but he calls himself Rocky, because that's the way his life has been—rocky and perilous and uphill at a dead run all the way. He's tired now, tired of running or wanting, of waiting for the breaks that come to others, but never to him, never to Rocky Valentine.

It's the story of a two-bit criminal who robs a pawnshop and kills the night watchman before he is shot by police. He wakes up to find himself seemingly uninjured and in the company of a friendly character named Pip, who tells Rocky that he is his guide. Pip proceeds to quote personal information from his notebook about Rocky's tastes and hobbies and has been instructed to grant him whatever he desires. Rocky demands that Pip give him his wallet. Pip says he has no wallet, but obligingly hands over a large sum of money and is willing to give Rocky as much as he wants. Pip takes Rocky to a luxury apartment containing beautiful clothes and meals served on a silver platter. Having never received anything for free in his life, Rocky demands to know what he must do to acquire all this money and luxury. Pip explains that it's all free, and he doesn't need to do anything. Rocky doesn't believe him and shoots Pip in the head, but it goes right through him, leaving him unharmed.

Rocky finally realizes he must be in Heaven and Pip must be his guardian angel. Later we see Rocky in a casino, surrounded by beautiful women and winning every game he plays. After returning to his apartment with Pip and the ladies, Rocky asks to see some of his former friends who have died. Pip says that won't be possible, as this "paradise" is Rocky's own private world, and none of the people are real except the two of them.

Rocky is puzzled as to why he was allowed into Heaven. "I must have done something good that made up for all the other stuff. But what? What did I ever do that was good?" Pip takes him to the Hall of Records, but it merely contains a list of his sins. Rocky remains mystified, but he decides that if God is okay with him being there, he won't bother worrying. A month goes by. He becomes bored by always having his desires satisfied and predictably winning at anything he attempts. He tells Pip, "If I gotta stay here another day, I'm gonna go nuts! I don't belong in Heaven, see? I want to go to the other place."

Pip replies, "Heaven? Whatever gave you the idea that you were in heaven, Mr. Valentine? This *is* the other place!" Pip then begins to laugh as Rocky comes to the realization that he is in Hell and unsuccessfully tries to escape his endless "paradise."

As I said in the first chapter, all that glitters is not gold. I lived in that idyllic American upper-class family in sunny California. Paradise on Earth isn't all it's cracked up to be. The Trump supporter who said we both want the same thing no doubt wants to live a life like the movie *Pleasantville*, the story of two siblings who wind up trapped in a 1950s black-and-white TV show, set in a small Midwestern town, where residents are seemingly perfect. Make America Great Again! No color, no conflict, no diversity, no music or art, no meaningful lives; just pleasant all the time.

But if I didn't have that colorful life, I would not have a story; I would not have written this book. Songs and poetry, art and writing are composed more about pain and triumph over adversity than pleasantry. Without people's suffering, I would not have had a greater purpose in my life—as a wellness counselor, an artist, a writer, a justice warrior, or just a friend with a sympathetic ear. Compassion, empathy, and forgiveness are Divine qualities, and we play out those roles for each other. We would miss the experience of those qualities if there weren't people in our lives who give us the opportunities to be our higher self as well as our lower self every once in a while. Redemption is Divine as well.

I believe that folks on the opposite side and I both want to be right. We need to be right; we want our beliefs and our traditions that identify who we are TO BE RIGHT! Because if they're not, then who are we? What is our place in the herd? What if everything they taught us to believe is a lie?

From my personal experience, living a lie is a frightening prospect. We want to feel safe, so we go along to belong. And in time we must bury our doubts, our questions, our imagination, and our individuality. We let the status quo dictate what is real, what is right—who is right and who is wrong. And to shore up our righteousness and avoid being exposed, those whom our tribe teaches us are wrong can become the enemy—the target to avoid or even eliminate.

Recently, I had another unexpected confrontation with a Trump supporter. After the encounter, I called my psychologist friend and told her the story. She stopped me and said, "Radhia, obviously your amygdala [primal brain] was aroused, and while I appreciate you wishing to discharge, if you continue you will ignite my amygdala, and then we both will perceive the situation from our primitive brain instead of our frontal cortex. I'm right in the middle of writing a chapter in my book, and I can't afford an activated amygdala." Ya gotta appreciate such a nerdy response at times like this. "Okay," I said, "I'll put my amygdala away. Tell me what you're writing." Ironically, she was writing about perceived enemies. Hmm! Like the one I just had an encounter with?

When we define another, whether through a pejorative nickname (I must admit, I wanted to refer to that Trump guy as a ... gee, so many to choose from!) or any derogative adjective, it automatically creates "the Enemy"—the "them" versus "us." So I have been trying to find compassion for "them;" and it's hard. I don't feel compassion right now. I feel anger, fear, and frustration. It's often advised to find common ground. But in this fraught time, when it comes to their ideas versus mine, I can't find common ground. Could a German citizen say to a Nazi sympathizer, "Oh, you wish to exterminate eleven million people—let's just agree to disagree"? I needed to break it down to its simplest emotions and start there.

... and there it was, the good old Venn Diagram!

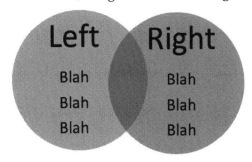

When I was in conversation with the Trump guy (let's call him Jack), we had some commonalities in the realm of conventional medicine. But after a while, the topic veered sharply to the right. It went from Big Pharma corporate influence to an immigrant invasion, paid for by George Soros. Huh?? I felt my first visceral reaction as my amygdala ignited and adrenaline surged up my spine. *Uh oh,* I thought. *We just took a sharp turn to crazy town.*

Jack's Viewpoint (This is what he said.)

Supposition: I (Radhia) and ALL LIBERALS:

1. Believe in open borders

2. We want diseased, illegal immigrants, drug and sex traffickers, and MS13 gang members to come to this country to receive free education, healthcare, and live off welfare, supported by real Americans' hard-earned tax money, while taking all their jobs, just so they can vote for our liberal agenda. Oh, and also we want to turn illegal immigrants into slaves. (Suddenly Jack weirdly defended illegal immigrants.) I think to him, "liberals" are even worse than his idea of illegal immigrants.

3. We want the freedom to kill fetuses to sell their body parts for money.

4. Eventually, all shall live as homosexuals and transgender persons, so we can get into the opposite-sex bathrooms and rape them. (Them being Jack and other nonliberals.)

5. Hillary Clinton and Barack Obama and now Joe Biden and Kamala Harris are Satan incarnate.

My Viewpoint

Supposition: This is a crazy person who has taken Trump and Fox News propaganda and swallowed it hook, line, and sinker. Jack and ALL TRUMPSTERS:

1.   Support taxing the middle class while giving tax breaks to corporations and the rich.

2.   Support removing as many regulations as possible to allow corporations once again to cause an economic recession like Wall Street did in 2008.

3.   Deny climate change, and let corporations continue to pillage the land and nature for profit until there is no way back and we all die, of war, famine, and climate catastrophes.

4.   Support Trump and his cabal of white Nationalists to roll back all civil, LGBTQ, and women's rights to the world of Jim Crow and *A Handmaid's Tale*.

5.   Will cause a second version of either the Civil War or Nazi Germany.

6.   Carry their AR-15s wherever they go so they can shoot liberals. Continue to bomb and mass murder freely.

7.   Donald Trump is Satan incarnate.

Initial Response: A quick gymnastic somersault into the cognitive dissonance pool. What does it matter, the truth will come out sooner or later, this really has nothing to do with me. Vote! Ah, sweet rationale! But wait—my amygdala is on fire. This is not helping. Return to original premise and embellish.

First Impulse: This is a crazy person who has… blah, blah, blah. Therefore, I am the enemy and he and his kind have all the guns and will eventually kill us. Irrational? I don't know, ask the survivors of the Tree of Life Synagogue. And thanks to technology, we can have our amygdala aroused anytime, anywhere, at the push of a button. Thanks, Zuckerberg. (Note: sometimes my amygdala likes to revert to sarcasm; sorry.)

Next Impulse: Try to change this person's perspective.

Method: Argue.

Result: Full amygdala detonation on both sides. We have now surrendered our frontal cortex completely, and our primal brains have resorted to grunting incoherently and throwing feces.

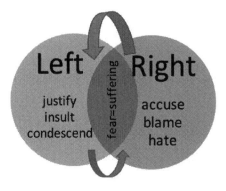

Interchangeable

Solution? VOTE, VOTE, VOTE!!!!! Right? But I realize that all voting does is change the power play (maybe). It does not fix the underlying problem and may make it worse. If we don't get a handle on this polarization, we may create the very things we are all afraid of. But how?

Return to the simplest common denominator and work with that, instead of trying to change their perspective in order to make ourselves comfortable. In other words, it's my responsibility to deal with my fears, thus relieve my own suffering.

Example:

Projection: I am afraid *you* are going to kill me. This posits an **Enemy.**

How does that feel? Terrifying.

Real fear: I am afraid to die. This is **Human.**

Common denominator? Aren't we all? Compassion.

Projection: I am afraid *you* are going to take my liberties away. **Enemy.**

Real fear: I am afraid to lose my liberties. **Human.**

Recommendation: Stay focused on common denominator rather than avoiding fear by deflecting onto a projected enemy.

A note on commonalities of Liberals and Conservatives:

Think of a refined porcelain teacup and a plain ceramic mug. **Reality.**

Both are beautiful, functional, and necessary, in the eyes of the beholder!

Projection

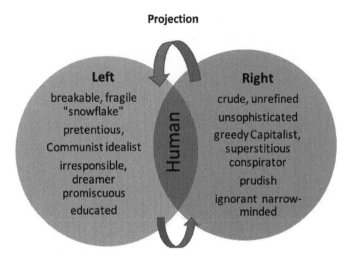

Interchangeable

I have a theory about why it seems so hard to talk to each other after a brief discussion with a client recently, who described a fundamental change in her son's personality after a stroke. She said he used to be very combative and argumentative but now he seems to be open and much more peaceful and accepting. I told her about a famous TED Talks episode by Jill Bolte Taylor called "My Stroke of Insight," in which Dr. Taylor, a brain biologist, tells the story of her experience of her own stroke. She starts by describing the two hemispheres of the brain and how they work.

> Our right brain hemisphere is all about this present moment, it's all about right here, right now. From the right hemisphere information in the form of energy streams in simultaneously through all of our sensory systems and then it explodes into this enormous collage of what this moment feels like, what it tastes like, smells

like, and what it sounds like. We are energy beings, connected to one another through the consciousness of our right hemisphere as one human family, and right here, right now we are brothers and sisters on this planet, here to make the world a better place.

Our left hemisphere thinks linearly and methodically. Our left hemisphere is all about the past and all about the future. Our left hemisphere is designed to take that enormous collage of the present moment and start picking out details, details, and more details about those details. It then categorizes and organizes all that information, associates it with everything in the past we've ever learned and projects it into the future, all of our possibilities. Our left hemisphere thinks in language. It's that ongoing brain chatter that connects me and my internal world to my external world. It's that little voice that says to me, "I am." And as soon as my left hemisphere voice says to me "I am," I become separate, I become a single solid individual, separate from the energy flow around me and separate from you.

My theory is that liberals ("snowflakes," artists, intellectuals, tree huggers, feed-the-hungry, justice-and-equality-for-all folks) are right-brain dominant. And conservatives, (capitalist, money, power, dog-eat-dog, survival-of-the-fittest, pragmatic, me-my-mine folks) are more left-brain dominant. Coming from those hemispheric perspectives, perhaps it is, in fact, physically impossible to hear each other. We literally cannot relate to each other, and that may just be the parallel universes in our own brains I mentioned in the introduction.

Like I said in my intro, this is not a how-to book to help you talk to your relatives at Thanksgiving. It is not meant to explain what is happening so everybody can have this epiphany and we all hold hands and sing "Kumbaya." This book is a warning! I did not write the Venn diagram analogy for Jack. I wrote it for me. I wrote it to help me keep my sanity and compassion in this tumultuous time. Because I'm never any good when my amygdala is a flambeau. And with my SNiG temperament being a mixture of one-part blood and two parts gasoline, it's not good to light a match around me.

In the Q and A at the film debut of *Holy Hell* at Sundance Film Festival, one person asked me, How did I heal? *Heal? That's a novel idea,* I thought. When I left the group, everything I was afraid would happen—did. My life was shattered. I lost my house, my clinic, my relationships, and I was so busy trying to stay alive and pick up the pieces that I didn't have time to consider the luxury of healing per se. But healing happens. Time does heal, and if we are patient, we will find our way to the other side.

For those who are beginning to wake up and trickle out of a cult, or for any other victims of a narcissist feeling raw and shaken, and wondering, *How did I give up all my principles and allow myself to be—duped?* I promised a few precious beads to help you navigate the pain and confusion. I first want to remind you that with all my sarcasm and pointing the finger at—well—just about everybody. I opened my kimono and coextended myself at almost every turn. Because, I get it! This is what we humans do. The first advice I can give you is to accept yourself where you are right now. You are a transforming being. You're not meant to remain stagnant in your experiences or beliefs. You're meant to grow from them into a more wise and evolved soul. You made the choices in your life because you believed they were the right thing at the time. Accept that!

Our whole life is a series of course corrections. You may have to sacrifice the herd you ran with, and it can be terrifying, I know. But you can never lose your true self and will even perhaps uncover it in the process. Try to find professional help or at least a compassionate person or group that will accept you and help you feel you are not alone. Because you are not.

One thing I learned was that just because I left the group, I didn't have to leave behind the good things I learned. For a long time after I left the Buddha-field I didn't want to meditate. Doing that spiritual practice was a traumatizing memory that was too fresh. I had to allow myself to go through a rebellious state to reclaim my power and separate completely from the things that reminded me of my powerlessness. Having led such a disciplined life for so long, I felt guilty and grappled with letting go of the commitment I'd made and the feeling of failure in myself. I struggled with the notion I was stupid, gullible, and weak—that I'd let it go way beyond what I knew was right. I felt I'd betrayed myself, rather than the actual betrayer having betrayed me. I came to realize that was still allowing him to control me.

I looked for things to take the place of my old habits. Instead of meditating, I took long walks. I immersed myself in nature as much as I could. I sat with my cat Sun, who knew I needed him and never left my side.

Try to find a creative outlet. For me, I painted and played the flute, formed a rock 'n' roll band. I wrote and created the concept for a web-based television network with 12 channels devoted to natural health and green living with my friend and business partner. I wrote and illustrated a children's novella and then a sci-fi novel and now this book. At first, I had no idea where this book was going, but Trump inspired me to use my experience to draw a parallel. Recently I described to a therapist my feeling of helplessness about what is happening to this country. I told her I felt paralyzed and didn't know what to do. She said, "Yes, you do. Do what you're doing.... Talk about it with people who will support you and allow you to have a safe place to express your fears, your anger, your grief; write about it, create and express yourself and your feelings."

Try to avoid jumping into a relationship with someone immediately after. That was a mistake I made, and it didn't end well. I hadn't realized how broken I was, and I relied on someone who was just as broken to shelter me from the pain and loneliness. When you have lived your life managing betrayal and abandonment, you build a protective wall around yourself that you don't even know is there. It just becomes such a part of you that you think it is you. The conscious mind will block the subconscious in an attempt to protect it from further trauma. We all do it. Some are just better at it. SNiG was a master at it, and the acorn doesn't fall far from the tree.

Comfort others who are seeking comfort. DO NOT argue or try to convince others to see the truth. They will find their way when they are ready. Trying to pull others away from the cult will only re-traumatize you. Be the compassionate example, but not the judge. This is hard to do. Once we wake up, we often feel compelled to strike out at those who remain and continue to enable the abuser. Be aware of that. It's a natural impulse, but it is counter to the goal of stopping them. Those who are ready to leave will find strength in you. They will not trust you if you appear to be rejecting them as friends or family members because they are not ready to leave. Be gentle with them and with yourself. As much as I am angry at the blind followers of Jaime or Trump, I still understand why they remain.

I know that when I was in the Buddha-field, there was nothing anyone could have said to me that would have made me change my mind. I've spent too much time in that cult with other members to know better than to even try. There are still people in Hawaii who will not read this, not see *Holy Hell*, not care about the truth, no matter what Jaime does. And nothing I could do or say will change that. It frustrates me and makes me feel helpless and angry to know he is still allowed to be victorious over his victims. They will continue to idolize him, and if something happens to either Jaime or Trump, the followers will make them a martyr. This infuriates me. I wrestle with my higher self and my very human self, and I have to love and accept both. I flip from anger and frustration to compassion and understanding and back again. I go from fear of the future to hope that this is the darkest hour before the dawn. And it will all be for a greater purpose.

But as I analyze my thoughts regarding our political divide, I realize that the more I express my disdain for the opposite side, it's a natural response for anyone to retreat to our accepting tribe for safety and security. Natural for "them" or for "us." Disdain only pushes us further into our cult of ideology.

One comforting thought is that everything has a rhythm. It flows out and in; everything has its tides; all things rise and fall; the pendulum-swing manifests in everything; the measure of the swing to the right is the equal measure of the swing to the left; rhythm compensates. This is known as the Law of Rhythm and is seen in the waves of the ocean, in the rise and fall of empires, in business cycles, even in the swaying of our thoughts from positive to negative.

In the book *The Fourth Turning*, authors Strauss and Howe look back five hundred years and uncover a distinct pattern: Modern history moves in cycles, each one lasting about the length of a long human life, each composed of four eras—or "turnings"—that last about twenty years and that always arrive in the same order.

There seems to be a 40-year cycle of cultural change in American society. The classic exploration of generational types and cycles, *The Fourth Turning*, identified a four-generational, 80-year cycle of profound crisis and transformation:

The order goes like this:

> "First comes a High, a period of confident expansion
> as a new order takes root after the old has been swept
> away. Next comes an Awakening, a time of spiritual
> exploration and rebellion against the now-established
> order. Then comes an Unraveling, an increasingly
> troubled era in which individualism triumphs over
> crumbling institutions. Last comes a Crisis—the
> Fourth Turning—when society passes through a
> great and perilous gate in history. Together, the four
> turnings comprise history's seasonal rhythm of growth,
> maturation, entropy, and rebirth".

For those who are from my generation, today's tumultuous times are nothing new to anyone who lived in the 60s and 70s. It's a kind of déjà vu. Race riots and demonstrations, the women's MeToo movement, narcissistic criminal dictators—Trump compared to 40 years ago Nixon or Hitler 40 years prior to that.

As one meme put it: *"This too shall pass. It may feel like a kidney stone, but it will pass."*

THE BUBBLE

THERE IS SOME GOOD NEWS. Some will come to the point of seeing the truth. When I finally decided that I had had enough of Jaime, the decision was so clear, so instantaneous, the best way I can describe is it was as though a bubble popped. To some this moment will never come, and the kamikazes will go down in flames with the leader. But to many it will.

For me, it happened on the Sunday after that Friday night movie, when I walked out and never looked back. It was 4:30, and I was standing at the sink in my kitchen, washing dishes. At 4:30 on any Sunday in the summer, I would have been on an outing. This was the first time in over two decades that I deliberately chose not to be there with everyone. I began to muse about where they'd gone and what they were doing in that moment. All at once I felt truly alone, and a little lost. I was imagining sitting at the lake, singing with everyone, and mixed feelings flooded my heart and head.

Suddenly the doorbell rang. I answered and there was a good friend of mine, Patrice, who was not part of the Buddhafield, but she knew most of us. Patrice was a wonderful, bohemian-type spirit—one who would be the weird character that the slogan "Keep Austin Weird" reflected. She had a big smile on her face and said, "Are you free right now?" The word struck me like a lightning bolt. "Free?" I said. I hesitated and took that word in with all its meaning. And my bubble popped.

I smiled and said, "Yes, I am free."

She grabbed my hand and put me in her car. She popped in an old Stevie Wonder CD, *Songs in the Key of Life*, turned it up, and we took off. I had no idea where we were going, and I didn't care. The first song that came on was "Love's in Need of Love" and the next song was "Have a Talk with God." A rush of joy came over me, and I laughed out loud at the irony of the whole thing. We drove out to the country, to a farm, where there was a huge gathering of other of Austin's weird community members. I walked around the grounds, listening to the live music, chatting with some, eating tasty hippie food, while sipping on a glass of red wine for the first time in twenty-five years. Thoughts of Jaime and the Buddha-filed were fading faster than the sunset that was washing the sky with warm, brilliant hues of gold, violet, and pink. I didn't really know how to interact with "regular" people—I still am challenged today. But as I ambled along the fence on the border of the property, I suddenly felt something brush my shoulder from behind. I looked around, and there was a beautiful Palomino horse walking with me. He knew!

It's strange to me that such an integral part of my life ended so abruptly; yet, other than talking about the ordeal with others, most of the time I have no feelings about it. I have no feeling about Jaime. I don't think about him; I don't miss him or hate him. I feel nothing—as though it were a movie, and when it was over, I stepped out of the dark theater into the light.

Shortly after that night the Buddha-field collapsed, and there was massive drama around me, with members calling and wanting answers. They wanted the truth and needed to confess their own nightmares of abuse. The "innies" were at war with the "outties," but I had emotionally disassociated from the group. Members would come to me, and when they heard the truth, out of the haze of their confusion, I saw clarity on many of their faces the moment their bubble popped. You could see it in their eyes, as though they had suddenly awakened from a paralyzing trance. Some were overcome with grief, some with anger; others just had to process.

It wasn't until ten years later, when a handful of us went to Sundance Film Festival for the premier of *Holy Hell*, that I and many of us saw our story and heard the details of the abuse of our brothers for the first time. After it was over, I went up on the stage with the others for the Q and A. As I blithely answered questions, I maintained that stoic persona SNiG gave me. The public was sympathetic, and I could feel the love they were offering to all of us. The compassionate audience of hundreds was the most healing gift Will could have given us. When we left the theater after the Q and A, I got into a bus and just burst into tears for so many reasons.

Curious people asked all kinds of questions in the Q and As, but the most obvious were: Did I still believe in God and Why did I stay?

In Chapter 3, I said that I don't believe in the Deity yarn. I believe, however, there is a single, intelligent Consciousness that pervades the entire Universe—the Universal Mind, the Alpha and the Omega, omnipotent, omnipresent, and omniscient. Albert Einstein said that "everything is energy;" that "a human being is a part of the whole called by us [the] Universe." The Universe is particles or matter and the frequency that holds them together. I am amused by those who refer to themselves as "Atheists"—another label, another identity, another club to belong to. To me it's a matter of semantics. The Universal Consciousness goes by many names. In the scientific world it is the Unified Field. In spiritual philosophy they refer to it as The All or as I refer to it, Universal Consciousness or just the Universe; and in religions most call it God, who goes by many names—Jehovah, Allah, and Brahman, just to name a few. Every one of us is a manifestation of this single Universal Consciousness.

The true nature of reality is non-dualistic. We are all connected—not only to each other, but to all of Nature and to everything in the Universe. While things may appear distinct, they are not separate. All is One. The same pattern expressed on all planes of existence, from the smallest electron to the largest star and vice versa, is Universal Consciousness. Therefore, to me, it is ludicrous to believe in the notion that we are exceptional over others. That would be impossible—you *are* others. Or, more precisely, there are no *others*.

Nothing rests; everything moves; everything vibrates. This is the law of vibration or frequency. Science has confirmed that everything in the Universe, including you and me, is pure energy vibrating at different frequencies. All things, all people, all creatures, even inanimate objects are frequencies—vibrations, consciousness—and we are all part of the whole of consciousness. I see this with my own eyes, especially in the wee hours of the morning. If I wake before the sun, I honestly can't see solid matter. All I see is everything in light particles, like Scotty in *Star Trek* beaming it up.

Think of it like a body. The brain doesn't oppose the heart or the liver or the fingernails. Everything has its role to contribute to the whole. The brain may have a greater function than the fingernails, but it would be foolish to pluck out the nails just out of spite. They still serve an important role, and *they thrive when they are well taken care of.* Even the simplest of creatures, such as the honeybee, is part of the grand design of consciousness, and without it, the whole balance of nature, including the human species, would die. When you realize that ultimately, it does not serve the individual or your human, animal, and plant family to compete with or seek to destroy each other, rather than work harmoniously together [the fundamental principle of "permaculture," but that's another story], using all that each has to offer, be it large or small, then—and only then—will we create a government that serves a higher civilization.

Take this book, for example. Everything starts with an idea—a thought. The printer laid thousands of words on the pages of this book to tell you my story. It took a lifetime to write this book. And now it's your book. Maybe you've been entertained, maybe you learned something new, maybe your amygdala was triggered; but look at the means by which we've delivered my collection of ideas. A book. A simple collection of symbols in ink, on pages bound together. And those thoughts manifest into a picture, whether it is on paper or a computer. Think about it. Where did the paper come from? Who cut the trees? Who transported them to the mill? Who built the road and the truck that the tree was carried on? Who gathered the minerals to make the chemicals that supplied the chemist with the materials to make a simple ink? Who taught you how to decipher these symbols, and don't even get me started on the computer.

Look around. Everywhere we are, everything we do—billions of people touch us a thousand times a day. Trillions of thoughts encumber our so-called reality—every second of our existence. Is individualism superior to collectivism, as Ayn Rand hypes? What an ignorant fallacy. Awareness of this Universe is often devoured by self-importance.

One thing that helps me cope with the present situation in our country and the world is understanding the Law of Polarity. Everything has its pair of opposites; opposites are identical, but different in degree. Things that appear as opposites are in fact only two extremes of the same thing. And all opposites are relative. That's how we relate to them and attach our emotional response to them. You cannot appreciate warmth until you know cold. Hot and cold are degrees of the same thing.

So right now, the country is clearly showing us what we don't want, in order to crystalize more clearly what we do want. Our thoughts automatically go out into the Unified Field and put frequency with matter and—create. There is no judgment, no right or wrong—just pure creation. The more powerful and consistent the thought/energy, the faster the manifestation. This is not magical thinking. This is science. In contrast, it's magical and infantile thinking to believe there is an invisible, paternal man/god out there, wrathfully judging whether he will help or hurt his supplicant—his very creation. The second most common question at the Q and As was: Why did I stay? In hindsight, I think there was something very secure and appealing about having a life that was simple and orchestrated for us. A set of rules and someone we thought we could trust to guide us through life. I loved my Buddha-field and consider them all my family and community. I served them for half of my adult life, and they served me.

On the other hand, I wasted a lot of time with this narcissist when my gut was telling me to leave long before I did. I stayed because I thought I had the security of community; I stayed because I believed that this community life afforded me a place to practice a deep spiritual discipline with like-minded individuals. I stayed because I truly desired union with God, and I hoped that Jaime's shenanigans would somehow lead me to that ultimate destination. If dropping my ego was the path to Nirvana, he had the vehicle. I stayed because I built bonds and relationships that I thought would break forever if I left; and if it wasn't for all of us exiting at once, that would have been the case. I stayed because I wanted to believe that things would change. I stayed because I believed that even if it was weird at times, there was nothing better "out there." I'm still not sure there is.

We definitely had our wonderful moments. We danced and sang and laughed and sat in silence for long blissful hours. We were all delightfully talented and creative, and we pulled together and built and produced some marvelous things. And good, bad, or indifferent, Jaime was the glue that held us together. I have never met anyone quite like the Buddha-field. We all seemed to have a quality about us that was different.

Our collective energy was dynamic and rare. We attracted one another out of this time and space to experience something that we collectively created.

We used to sing the song *"Those were the days my friends* [weird and wondrous], *we thought they'd never end!"*

I have discovered many things since I left the Buddha-field.

1) There is life after the Buddha-field. I will survive.

2) If I'm open to it, my world is teeming with beautiful and profound teachers and teachings.

3) I see that my concepts of God and spirituality were in fact confused at best, in some cases downright fallacious.

4) *Life* is the mystery school if you are awake to it.

5) The relationships that were meant to be will always be.

6) It *is* about the adventure, not the goal!

7) The notion that we must strive to be someone greater than ourselves, more holy, more illumined, more perfect is erroneous thinking.

8) The old paradigm of master/disciple relationship is dead and dying. The last vestiges of an immature society that needs a paternal intermediary between you and your God-self is collapsing, and a new consciousness is rising from the ashes.

9) Who am I? An artist, musician, writer, equestrian, entrepreneur, nutritionist, holistic counselor, legislative representative—okay, I'm only kidding. Like the last words my mother said to me, "That's what you do, not who you are." Who am I? I am a sliver of the unified field, apparently made of stardust, mostly. I am here because...I'll let you know after I'm finished.

10) Those who stay behind in the illusion of their identities will continue to create their purgatory until they either free themselves from their bondage or perish from this earthly life

and discover it's all a great cosmic game. We are the players and the played.

I wish you freedom, joy, and light as you play and I thank you for sharing this journey with me.

APPENDIX

QANON ARREST-EXECUTION LIST
JUNE 13, 2020 & JUNE 28, 2020

George Soros ARRESTED & EXECUTED

   (Executed a while ago. No date given)

Courtney Cox ARRESTED WAITING TRIBUNAL

Mathew Leblanc ARRESTED & EXECUTED

David Schwimmer ARRESTED & EXECUTED

Lisa Kudrow ARRESTED & EXECUTED

Mathew Perry ARRESTED & EXECUTED

Helen Hunt ARRESTED & EXECUTED

Calista Flockhart ARRESTED & EXECUTED

Vin Diesel ARRESTED & EXECUTED

Barbra Streisand ARRESTED & EXECUTED

Brad Pitt ARRESTED & EXECUTED

Angelina Jolie ARRESTED & EXECUTED

Billy Bob Thornton ARRESTED & EXECUTED

Christopher Bridges ARRESTED & EXECUTED

Gal Gadot ARRESTED & EXECUTED

Leonard Goldberg Producer ARRESTED & EXECUTED

Chrissy Teigen ARRESTED WAITING TRIBUNAL

Alecia Beth Moore "Pink" ARRESTED WAITING TRIBUNAL

Justin Timberlake ARRESTED WAITING TRIBUNAL

Kathy Griffin ARRESTED WAITING TRIBUNAL

Mick Jagger ARRESTED WAITING TRIBUNAL

Howie Mandell ARRESTED WAITING TRIBUNAL

Anthony Fauci ARRESTED & RELEASED FOR A TIME TO
HELP TRUMP. (Other sources show Fauci EXECUTED)

Andrew McCabe ARRESTED & SERVING LIFE

Barack Obama ARRESTED & EXECUTED

Michelle (Michael) Obama ARRESTED & EXECUTED

Bill Gates DECEASED (HUNG, 2013)

Melinda Gates DECEASED (HUNG 2013)

BILL & MELINDA WERE HUNG IN INDIA BY PARENTS
OF VACCINE- INJURED CHILDREN (PARALYZED /
DEATH).

Mike Pence ARRESTED & EXECUTED
(EXECUTED JULY 4, 2019 AFTER ATTEMPTING TO
ASSASSINATE TRUMP 2X. PENCE RAPED & KILLED
186 BABIES).

Huma Abedine ARRESTED & EXECUTED

John Brennan ARRESTED & SERVING LIFE

George H.W. Bush ARRESTED & EXECUTED

George W. Bush ARRESTED & EXECUTED

   (CONFESSIONS AND BUSH JUNIOR & SENIOR'S 9/11

   TRIBUNAL WILL BE RELEASED JANUARY 2021).

Laura Bush ARRESTED & EXECUTED

Jeb Bush ARRESTED & EXECUTED

Dick Cheney ARRESTED & EXECUTED

James Baker ARRESTED & EXECUTED

James Clapper ARRESTED & SERVING LIFE

Hillary Clinton ARRESTED & EXECUTED

   (EXECUTED 9/11/2016)

Bill Clinton ARRESTED & EXECUTED

James Comey ARRESTED & SERVING LIFE

Paul Ryan ARRESTED & AT GITMO

Diane Feinstein EXILED TO CHINA

Eric Holder ARRESTED & SERVING LIFE

John Kerry ARRESTED & SERVING LIFE

Loretta Lynch ARRESTED & SERVING LIFE

Lisa Page ARRESTED & SERVING LIFE

Tony Podesta ARRESTED & EXECUTED

John Podesta ARRESTED & AT GITMO

Samantha Powers ARRESTED & SERVING LIFE

Harry Reid ARRESTED & SERVING LIFE

Susan Rice ARRESTED & SERVING LIFE

Donald Rumsfeld ARRESTED & EXECUTED

Adam Schiff ARRESTED & EXECUTED

Eric Schmidt ARRESTED & AT GITMO

Debbie Wasserman-Shultz ARRESTED & AT GITMO

Maxine Waters ARRESTED & AT GITMO

Sally Yates ARRESTED & AT GITMO

Nancy Pelosi ARRESTED & AT GITMO

Chuck Schumer ARRESTED & AT GITMO

Ruth Bader Ginsburg ARRESTED & EXECUTED

Peter Strzok ARRESTED & AT GITMO

Elijah Cummings ARRESTED & EXECUTED

Jacinda Adern ARRESTED & UNDER HOUSE ARREST

Tom Hanks ARRESTED & EXECUTED

Rita Wilson Hanks ARRESTED & EXECUTED

Madonna ARRESTED & EXECUTED

Lady Gaga ARRESTED & EXECUTED

Oprah Winfrey ARRESTED & WAITING TRIBUNAL

Ellen Degeneres ARRESTED & ON HOUSE ARREST & FACING EXECUTION

Stephen Spielberg ARRESTED & EXECUTED

Harvey Weinstein ARRESTED & IN PRISON (SERVING LIFE FOR SHARING ALL ABOUT HOLLYWOOD)

Jeffrey Epstein ARRESTED & SERVING LIFE IN PRISON (SERVING LIFE FOR SHARING ALL ABOUT ISLAND)

Pope Francis ARRESTED & EXECUTED

All Cardinals At Vatican ARRESTED & EXECUTED

Queen Elizabeth ARRESTED & EXECUTED

Phillip Windsor ARRESTED & EXECUTED

Charles Windsor ARRESTED & EXECUTED

Justin Trudeau ARRESTED & ON HOUSE ARREST

Scott Morrison ARRESTED & ON HOUSE ARREST

Harry Windsor ARRESTED & EXECUTED (NOT THE REAL HARRY)

Meghan Markle ARRESTED & EXECUTED (TRANSGENDER CIA)

Meryl Streep ARRESTED & ON HOUSE ARREST

Robert De Niro ARRESTED & EXECUTED

Richard Gere ARRESTED & ON HOUSE ARREST

Joe Biden ARRESTED & EXECUTED

Hunter Biden ARRESTED & EXECUTED

John Mccain ARRESTED & EXECUTED

Roy Horn of Sigfreid & Roy ARRESTED & EXECUTED

Troy Sneed (Singer) ARRESTED & EXECUTED

Fred The Godson (Rapper) ARRESTED & EXECUTED

Joel Rogosin (Writer) ARRESTED & EXECUTED

Matthew Seligman (Musician) ARRESTED & EXECUTED

Charles Gregory ARRESTED & EXECUTED

Hilary Heath ARRESTED & EXECUTED

Hal Wilner (Producer) ARRESTED & EXECUTED

John Prine (Singer) ARRESTED & EXECUTED

Lee Fierro ARRESTED & EXECUTED

Adam Schlesinger ARRESTED & EXECUTED

Joe Diffie ARRESTED & EXECUTED

Mitt Romney ARRESTED & AT GITMO

Britney Spears ARRESTED SERVING LIFE

Christina Aguilera ARRESTED SERVING LIFE

Miley Cyrus ARRESTED SERVING LIFE

Bette Midler ARRESTED SERVING LIFE

Robert Downey Jr. ARRESTED & EXECUTED

Dwayne Johnson (The Rock) ARRESTED & EXECUTED

George Clooney ARRESTED & EXECUTED

Adam Sandler ARRESTED & EXECUTED

Nicolas Cage ARRESTED & EXECUTED

Kevin Spacey ARRESTED & EXECUTED

Charlie Sheen ARRESTED & EXECUTED

Ashton Kutcher ARRESTED SERVING LIFE

Kyriakos Mitsotakis PM Greece ARRESTED WAITING
TRIBUNAL

Panagiotis Pikrammenos Deputy PM ARRESTED WAITING
TRIBUNAL

Celine Dion ARRESTED & EXECUTED

Don Lemon ARRESTED WAITING TRIBUNAL

Chris Cuomo ARRESTED WAITING TRIBUNAL

Kamala Harris ARRESTED WAITING TRIBUNAL

Elizabeth Warren ARRESTED WAITING TRIBUNAL

Nydia Velázquez ARRESTED WAITING TRIBUNAL

Ilhan Omar ARRESTED WAITING TRIBUNAL

Alexandria Ocasio-Cortez ARRESTED WAITING TRIBUNAL

Rashida Tlaib ARRESTED WAITING TRIBUNAL

Quentin Tarantino ARRESTED & EXECUTED

Michael Moore ARRESTED & EXECUTED

Jerry Nadler ARRESTED & AT GITMO

Bernie Sanders ARRESTED & AT GITMO

Boris Johnson ARRESTED & EXECUTED

Jimmy Kimmel ARRESTED WAITING TRIBUNAL

Alec Baldwin ARRESTED & EXECUTED

William Baldwin ARRESTED & EXECUTED

Jack Nicholson ARRESTED & EXECUTED

Johnny Depp ARRESTED & EXECUTED

Will Smith ARRESTED & EXECUTED

Bruce Willis ARRESTED & EXECUTED

Demi Moore ARRESTED & EXECUTED

Martin Scorsese ARRESTED & EXECUTED

King Harald V Of Norway ARRESTED & EXECUTED

Queen Sonja Of Norway ARRESTED & EXECUTED

Erna Solberg PM of Norway ARRESTED & IN PRISON

Stefan LöFven PM of Sweden ARRESTED & EXECUTED

Carl Xvi Gustaf King of Sweden ARRESTED & EXECUTED

Silvia Renate Sommerlath Gustaf Queen Of Sweden
ARRESTED & EXECUTED

Angela Merkel Chancellor of Germany ARRESTED &

EXECUTED (HITLER'S DAUGHTER)

Frank-Walter Steinmeier President of Germany ARRESTED &

EXECUTED

Sauli Niinistö Pres. of Finland ARRESTED & WAITING

TRIBUNAL

Sanna Marin PM of Finland ARRESTED & WAITING

TRIBUNAL

Emmanuel Macron Pres. of France ARRESTED & EXECUTED

Édouard Philippe PM of France ARRESTED & EXECUTED

John Bolton National Security Advisor ARRESTED &

WAITING TRIBUNAL

Ghislaine Maxwell ARRESTED & SERVING LIFE (EPSTEIN'S

HANDLER. SERVING LIFE FOR SHARING ALL)

Steve Bing MURDERED

Marina Abramovic ARRESTED & EXECUTED

FrançOis Legault PM of Quebec ARRESTED & ON HOUSE

ARREST

Recep Tayyip ErdoğAn Pres of Turkey ARRESTED &

EXECUTED

Keanu Reeves ARRESTED & EXECUTED

Justin Bieber ARRESTED & EXECUTED

John Travolta ARRESTED & EXECUTED

Tom Cruise ARRESTED & EXECUTED

John Huntsman Former Ambassador to China ARRESTED

WAITING TRIBUNAL

Alec Baldwin ARRESTED & EXECUTED

Anderson Cooper ARRESTED & EXECUTED

Ben Affleck ARRESTED & EXECUTED

Beyoncé ARRESTED & EXECUTED

Bill Murray ARRESTED & EXECUTED

Courtney Love ARRESTED & EXECUTED

Gwen Stefani ARRESTED & EXECUTED

James Franco ARRESTED & EXECUTED

James Gunn ARRESTED & EXECUTED

Jim Carrey ARRESTED & EXECUTED

John Cusack ARRESTED & EXECUTED

John Legend ARRESTED & EXECUTED

Katy Perry ARRESTED & EXECUTED

Lynn Forester De Rothschild ARRESTED & EXECUTED

Naomi Campbell ARRESTED & EXECUTED

Pharrell Williams ARRESTED & EXECUTED

Seth Green ARRESTED & EXECUTED

Shawn Carter Jay-Z ARRESTED & EXECUTED

Stephen Tyler ARRESTED & EXECUTED

Will Ferrell ARRESTED & EXECUTED

Woody Allen ARRESTED & EXECUTED

John Davison "Jay" Rockefeller IV ARRESTED & EXECUTED

Sadiq Khan ARRESTED & EXECUTED

Matt Hancock ARRESTED & EXECUTED

Tony Blair ARRESTED & EXECUTED

Richard Branson ARRESTED & EXECUTED

Leo Eric Varadkar PM of Ireland ARRESTED & EXECUTED

David Cameron Former UK PM ARRESTED & EXECUTED

Prif Weinidog Cymru Wales PM ARRESTED & EXECUTED

Jordana Brewster ARRESTED & EXECUTED

Sandra Bullock ARRESTED & EXECUTED

All Royalties have either been removed, arrested, or executed around the world.

All Prime Ministers have been removed, arrested, or executed around the world.

BIBLIOGRAPHY

1. *Holy Hell* video: https://www.amazon.com/ HOLY-HELL-Will-Allen/dp/B01KP1QRGE

2. *The Most Dangerous Superstition, (2ⁿᵈ Edition)*, 2012, By Larken Rose, https://www.amazon.com/ Most-Dangerous-Superstition-Larken-Rose/ dp/145075063X

3. *Diagnostic and Statistical Manual of Mental Disorders (5ᵗʰ edition)* by American Psychiatric Assc. https://www. amazon.com/American-Psychiatric-Association/e/ B00LZF2ELC/ref=dp_byline_cont_pop_book_1

4. *Combating Cult Mind Control,* by Steven Hassan, https://www.amazon.com/Combating- Cult-Mind-Control-Destructive-ebook/dp/ B00V9DU340

5. *The Sociopath Next-door* by Martha Stout, PhD, https:// www.amazon.com/Sociopath-Next-Door-Martha-Stout/ dp/0767915828

6. *Mad Men series.* www.amcplus.com/madmen

7. *David and Goliath*, by Malcolm Gladwell, *https://www. amazon.com/David-Goliath-Underdogs-Misfits-Battling-ebook/ dp/B00BAXFAOW*

8. *St. Theresa; Story of a Soul*, https://www.amazon.com/ Story-Soul-Autobiography-Translation-Manuscripts/ dp/0935216588

9. *Leave it to Beaver* series;

10. *Be Here Now by Ram Das*, https://www.amazon.com/ Be-Here-Now-Ram-Dass/dp/0517543052

11. *The Mustard Seed: Discourses on the Sayings of Jesus, Taken from the Gospels According to Thomas.* By Bhagwan Shree Rajneesh. https://www.amazon. com/Mustard-Seed-Discourses-Sayings-According/dp/0060667850

12. *The Razors Edge, by W Somerset Maugham,* https://www. amazon.com/Razors-Edge-W-Somerset-Maugham/dp/1400034205

13. *Atlas-Shrugged* by Ayn-Rand; https://www.amazon.com/Atlas-Shrugged-Ayn-Rand/dp/0451191145

14. *National Velvet;* http://www.tcm.com/tcmdb/title/84601/national-velvet/

15. P_D_Ouspensky, https://www.goodreads.com/author/show/16227499.P_D_Ouspensky

16. George Gurdjieff: https://www.amazon.com/Books-George-Gurdjieff/s?rh=n%3A283155%2Cp_27%3AGeorge+Gurdjieff

17. *A Dream of Passion: The Development of the Method,* by Lee Strasberg, https://www.amazon. com/s?k=Strasberg&i=stripbooks&ref=nb_sb_noss_2

18. *Narcissism Book of Quotes: A Selection of Quotes from the Collective Wisdom of Over 12,000 Individual Discussions* by Sam Vaknin:

19. https://www.amazon.com/Smear-Shady-Political-Operatives-Control/dp/0062468162

20. https://www.amazon.com/Russian-Diary-Journalists-Account-Corruption-ebook/dp/B000SEKKYE

21. *When Prophecy Fails* by Leon Festinger, https://www. amazon.com/When-Prophecy-Fails-Leon-Festinger/dp/1578988527

22. *The Lucifer Effect,* by Philip Zimbardo, https://www. amazon.com/The-Lucifer-Effect-Philip-Zimbardo-audio/ dp/B004USSERO

23. The Power Worshipers, by Katherine Stewart, https://www.amazon.com/Power-Worshippers-Dangerous-Religious-Nationalism/ dp/1635573432

24. https://www.amazon.com/ Single-Girl-Helen-Gurley-Brown/dp/B000PGLP9Y

25. https://www.tcm.com/tcmdb/title/16095/ sex-and-the-single-girl

26. *Too Much and Never Enough* by Mary Trump, https://www.amazon.com/ Too-Much-Never-Enough-Dangerous/dp/1982141468

27. *Trump on the Couch, Inside the Mind of the President,* by Justin A. Frank.

REFERENCES

Introduction

1. *The Most Dangerous Superstition*, (2nd Edition), 2012, By Larken Rose, https://www.amazon.com/Most-Dangerous-Superstition-Larken-Rose/dp/145075063X

2. *Diagnostic and Statistical Manual of Mental Disorders (5th edition)* by American Psychiatric Assc. https://www.amazon.com/American-Psychiatric-Association/e/B00LZF2ELC/ref=dp_byline_cont_pop_book_1

3. *Combating Cult Mind Control*, by Steven Hassan, https://www.amazon.com/Combating-Cult-Mind-Control-Destructive-ebook/dp/B00V9DU340

4. *The Sociopath Next-door* by Martha Stout, PhD, https://www.amazon.com/Sociopath-Next-Door-Martha-Stout/dp/0767915828

Section 1
Chapter 2

5. *David and Goliath*, by Malcolm Gladwell, https://www.amazon.com/David-Goliath-Underdogs-Misfits-Battling-ebook/dp/B00BAXFAOW

Chapter 4

6. Mont Pelerin Society; www.MontPelerin.org

7. The Fairness Doctrine; https://www.britannica.com/topic/Fairness-Doctrine

Section 2
Chapter 7

8. https://www.mentalfloss.com/article/536260/whats-really-happening-when-we-see-stars-after-rubbing-our-eyes

9. Diagnostic and Statistical Manual of Mental Disorders 5th edition, https://www.amazon.com/Diagnostic-Statistical-Manual-Mental-Disorders/dp/0890425558

10. https://www.cnn.com/videos/politics/2017/08/18/trump-albany-rally-winning-sot.cnn

11. https://time.com/4473972/donald-trump-mexico-meeting-insult/

12. https://qz.com/1686214/fake-news-is-a-fascist-invention/

13. https://www.bbc.com/news/world-europe-19591179

14. https://www.indiatoday.in/india/north/story/narendra-modi-the-game-changer-biography-sudesh-k.-verma-192071-2014-05-06

15. https://media.defense.gov/2019/Apr/11/2002115482/-1/-1/0/17SADDAMISIRAQ.PDF

16. https://www.apa.org/pubs/books/Threat-To-Democracy-Intro-Sample.pdf

17. http://www.prem-rawat-reviewed.org/history.html

18. https://en.wikipedia.org/wiki/Shaktipat

19. https://www.eastern-spirituality.com/glossary/spirituality-terms/m-definitions/muktananda-swami-muktananda

20. https://www.yogapedia.com/definition/6658/blue-pearl

21. *The Narcissistic Delusional Guru—Definition* http://www.kheper.net/index.htmhttps://en.wikipedia.org/wiki/Never_Give_a_Sucker_an_Even_Break#:~:text=Never%20Give%20a%20Sucker%20an%20Even%20Break%20(known%20in%20some,the%20pseudonym%20%22Otis%20Criblecoblis%22.

22. Jim Baker https://www.history.com/this-day-in-history/jim-bakker-is-indicted-on-federal-charges

23. Henry Lyon;https://www.washingtonpost.com/wp-srv/national/daily/feb99/lyons28.htm

24. Sun Myung; https://en.wikipedia.org/wiki/United_States_v._Sun_Myung_Moon

25. David Yongii Cho, https://www.christianitytoday. com/news/2014/february/founder-of-worlds-largest-megachurch-convicted-cho-yoido.html

26. Bernie Madoff, https://corporatefinanceinstitute.com/ resources/knowledge/other/bernie-madoff/

27. Forbes, Nov 24, 2015, https://www.forbes.com/sites/ steveolenski/2015/11/24/donald-trumps-real-secret-to-riches-create-a-brand-and-license-it/#2e5dc9d73622

28. *'MAFIA' Don: Donald Trump's 40 years of Mob ties.* by HB Glushakow https://www.amazon.com/ MAFIA-Don-Donald-Trumps-years/dp/1537454692

29. https://www.washingtonpost.com/politics/2016/ live-updates/general-election/real-time-fact-checking-and-analysis-of-the-first-presidential-debate/fact-check-has-trump-declared-bankruptcy-four-or-six-times/

30. https://www.propublica.org/article/trump-inc-podcast-never-before-seen-trump-tax-documents-show-major-inconsistencies

31. https://www.vanityfair.com/news/2019/08/ trump-organization-undocumented-workers

32. https://www.app.com/story/ news/politics/2016/07/05/ trump-lambasted-casino-regulators/85928852/

33. https://www.americanbar.org/content/dam/aba/ publishing/antitrust_source/apr16_skitol_4_11f. authcheckdam.pdf

34. https://www.wsj.com/articles/donald-trumps-business-plan-left-a-trail-of-unpaid-bills-1465504454

35. https://www.businessinsider.com/25-million-settlement-reached-in-fraud-lawsuit-against-trump-university-2018-4

36. https://www.businessinsider.com/trump-campaign-spent-55000-of-donor-funds-to-buy-thousands-of-copies-of-his-own-book-2016-8

37. https://www.factcheck.org/2016/06/expert-voice-analyst-its-trump/

38. https://www.bolderadvocacy.org/2018/06/29/the-trump-lawsuit-a-teachable-moment-for-nonprofits/

39. https://www.bloomberg.com/features/2016-donald-trump-golf-cuba/

40. https://www.postandcourier.com/news/trump-directed-ukraine-quid-pro-quo-key-witness-says/article_bf690c8a-0c70-11ea-974e-9fd11df32505.html

41. https://www.acslaw.org/projects/the-presidential-investigation-education-project/other-resources/key-findings-of-the-mueller-report/

42. https://www.reuters.com/article/us-usa-trump-cohen/fbi-documents-point-to-trump-role-in-hush-money-for-porn-star-daniels-idUSKCN1UD18D

43. https://www.justice-integrity.org/1449-trump-s-multiple-sex-scandals-endanger-u-s-national-security

Chapter 8

44. *The Sociopath Next Door*, by Martha Stout, https://www.amazon.com/Sociopath-Next-Door-Martha-Stout/dp/0767915828

45. https://en.wikipedia.org/wiki/Federico_Fellini

46. La Dolce Vida https://www.imdb.com/title/tt0053779/

47. Satyricon https://en.wikipedia.org/wiki/Fellini_Satyricon

48. Holy Hell https://www.imdb.com/title/tt5278464/

49. https://en.wikipedia.org/wiki/Sand_mandala

50. *Pure Land Buddhism* https://www.learnreligions.com/pure-land-buddhism-450043

51. https://en.wikipedia.org/wiki/Agrippina_the_Younger

52. *Warren Jeffs* https://archive.sltrib.com/article.php?id=52354441&itype=cmsid

53. *Swami Preminanda*; https://frontline.thehindu.com/other/article30214981.ece

54. *Theodore Renaldo* https://hj.gamakmoon.ru/40

55. Adam Schiff speech https://www.youtube.com/watch?v=h8kAeQA4HdA

56. https://www.whitehouse.gov/briefings-statements/president-donald-j-trump-award-medal-freedom-072120/

57. http://relevantscience.blogspot.com/2017/07/trump-seems-much-better-at-branding.html

58. https://www.nytimes.com/interactive/2017/07/18/upshot/trump-seems-much-better-at-branding-opponents-than-at-marketing-policies.html

59. https://www.cambridge.org/core/books/becoming-madam-chancellor/personal-is-the-political/DCF2378AE79AB2B38329DF8B6FAE427E/core-reader

60. https://www.cnn.com/videos/tv/2016/12/01/gingrich-camerota-crime-stats-newday.cnn

61. https://scholarworks.arcadia.edu/cgi/viewcontent.cgi?article=1011&context=senior_theses

Chapter 9

62. *Carl C Bell,* https://www.ncbi.nlm.nih.gov/pmc/articles/PMC2552506/

63. https://twitter.com/mhelcat/status/896433170119307264

64. https://naacp.org/latest/john-r-lewis-voting-rights-act-2020/

65. https://naacp.org/latest/john-r-lewis-voting-rights-act-2020/

66. https://giffords.org/blog/2020/04/why-wont-the-senate-pass-the-violence-against-women-act/

67. https://www.congress.gov/bill/103rd-congress/senate-bill/11

68. https://abcnews.go.com/Politics/blame-abc-news-finds-17-cases-invoking-trump/story?id=58912889

69. https://www.thenationalnews.com/world/the-americas/donald-trump-my-rhetoric-brings-people-together-1.895712

70. https://thehill.com/homenews/administration/456519-trump-i-think-my-rhetoric-brings-people-together

71. https://www.facebook.com/watch/?v=417747466100019

72. https://www.youtube.com/watch?v=JmaZR8E12bs

73. https://www.vox.com/2017/8/12/16138358/charlottesville-protests-david-duke-kkk

74. https://abcnews.go.com/Politics/blame-abc-news-finds-17-cases-invoking-trump/story?id=58912889

75. https://thehill.com/homenews/administration/456519-trump-i-think-my-rhetoric-brings-people-togetherVV

76. https://thehill.com/homenews/senate/543050-gop-senator-says-he-didnt-feel-unsafe-during-riot-but-would-have-if-blm

77. https://www.cbs58.com/news/it-is-beyond-racist-wisconsin-leaders-respond-to-ron-johnsons-comments-on-capitol-riot

78. https://www.saltradioministries.com/post/covfefe-its-actually-a-real-word-and-this-is-what-it-means

79. https://www.youtube.com/watch?v=J53Ajl5_Bg0

80. https://www.billboard.com/articles/columns/pop/7565904/donald-trump-mispronounce-beyonce-name-video

81. https://www.youtube.com/watch?v=jwQHHNWwfi8

82. https://www.reddit.com/r/esist/comments/7a6w90/trump_cant_even_bring_himself_to_admit_he/

83. https://meaww.com/donald-trump-mt-rushmore-rally-specch-ulysses-ulyssius-mispronounce-mocked-twitter-fans-react

84. https://www.youtube.com/watch?v=meNOKSyDFRk

85. https://www.youtube.com/watch?v=WnYWN-hvHX4

86. https://www.ibtimes.com/donald-trump-lambasted-mispronouncing-sanctuary-potus-deteriorating-speech-linked-2917496

87. https://www.youtube.com/watch?v=kwcploTZbKA

88. https://www.youtube.com/watch?v=EJQ9hknvaQM

89. https://www.independent.co.uk/news/world/americas/us-politics/trump-speech-veterans-student-debt-isis-a9074261.html

90. https://m.dailyhunt.in/news/india/english/the+free+press+journal-epaper-fpressjr/from+swami+vivekanon+non+to+soo+chin+tendulkar+us+president+donald+trump+s+epic+mispronunciations+of+indian+icons-newsid-n167606854

91. https://www.youtube.com/watch?v=qUPsNgmXR7M

92. https://www.youtube.com/watch?v=4icGgFxVueQ

93. https://www.nytimes.com/interactive/2016/01/28/upshot/donald-trump-twitter-insults.html

94. https://www.bongocelebrity.com/donald-trumps-wealth-is-fools-gold/

95. https://www.macleans.ca/news/world/the-definitive-list-of-every-person-donald-trump-has-called-a-loser/

96. https://www.washingtonpost.com/politics/under-trump-coronavirus-scientists-can-speak--as-long-as-they-toe-the-line/2020/04/22/a0a67c12-84b9-11ea-878a-86477a724bdb_story.html

97. https://www.washingtonpost.com/opinions/mr-president-take-all-the-executive-time-you-need/2019/02/04/88ab921a-28bb-11e9-8eef-0d74f4bf0295_story.html

98. https://www.vanityfair.com/style/2017/01/donald-trump-orange-skin-tan

99. https://slate.com/culture/2016/11/heres-everything-samantha-bee-has-called-donald-trump.html

100. https://www.britannica.com/topic/Narcissus-Greek-mythology

101. https://www.psychologytoday.com/us/blog/life-after-50/201812/trumps-temper-tantrums

102. "The Strange Case of Dr. Jekyll and Mr. Trump," 2018 *Chicago Tribune,* https://www.chicagotribune.com/opinion/editorials/ct-edit-trump-mueller-cohen-stormy-20180410-story.html

Chapter 10

103. https://theintercept.com/2020/07/09/the-trump-child-abuse-scandal/

104. https://www.amazon.com/Smear-Shady-Political-Operatives-Control/dp/0062468162

105. https://www.amazon.com/Russian-Diary-Journalists-Account-Corruption-ebook/dp/B000SEKKYE

106. https://www.bbc.com/news/uk-19647226

107. https://www.4freerussia.org/tag/vladimir-putin/

108. https://www.washingtonpost.com/politics/2019/11/16/transcript-marie-yovanovitchs-nov-testimony-front-house-intelligence-committee/

109. https://en.wikipedia.org/wiki/Id,_ego_and_super-ego

110. https://www.washingtonpost.com/politics/trump-celebrates-end-of-impeachment-with-angry-raw-and-vindictive-62-minute-white-house-rant/2020/02/06/78cd95ee-4914-11ea-b4d9-29cc419287eb_story.html

111. https://www.latimes.com/opinion/story/2019-11-15/
column-witness-intimidation-trump-marie-yovanovitch

112. https://www.rollcall.com/2019/11/21/trump-comes-
out-swinging-but-fiona-hill-fights-back-in-dramatic-
impeachment-finale/

113. https://www.politico.com/news/2019/11/08/
fiona-hill-impeachment-testimony-released-067908

114. https://www.rev.com/blog/transcripts/impeachment-
hearings-first-day-transcript-bill-taylor-george-kent-
testimony-transcript

115. https://www.pbs.org/newshour/politics/read-michael-
mckinleys-full-testimony-in-trump-impeachment-inquiry

116. https://www.theatlantic.com/ideas/archive/2019/10/
experts-strike-back/600136/

117. https://www.nytimes.com/2019/10/18/opinion/
gordon-sondland-testimony-trump.html

118. https://www.cnn.com/2020/07/08/politics/vindman-
retiring-alleged-white-house-retaliation/index.html

119. https://www.militarytimes.com/news/your-
army/2020/02/10/lt-col-vindmans-former-army-
commander-pushes-back-on-trumps-decision-to-dismiss-
officer-from-national-security-council-staff/

120. https://www.cnbc.com/2020/02/07/trump-
impeachment-witness-vindman-escorted-out-of-white-
house.html

121. https://www.businessinsider.com/yevgeny-vindman-ousted-white-house-same-time-as-alex-2020-2

122. https://www.businessinsider.com/republicans-shocked-angered-by-mitt-romney-conviction-vote-2020-2

123. https://www.koamnewsnow.com/i/right-wing-media-condemn-mitt-romney-after-gop-senator-casts-vote-to-convict-trump/

124. https://www.psychologytoday.com/us/blog/the-time-cure/201709/the-dangerous-case-donald-trump

125. https://www.washingtonpost.com/outlook/trump-lied-to-me-about-his-wealth-to-get-onto-the-forbes-400-here-are-the-tapes/2018/04/20/ac762b08-4287-11e8-8569-26fda6b404c7_story.html

126. https://www.youtube.com/watch?v=xnhJWusyj4I

127. https://www.vox.com/2020/3/25/21193803/trump-to-governors-coronavirus-help-ventilators-cuomo

128. https://www.dailymail.co.uk/news/article-9188251/Fauci-says-Trumps-COVID-19-disinfectant-claim-dangerous.html

Chapter 11

129. https://en.wikipedia.org/wiki/Cognitive_dissonance

130. https://www.verywellmind.com/what-is-cognitive-dissonance-2795012

131. https://www.washingtonpost.com/outlook/
the-psychological-phenomenon-that-blinds-trump-
supporters-to-his-racism/2019/07/18/29789344-a8ac-
11e9-ac16-90dd7e5716bc_story.html

132. *When Prophecy Fails, by Leon Festinger, https://www.amazon.
com/When-Prophecy-Fails-Leon-Festinger/dp/1578988527*

133. https://onlinelibrary.wiley.com/doi/10.1111/pops.12647

134. *The Lucifer Effect,* by Philip Zimbardo, https://www.
amazon.com/The-Lucifer-Effect-Philip-Zimbardo-audio/
dp/B004USSERO/

Chapter 12

135. https://www.cnbc.com/2019/08/21/i-am-the-chosen-
one-trump-proclaims-as-he-defends-china-trade-war.
html

136. https://apnews.com/article/
f49879eeba44433f9a35b8d5c9cfac8f

137. Dictators and their Followers: A Theory of Dictatorship
(University of Warsaw), author Dr. Gustav Bychowski

Chapter 13

138. https://en.wikipedia.org/wiki/
Donald_Trump_sexual_misconduct_allegations

139. https://www.forbes.com/sites/
lisettevoytko/2020/07/21/heres-every-time-donald-
trump-and-ghislaine-maxwell-have-been-photographed-
together/?sh=353daa9e183d

140. Bonewit's Cult Danger Evaluation Form; http://
www.wellspringcoven.com/blog/2019/7/26/
the-advanced-bonewits-cult-danger-evaluation-form

141. https://www.politico.com/agenda/
story/2017/12/29/138-trump-policy-
changes-2017-000603

142. www.aboutthetruth.com

Chapter 14

143. https://www.businessinsider.com/
women-accused-trump-sexual-misconduct-list-2017-12

144. In case number 1:16-cv-04642, document 1 Filed 06/20/16
In the United States District Court Southern District of
New York, Jane Doe, proceeding under a pseudonym,
Plaintiff v. Donald J. Trump and Jeffrey E. Epstein.
https://www.scribd.com/doc/316341058/Donald-
Trump-Jeffrey-Epstein-Rape-Lawsuit-and-Affidavits?fbcl
id=IwAR0sTCPQYbCqLh4HBEDos2nYOamRT7SLdfNQ
J4D-YcTPfYrAypdvYgEwG9g

145. https://www.nytimes.com/2019/11/04/nyregion/jean-
carroll-sues-trump.html

146. https://www.bustle.com/p/harvey-weinsteins-i-
came-of-age-quote-is-getting-dragged-by-women-on-
twitter-2806013

147. https://www.nytimes.com/2020/10/27/nyregion/
nxivm-cult-keith-raniere-sentenced.html

148. https://time.com/4971529/
harvey-weinstein-sexual-harassment-jay-z-fake-quote/

149. https://www.amazon.com/
Single-Girl-Helen-Gurley-Brown/dp/B000PGLP9Y

150. https://www.tcm.com/tcmdb/title/16095/
sex-and-the-single-girl

151. https://www.nytimes.com/2020/10/27/nyregion/
nxivm-cult-keith-raniere-sentenced.html

152. https://www.pewresearch.org/politics/2018/08/09/
an-examination-of-the-2016-electorate-based-on-
validated-voters/

153. https://en.wikipedia.org/wiki/Becky_(slang)https://
www.imdb.com/title/tt0042114/https://www.amazon.
com/Jesus-John-Wayne-Evangelicals-Corrupted/
dp/1631495739

154. https://www.amazon.com/Trump-Finally-Someone-
Balls-Shirt/dp/B07FM6KQXW https://www.
youtube.com/watch?v=Fcux4JawwP0https://
www.theatlantic.com/politics/archive/2016/08/
the-era-of-the-bitch-is-coming/496154/

155. https://www.salon.com/2020/01/16/
that-expression-trump-keeps-using-partner/

156. "I love the poorly educated" https://www.youtube.com/
watch?v=Vpdt7omPoa0

Chapter 15

157. Rama; https://www.washingtonpost.com/archive/local/1998/04/15/controversial-guru-frederick-p-lenz-iii-dies-at-48/6d30fcea-3de3-4d0e-9971-15ef8442e1b1/

158. https://www.politifact.com/factchecks/2020/jun/24/priorities-usa-action/trump-positive-coronavirus-tests-slowdown-look-bad/

159. https://www.washingtonpost.com/politics/2020/07/13/white-houses-maligning-anthony-fauci-annotated/

160. https://khn.org/morning-breakout/trump-administration-orders-hospitals-to-bypass-cdc-with-data-on-covid/

161. https://billmoyers.com/story/follow-the-money-covid-19-data-and-trump-campaign-edition/

162. https://www.axios.com/trump-coronavirus-testing-overrated-cf847872-20d0-48b1-95dd-34af301642c0.html

163. https://www.independent.co.uk/news/world/americas/trump-twitter-democrat-cities-rot-retweet-a9674106.html

164. Trump's first cabinet meeting; https://www.youtube.com/watch?v=6ARgUIpM6f0
https://www.c-span.org/video/?429863-1/president-touts-accomplishments-cabinet-meeting

Section 3
Chapter 16

165. https://www.theparisreview.org/blog/2018/05/21/why-are-we-so-fascinated-by-cults/

166. https://www.merriam-webster.com/dictionary/cult

167. http://www.eaec.org/cults.htm

168. https://www.theatlantic.com/national/archive/2014/06/the-seven-signs-youre-in-a-cult/361400/

169. http://skepticsannotatedbible.com/sex/long.html

170. Holy Bible: Genesis 9:24.

171. Holy Bible: Genesis 19:30-38

172. Deuteronomy 21:11-14

173. https://www.amazon.com/Combating-Cult-Mind-Control-Destructive-ebook/dp/B00V9DU340

174. https://www.vice.com/en_us/partners/strange-angel/this-buff-speedo-wearing-guru-started-a-1980s-sex-cult

175. https://www.amazon.com/End-Faith-Religion-Terror-Future/dp/0393327655/

Chapter 18

176. https://www.amazon.com/Republic-Lost-Version-Lawrence-Lessig/dp/1455537012

177. https://priceonomics.com/when-lobbying-was-illegal/

178. https://www.nytimes.com/2014/10/19/books/review/zephyr-teachouts-corruption-in-america.html

179. https://www.fec.gov/legal-resources/court-cases/citizens-united-v-fec/

180. https://www.fec.gov/updates/mccutcheon-v-fec-supreme-court-finds-aggregate-biennial-limits-unconstitutional/

181. https://publicintegrity.org/politics/the-mccutcheon-decision-explained-more-money-to-pour-into-political-process/

182. https://www.nbcnews.com/meet-the-press/video/conway-press-secretary-gave-alternative-facts-860142147643

183. https://www.nytimes.com/2016/08/07/opinion/sunday/clintons-fibs-vs-trumps-huge-lies.html

184. https://www.politifact.com/personalities/hillary-clinton/

185. https://www.politifact.com/article/2016/nov/09/fact-checking-donald-trump-2016/

186. https://www.nytimes.com/2016/08/07/opinion/sunday/clintons-fibs-vs-trumps-huge-lies.html

187. https://www.theworldweekly.com/reader/view/2930/hillary-clinton-receives-a-boost-as-the-benghazi-report-clears-her

188. https://www.newstalkflorida.com/featured/gops-fear-loathing-hillary-clinton-cost-100-million/

189. https://www.fbi.gov/news/pressrel/press-releases/statement-by-fbi-director-james-b-comey-on-the-investigation-of-secretary-hillary-clinton2019s-use-of-a-personal-e-mail-system

190. https://www.splcenter.org/fighting-hate/extremist-files/group/proud-boys

191. https://www.wbur.org/onpoint/2020/07/10/the-origins-of-the-extremist-boogaloo-movement

Chapter19

192. https://www.youtube.com/watch?v=pxBQLFLei70

Chapter 20

193. https://www.youtube.com/watch?v=38DY30I73lg

194. https://uscode.house.gov/view.xhtml?req=granuleid:USC-prelim-title18-section611&num=0&edition=prelim

195. https://www.foxbusiness.com/politics/hillary-clinton-would-double-taxes-on-short-term-capital-gains

196. https://www.brookings.edu/blog/up-front/2018/10/16/the-middle-class-needs-a-tax-cut-trump-didnt-give-it-to-them/

197. https://www.aeaweb.org/articles?id=10.1257/aer.20140913

198. https://cdn.factcheck.org/UploadedFiles/AER_revision.pdf

199. https://www.forbes.com/sites/realspin/2016/11/07/trump-is-right-about-one-thing-the-economy-does-better-under-the-democrats/#787f20976786

200. https://www.govtrack.us/congress/bills/114/s862/summary

201. https://taxfoundation.org/details-and-analysis-hillary-clinton-s-tax-proposals-october-2016/

202. https://presidentialwm.com/blog-2020/an-ugly-sunset-what-will-happen-if-the-tax-cuts-and-jobs-act-expires/

Chapter 21

203. https://www.history.com/this-day-in-history/patty-hearst-kidnapped#:~:text=On%20February%204%2C%20 1974%2C%20Patty,neighbor%20who%20tried%20to%20 help.

204. https://www.amazon.com/American-Heiress-Kidnapping-Crimes-Hearst/dp/0345803159

205. https://www.npr.org/2016/08/03/488373982/whose-side-was-she-on-american-heiress-revisits-patty-hearst-s-kidnapping Cialdini, R. B.; Goldstein, N. J. (2004). "Social influence: Compliance and conformity" (PDF). *Annual Review of Psychology*. 55: 591–621. doi:10.1146/annurev.psych.55.090902.142015. PMID 14744228.

206. http://worldcat.org/identities/lccn-n50017706/

207. *Born in Blood: The Lost Secrets of Freemasonry,* by John J. Robinson; https://www.amazon.com/Born-Blood-Lost-Secrets-Freemasonry/dp/1590771486

208. https://www.amazon.com/Glorious-Cause-American-Revolution-1763-1789/dp/019531588X

209. Godless Constitutions; https://www.123helpme.com/essay/The-Godless-Constitution-90278

210. https://springwolf.net/2012/09/27/religious-awareness-in-america/

Chapter 22

211. https://kristindumez.com/

212. "Test for an Unfaithful Wife" Holy Bible, (Numbers 5:11-31).

213. Genesis 2:7, *God, Holy Bible*

214. Ezekiel 37:5, *Holy Bible*

215. https://www.npr.org/templates/story/story.php?storyId=120746516

216. https://www.washingtonpost.com/investigations/amy-coney-barrett-people-of-praise/2020/10/06/5f497d8c-0781-11eb-859b-f9c27abe638d_story.html

Chapter 23

217. https://qz.com/1561835/loyalty-rats-and-family-the-cohen-hearings-strong-mob-vibes/

Chapter 24

218. https://www.amazon.com/Lot-People-Are-Saying-Conspiracism/dp/0691188831

219. https://www.justsecurity.org/72339/qanon-is-a-nazi-cult-rebranded/

220. https://www.washingtonpost.com/news/the-intersect/wp/2014/09/25/absolutely-everything-you-need-to-know-to-understand-4chan-the-internets-own-bogeyman/

221. https://www.filmsforaction.org/articles/6-reasons-so-many-spiritual-people-have-been-fooled-by-qanon/

222. https://www.politicalresearch.org/2016/08/18/dominionism-rising-a-theocratic-movement-hiding-in-plain-sight

223. *The Road to 9/11: Wealth, Empire, and the Future of America* by Peter Dale Scott, https://www.amazon.com/Road-11-Wealth-Empire-America/dp/0520258711

224. *In Deep: the FBI, the CIA, and the Truth about America's "Deep State,"* by David Rohde, https://www.amazon.sg/Deep-Truth-about-Americas-State/dp/1324003545

Chapter 25

225. https://www.filmsforaction.org/articles/6-reasons-so-many-spiritual-people-have-been-fooled-by-qanon/

226. https://www.politicalresearch.org/2016/08/18/dominionism-rising-a-theocratic-movement-hiding-in-plain-sight

227. *The Road to 9/11: Wealth, Empire, and the Future of America* by Peter Dale Scott, https://www.amazon.com/Road-11-Wealth-Empire-America/dp/0520258711

228. *In Deep: the FBI, the CIA, and the Truth about America's "Deep State,"* Rohde, https://www.amazon.com/Deep-Truth-about-Americas-State-ebook/dp/B07TK261HR

229. *Act of 1871*, also known as the Ku Klux Klan Act, https://history.house.gov/Historical-Highlights/1851-1900/hh_1871_04_20_KKK_Act/

230. https://www.insider.com/marjorie-taylor-greene-jewish-lasers-space-conspiracy-theories-theory-history-2021-2

231. https://www.britannica.com/biography/Buddha-founder-of-Buddhism/The-first-disciples

Chapter 26

232. https://www.law.umich.edu/special/exoneration/Pages/casedetail.aspx?caseid=5156

233. https://www.azcentral.com/story/travel/ arizona/2019/10/01/sedona-chapel-of-the-holy-cross-vandalism-qanon-supporter-arrested/3826336002/

234. https://www.inquisitr.com/1125232/katy-perry-worshipped-satan-at-the-grammys-with-some-help-from-the-beatles/

235. https://wppow.storyhorse.de/mark-dice-beyonce.html

236. https://www.thedailybeast.com/ why-american-christians-love-satan

237. https://today.yougov.com/topics/ lifestyle/articles-reports/2013/09/17/ half-americans-believe-possession-devil

238. https://www.scientificamerican.com/article/ psychological-power-satan/

Chapter 27

239. https://www.chicagoreader.com/Bleader/ archives/2018/04/06/former-chicago-gossip-columnist-liz-crokin-is-now-a-star-among-far-right-conspiracy-theorists

240. https://www.nytimes.com/2020/07/31/style/karen-name-meme-history.html

241. https://reason.com/2015/06/08/ sex-traffickers-kidnap-at-hobby-lobby/

242. https://www.justice.gov/usao-dc/pr/north-carolina-man-sentenced-four-year-prison-term-armed-assault-northwest-washington

243. https://www.smh.com.au/world/north-america/false-antifa-claims-spread-amid-wave-of-social-media-hoaxes-20200603-p54z68.html

244. https://datasociety.net/wp-content/uploads/2019/09/Source-Hacking_Hi-res.pdf

Chapter 28

245. https://www.washingtonpost.com/business/technology/baseless-wayfair-child-trafficking-theory-spreads-online/2020/07/16/f5206c10-c7aa-11ea-a825-8722004e4150_story.html

246. https://www.nytimes.com/2019/07/21/nyregion/gambino-shooting-anthony-comello-frank-cali.html

247. https://www.dailykos.com/stories/2021/1/28/2012494/-A-List-of-All-the-Pro-Trump-Terrorists-So-Far

248. https://thehill.com/homenews/house/537391-mccarthy-on-qanon-i-dont-even-know-what-it-is

249. https://www.mediamatters.org/qanon-conspiracy-theory/qanon-may-be-coming-congress-and-journalists-need-be-ready

Chapter 29

250. https://www.sciencealert.com/swearing-is-a-sign-of-more-intelligence-not-less-say-scientists

251. https://www.apa.org/monitor/2009/12/consumer.aspx

252. https://en.wikipedia.org/wiki/Liberalism

253. https://www.cambridge.org/core/journals/central-european-history/article/an-american-fuhrer-nazi-analogies-and-the-struggle-to-explain-donald-trump/25CBE639F23D2D80870EA4D3F1E6D566

254. *Democracy in Chains: The Deep History of the Radical Right's Stealth Plan for America* by Nancy MacLean, https://www.amazon.com/Democracy-Chains-History-Radical-Stealth/dp/1101980966

255. *Dark Money* by Jane Mayer, https://www.amazon.com/Dark-Money-History-Billionaires-Radical/dp/0307947904

256. https://www.haaretz.com/us-news/.premium-how-did-the-term-globalist-became-an-anti-semitic-slur-blame-bannon-1.5895925

257. https://www.newyorker.com/news/daily-comment/in-orlando-trump-kicks-off-his-reelection-campaign-with-an-old-divisive-message

258. https://www.washingtonpost.com/politics/2019/06/20/republicans-have-been-tying-democrats-socialism-years-trump-is-going-all-tradition/

259. https://www.britannica.com/topic/Kali

Chapter 30

260. https://www.ar15.com/forums/General/
We-ll-Get-F-ing-Torn-Apart-in-2022/5-2387679/

261. http://www.azerta.cl/en/es-la-economia-estupido/

262. https://www.theatlantic.com/
magazine/archive/2018/11/
newt-gingrich-says-youre-welcome/570832/

263. https://www.wbur.org/hereandnow/2016/07/19/
gerrymandering-republicans-redmap

264. https://www.history.com/topics/american-revolution/
tea-act

265. https://variety.com/2020/digital/news/
twitter-trump-limit-interaction-election-1234852363/

266. https://www.businessinsider.com/georgia-election-
vote-certification-brad-raffensperger-recount-trump-
biden-2020-12

267. https://www.npr.org/sections/biden-transition-
updates/2020/11/28/939645865/biden-gains-votes-in-
recount-of-milwaukee-county-requested-by-trump

268. https://www.washingtonpost.com/
politics/2020/12/14/most-remarkable-rebukes-trumps-
legal-case-judges-he-hand-picked/

269. https://apnews.com/article/criminal-investigations-dallas-ken-paxton-coronavirus-pandemic-crime-3657864db01b3e2525f53f8f52 3af316

270. https://www.businessinsider.com/sidney-powell-urging-executive-order-to-seize-voting-machines-nyt-2020-12

271. https://www.youtube.com/watch?v=NYnHfF5KGrw

272. https://www.psychiatry.org/newsroom/goldwater-rule

273. https://www.scientificamerican.com/article/psychiatrists-debate-weighing-in-on-trumps-mental-health/

Chapter 31

274. https://www.theholocaustexplained.org/the-nazi-rise-to-power/the-nazi-rise-to-power/

275. https://www.tandfonline.com/doi/abs/10.1080/00335630500157516

276. https://www.politifact.com/article/2018/apr/18/true-alex-jones-said-no-one-died-sandy-hook-elemen/

277. https://www.snopes.com/fact-check/alex-jones-biden-removed/

278. https://abcnews.go.com/US/shot-competing-protesters-clash-washington-state/story?id=74697209

279. https://www.ctvnews.ca/world/these-are-some-of-the-extremist-groups-responsible-for-the-violence-on-capitol-hill-1.5259142

280. https://www.usatoday.com/story/opinion/2021/03/02/cpac-2021-stage-design-public-high-five-white-supremacy-column/6883518002/

281. https://www.businessinsider.com/matt-gaetz-george-floyd-protesters-antifa-hunt-them-down-2020-6

282. https://www.cruz.senate.gov/?p=press_release&id=5147

283. https://www.justice.gov/opa/pr/attorney-general-william-p-barrs-statement-riots-and-domestic-terrorism

284. https://en.wikipedia.org/wiki/Gaslighting

285. https://theconversation.com/how-should-we-protest-neo-nazis-lessons-from-german-history-82645

Made in the USA
Columbia, SC
04 July 2021

41290348R00237